TIMOTHY HAMPTON

Introduction: Baroques

We need topographers to give faithful narrations of the places they
have been.

—Montaigne

Near the end of the second book of his *Essais* Montaigne tells of being
shown a monstrous child consisting of two bodies joined by a single
head. "They were joined face to face, and as if the smaller child were
trying to embrace a bigger one around the neck." His initial reaction, he
says, was to interpret the child's deformity as an emblem of France,
whose body politic was monstrously torn between warring factions of
Catholics and Protestants. Montaigne states that the monstrous child
might provide "a favorable prognostic to the king that he will maintain
under the union of his laws these various parts and factions of our
state."[1] Once he has playfully considered this interpretation, however,
Montaigne sets it aside and asserts that the monster merely seems
strange because human understanding is limited. In fact, he says, in the
eyes of God nothing is monstrous.

The richly suggestive figure of the child described by Montaigne—a
"natural" freak made monstrous by cultural perception, a body signifying France itself—might serve as a guiding image for this issue of *Yale
French Studies*, with its dual concern for the Baroque and for problems
of space, or what I am calling "topography." For not only has the
Baroque traditionally been understood as a site inhabited by freaks—
from the grotesques of late sixteenth- and seventeenth-century architectural decoration to the extravagant linguistic constructions of
Góngora and the German *Trauerspiel*—but it has itself been a historiographical monstrosity—a phenomenon defying conventional categories of periodization and description.

The Baroque provides us with that rarest of phenomena these

1. I cite Donald Frame's translation of Montaigne's *Essays* (Stanford: Stanford University Press, 1985), 538.

YFS 80, *Baroque Topographies,* ed. Timothy Hampton, © 1991 by Yale University.

1

days—a body of texts with no theory. As any student of the history of criticism knows, it was in the 1950s, during the heyday of stylistics and of New Criticism, that the study of Baroque culture and of the Baroque as a critical concept came into vogue.[2] However, with the advent of various types of structuralist analysis the attention of students of early modernity turned elsewhere. My intention here is neither to try to revive the critical categories that promoted the study of the Baroque, nor even to define the notion. It may be more useful to explore its ambiguities and their methodological interest. It is clear, in any case, that despite its disappearance the Baroque has shadowed ghostlike around much recent thought. One need only point out the importance for poststructuralist criticism, theory and historiography of analyses concerned with historical structures and texts traditionally labeled Baroque. Michel Foucault's influential work on early seventeenth-century models of representation and on seventeenth-century institutions of normalization, Walter Benjamin's often mentioned but rarely studied thesis on the German Baroque *Trauerspiel*, and Michel de Certeau's studies of mystical discourse, to name only the most famous, all suggest the importance of the Baroque in both the genesis of modernity and the critical vocabulary of what has come to be called postmodernism. Indeed, some writers have even spoken recently of a "neo-Baroque" characterizing modernity, or of a post-modern Baroque.[3]

A major problem faced by any attempt to reconsider the Baroque is the ubiquity and meaninglessness of the term itself. The application of labels to historical moments and groups of texts inevitably raises questions about the way in which cultural history creates norms and crite-

2. For accounts of the history of the Baroque see René Wellek, "The Concept of Baroque in Literary Scholarship," in his *Concepts of Criticism* (New Haven: Yale University Press, 1963), 69–127; as well as Marc Fumaroli's introduction to the re-edition of Victor L. Tapié's *Baroque et classicisme* (Paris: Livre de Poche, 1980).

3. See Michel Foucault, *The Order of Things* (New York: Vintage, 1970), pt. 1; *Madness and Civilization*, trans. Richard Howard (New York: Vintage, 1965), chapters 1–3; and *Discipline and Punish*, trans. Alan Sheridan (New York: Vintage, 1979), pts. 1 and 2; Walter Benjamin, *The Origin of German Tragic Drama*, trans. by John Osborne (London: New Left Books, 1977); as well as Michel de Certeau, *La Fable Mystique* (Paris: Gallimard, 1982) and *L'Ecriture de l'histoire* (Paris: Gallimard, 1984). It is also worth recalling in this context the important "structuralist" essays by Gérard Genette on d'Urfé and Sponde in his *Figures I* (Paris: Editions du Seuil, 1966). For the notion of a "neo-Baroque," see the final sections of Gilles Deuleuze's *Le Pli: Leibniz et le Baroque* (Paris: Les Editions de Minuit, 1988), as well as two works by Christine Buci-Glucksmann, *La Raison baroque. De Baudelaire à Benjamin* (Paris: Galilée, 1984), and *La Folie du voir. De l'esthétique baroque* (Paris: Galilée, 1986).

ria of exclusion. Labeling homogenizes. Certainly, the appearance of the term Baroque in the title of this volume is in no way dictated by the texts studied. Any one of a number of labels might have worked. Yet the use of the notion of the Baroque (and in what follows, the word should be read as implicitly set apart by quotation marks) has been characterized from its earliest days by uncertainty. The methodological interest of the term may lie in its very imprecision.

Students of the Baroque have traditionally used the word to refer to both a particular historical moment (Europe and Latin America in the late sixteenth and early seventeenth centuries) and a particular mode of representation employing paradox, illusionism, preciosity, the thematics of melancholy and so on. The Baroque is seen as a moment of transition between, for example, the religious struggles of the Reformation and the consolidation of the absolutist state.[4] No less frequently, however, it is studied as an aesthetics of conflict which is contrasted to both the harmonious ideals of Ciceronian humanism and the neoclassical orthodoxy of Boileau. The problem, of course, is to link the notion of the Baroque as a historical label (with its concern for such problems as the genesis of absolutism, the institution of the Counter Reformation, the rise of salon culture, the birth of the capital, and so on) to a model of the Baroque as a particular set of stylistic traits or tropological combinations that transcend the moment of their production and immediate reception. Only an analysis that concerns itself with a general economy of representation, with an attention to the circulation of signs *between* aesthetics and politics, text and history, might begin to rethink this dichotomy without falling into facile categorizations.

Originally a term describing a misshapen pearl, the adjective "barocco" was used from the time of Saint-Simon to refer to whatever was bizarre, strange, or shocking. The supplement to the *Encyclopédie* included a note by Rousseau describing as "Baroque" any music that was confused and dissonant. Like Montaigne's monstrous child, the Baroque seems at once misshapen and a creation of those who contemplate it. Yet uncertainty over what the Baroque is or might be is articulated in the very book that gave birth to modern studies of the phenomenon, Heinrich Wölfflin's *Renaissance and Baroque* of 1888. In

4. For this reading of the Baroque as a particular historical moment see José Antonio Maravall's suggestive study of seventeenth-century Spain, *The Culture of the Baroque*, trans. Terry Cochran (Minneapolis: University of Minnesota Press, 1986), as well as the collection entitled *L'Etat Baroque, 1610–1652*, ed. Henry Méchoulan (Paris: Vrin, 1985).

the preface to his study Wölfflin recognizes the difficulty of reducing the Baroque to the limited framework required by historical analysis. Wölfflin states that he wants to study the rise of a particular artistic style ("that style into which the Renaissance resolved itself"), but that the object of his interest is so incoherent and fluid as to resist a unified treatment: "The Baroque changed so much that it is difficult to think of it as a single whole. Beginning and end have little resemblance to each other and it is difficult to distinguish any continuity."[5] This historical disunity is matched by a geographical paradox, since he sees the Baroque as being both pan-European and "exclusively Roman." The Baroque is both one and many, both everywhere and only in Rome. As an object of study it is a monstrosity, with the disunity of its beginning and end recalling less Montaigne's freakish child than Horace's famous characterization of the exorbitant in art as a woman's head attached to a fish's body.

Wölfflin's study takes as its point of departure Roman architecture in the late sixteenth century. It relates the Roman style to the ideals represented by the high humanist architecture of the *quattrocento*. The notion of a French literary Baroque is first developed in Jean Rousset's *La Littérature de l'âge baroque en France: Circé et le paon* of 1954. Like Wölfflin, Rousset defines the Baroque through reference to another phenomenon. He relates it, however, not to what precedes it but to what follows it, to the French classicism that has traditionally dominated considerations of the seventeenth century. By defining the Baroque against classicism, Rousset aims to present it as a force of subversion, as a monstrous or demonic element excluded by traditional accounts of early modernity. He begins his reevaluation with a gesture of geographical displacement. Like Wölfflin he admits that the Baroque is a notion that is extremely difficult to define. Only in the work of Bernini, Borromini, and Pietro da Cortona can one find "a pure and indisputable notion of the Baroque."[6] But for Rousset this methodological limitation becomes an ideological strength. For to the extent that one can speak of Baroque literature or art in France, says Rousset, one must do so with constant reference to developments beyond the French border: "its sources and its centers of activity are abroad" (Rousset: *Circé*, 9). This interest in non-French literature aims

5. Heinrich Wölfflin, *Renaissance and Baroque*, trans. Kathrin Simon (Ithaca: Cornell University Press, 1984), 16.
6. Jean Rousset, *La Littérature de l'âge baroque en France: Circé et le paon* (Paris: José Corti, 1954), 8. Translations mine. Hereafter cited in the text.

Yale French Studies

Baroque Topographies: Literature/History/Philosophy

Yale French Studies

Timothy Hampton, *Special editor for this issue*
Liliane Greene, *Managing editor*
Editorial board: Ora Avni (Chair), Hilari Allred, Sahar
   Amer, Peter Brooks, Shoshana Felman, Denis
   Hollier, Didier Maleuvre, Christopher Miller, Kevin
   Newmark, Charles Porter, Allan Stoekl
Staff: Cynthia J. Mesh
Editorial office: 80–90 Wall Street, Room 308.
Mailing address: 2504A-Yale Station, New Haven,
   Connecticut 06520.
Sales and subscription office:
   Yale University Press, 92A Yale Station
   New Haven, Connecticut 06520
   Published twice annually by Yale University Press

Designed by James J. Johnson and set in Trump
Medieval Roman by The Composing Room of
Michigan, Inc.
Printed in the United States of America by the Vail-
Ballou Press, Binghamton, N.Y.

ISSN 044-0078
ISBN for this issue 0–300–05066–6

to undermine the myopic imperialism of traditional French academic criticism, with its fixation on the seventeenth century as "the great century," as the century, to use Voltaire's term, of Louis XIV. In fact, Rousset takes aim at the canonical narrative history of French literature, Gustave Lanson's *Histoire de la littérature française*, when he states as his intention a reevaluation of "certain currents and certain poets that Lanson would not know what to do with" (*Circé*, 8). In this context the Baroque becomes the excluded, the repressed, that which the official history of the literature cannot accept. And the value placed by Rousset on Italian and Spanish literature turns France from a Mecca into a province, displacing it to the edge of the literary empire.

Rousset defines the Baroque as a set of themes or phenomenological motifs which nevertheless enjoy historical specificity: "an entire period, which runs approximately from 1580 to 1670, from Montaigne to Bernini, recognizes itself in a series of themes that are proper to it: change, inconstancy, the trompe-l'oeil and decoration, the funerary spectacle, the flight of time and the world's instability" (*Circé*, 8). These "themes" (which in fact intertwine thematic and generic concerns), can be summed up in two images, the famous emblems of Circe and the Peacock, also described as "movement and background" [le mouvement et le décor].

The various references to the classicism of Louis XIV, the "pure Baroque" of Bernini, Borromini, and Pietro da Cortona, and the specific delineation of the limits of the Baroque as 1580–1670 (the former date falling, it should be noted, long before the birth of any of the "pure Baroque" artists just mentioned) restate in specific terms the methodological question of whether the Baroque is to be understood as a historical moment defined by particular political and social relationships or as an aesthetic project. Rousset seems to want it both ways. On the one hand, he argues that the works of Bernini, Borromini, and Pietro da Cortona permit one to describe a "Baroque ideal" against which other works are to be measured for stylistic similarities. In this formulation the Baroque is perceived ahistorically, as a series of stylistic attempts to approach a linguistic ideal. Yet at the same time, the Baroque is imagined as a period, as the "Baroque Age" of the book's title. To resolve the tension between these two models for understanding the Baroque, Rousset takes refuge in an interesting image. The purpose of his study, he says, is to "displace the perspective" on the seventeenth century. In the "light" [*éclairage*] of this new perspective, the classical seventeenth century will not be darkened ("nullement obscurci"), but it will seem less homogenous and less linear: "au lieu d'un siècle en évolution progressive et monochrome, on verrrait se dessiner plusieurs XVIIe siècles parallèles" (*Circé*, 9). [In place of a century evolving progressively and monochromatically, one might see drawn several parallel seventeenth centuries]. The tension in Rousset's preface between narrative historiography and the imaginary space of stylistic variation is resolved in the image of a painting that reveals, under new light, a set of multiple progressions. Not only is the Baroque defined by painting, it is itself a work of art. The seventeenth century becomes a kind of historical fresco that is both unified (within a frame) and multiple ("several seventeenth centuries"), both static and mobile, both spatial and narrative, both monstrous and familiar.

On one level, this aestheticizing depiction of the Baroque seems to elide all consideration of historical, political, and social concerns. It places the Baroque in history only to the extent that it frames it by two specific years and claims that the Baroque provides "an entire period" with themes in which it can "recognize" itself. Yet it is this very scene of recognition that provides the ground for a reconsideration of the Baroque. For the scene of recognition that Rousset evokes—the scene in which a given historical moment confronts its own representations—is anything but innocent. On the contrary, the achievement of recent cultural theorists, from Althusser to Foucault to Bourdieu— those thinkers who separate us from Rousset—is to have opened perspectives on the politics of recognition, on the ways in which encounters between cultural texts and specific historical subjects (whom Rousset here ignores when he speaks of "an entire period") are defined by power. The encounter between a subject and a text in which she or he is to find self-recognition constitutes that moment at which subjectivity is defined and circumscribed by the discourses of power, whether political or aesthetic. It is through recognition that people become the subjects of political and social systems.

For the France of the late sixteenth and seventeenth centuries these recognition scenes (like Montaigne's encounter with the monstrous child) must be located in the aftermath of the great upheavals of thirty years of religious conflict. The crisis of public and political life signaled by these religious struggles was followed by a period of national reconstruction under Henry IV and Louis XIII. This period of "unification," however, was characterized by a battle no less vicious in its way than the religious wars. For the provincial nobility found its traditional autonomy endangered by the power of the newly centralized monarchy. The violent transformations that mark the period after the wars of religion involve a radical restructuring of every level of political, cultural, religious, and social experience and bring to prominence a whole new set of cultural forms and spaces, from the private library to the theater to the pastoral novel.

Perhaps nowhere are the stakes of this transformation more succinctly evoked than in the fourth act of Corneille's tragi-comedy *Le Cid*, where the female protagonist Chimène implores her king to sanction a duel between her lover Rodrigue (who is also the killer of her father) and anyone who might challenge him for her hand. The king resists: "Cette vieille coutume en ces lieux établie, / Sous couleur de punir un injuste attentat, / Des meilleurs combattants affaiblit un État".[7] [That ancient custom established in these parts, / Under the guise of punishing unjust deeds, / Deprives the State of its best soldiers]. The contrast in this passage between "these parts" and "the State" links the development of Baroque culture to the organization of space. With admirable concision Corneille defines the nobility's struggle against royal power as an issue involving the definition of place, as a fight between conflicting ways of defining the same territory. The political and social restructuring that accompanies the rise of absolutism here involves a renaming, as the same site ("ces lieux") is recharted and relabeled. The domain of custom, the space in which the traditional nobility plays out its intrigues of vengeance and honor, is reimagined as a building block of the unified nation state, with its need for standing armies and mapped territory. Corneille's contrast of "place" and "State" might be seen as a synechdoche for the entire geographical, political, psychological and social realignment that marks France after the wars of religion—a realignment whose emblems might include the country villa of Richelieu or the new topography of Paris under Henri IV, with its Palais Royal, its Place des Vosges, and its Pont Neuf.

Nor is this realignment merely geographical or chorographic. In the preface to his book *The Hero*, one of the most important manuals of comportment of the seventeenth century, the Spanish Jesuit Baltasar Gracián tells his reader that learning to survive at court involves "not political reason or economic reason, but a reason of state of yourself."[8]

---

7. I cite and translate from André Stegmann's edition of Corneille's *Oeuvres complètes* (Paris: L'Intégrale, 1963), lines 1405–07.

8. "Aquí tendrás una no política ni aun económica, sino una razón de estado de ti mismo," my translation from Baltasar Gracián, *Obras Completas*, ed. Arturo del Hoyo (Madrid: Aguilar, 1960), 6. Gracián's works were widely circulated in France in translations by Amelot de la Houssaie.

Gracián projects the rational direction of the state onto the individual subject. In this formulation the self is a space, a territory that can be conquered and structured according to the same rules used by the state to conquer its subjects and enemies. But Gracián's very vocabulary suggests that the rational techniques of statecraft can be appropriated by the subject and turned back against domination, that the prudent man is defined by a political logic that he can nonetheless use for his own ends. The subject, too, is a state. Neither the Renaissance notion that the self is a mere microcosmic reflection of the universe, nor yet the model of the private Cartesian subject, Gracián's formulation suggests a complex interrelationship between an unsettled subjectivity and political power, between self-representation and the brute violence of pure force.[9]

The topographical concerns of Corneille, Gracián, and, more distantly, Montaigne (whose monstrous child, it should be recalled, suggests the body of France) thus refer to both a geographical struggle (the consolidation of royal power for Corneille, the survival of the subject in the closed world of the court for Gracián) and a symbolic battle over the imaginary space that is culture itself. And it is here that the historical struggles of the late sixteenth and early seventeenth century link up with the methodological question of how contemporary cultural criticism might reconsider the Baroque. For as recent theorists of the politics of discourse have reminded us, the problem of discursive originality may be best understood as a problem of location, as a question of territoriality. The subject's struggle to speak is the struggle to forge a site for itself within the web of discourses in which it is caught, to create what Michel de Certeau calls "the fiction of one's own place."[10] It is this topographical impulse (much more than the concern with "metamorphosis" privileged by Rousset) that speaks most directly to

9. For a discussion which defines the perimeters of "Baroque" political action as, on the one hand, the mere representation of state power and, on the other hand, the violence of the originary "coup d'état," see "Pour une théorie 'Baroque' de l'action politique," Louis Marin's introduction to his edition of Gabriel Naudé's, *Considérations politiques sur les coups d'état* (Paris: Les Editions de Paris, 1989). On Gracián's "spatialization" of the self see the discussion of Vladimir Jankélevitch in *La Manière et l'occasion* (Paris: Editions du Seuil, 1980), 18ff. On the "fixed" or "settled" space of the "Classical" subject see Louis van Delft, "Moralistique et topographie: *Caractères* et *lieux* dans l'anthropologie classique," *Französiche Klassik*, ed. Fritz Nies and Karlheinz Stierle (Munich: Wilhelm Fink, 1985), 61–75.

10. Michel de Certeau, *The Practice of Everyday Life*, trans. Steven Rendall (Berkeley: University of California Press, 1988), 118. De Certeau's entire discussion of "Spatial Stories" is extremely suggestive in this regard.

the present moment, in which the thematics of temporality so dear to high modernism have begun to be replaced by new types of analysis concerned with problems of marginality.[11] In this context it may be most useful to imagine the Baroque as a series of exchanges (thematized in encounters of subjects and texts) between various types of representation—political, literary, historiographical, philosophical. These exchanges define the emergence of various material and imaginary sites (academies, salons, theaters, the folds of Leibnizian philosophy, the uncertain location of the Cartesian subject) that provide the terrain for the very invention of modernity. The essays in this volume explore this monstrous territory.

11. For discussions of the central importance of notions of space for postmodernism, see Fredric Jameson's essay "Postmodernism, or The Cultural Logic of Late Capitalism," *New Left Review* 146 (1984), 53–92, as well as the recent book by Edward W. Soja, *Postmodern Geographies: The Reassertion of Space in Critical Social Theory* (London: New Left Books, 1989).

I. Scenes of Writing

EDWIN M. DUVAL

The Place of the Present: Ronsard, Aubigné, and the "Misères de ce Temps"

To sixteenth-century Frenchmen the year 1562 appeared as the greatest turning point in the history of France. No event, with the possible exception of the Treaty of Troyes in 1420, had ever seemed so politically consequential as the outbreak of full-scale civil war on native soil. And no armed conflict—whether foreign war, feudal power struggle, or peasant revolt—had ever matched the horror of a fight to the death between compatriots, neighbors, and brothers. In 1562 the future, even the existence of the nation, seemed to hang in the balance.

In two of the best-known literary treatments of the civil war and its attendant "misères" Pierre de Ronsard and Agrippa d'Aubigné gave powerful expression to the sense of crisis universally associated with 1562. Their complete agreement on the importance of that single date is all the more remarkable for the fact that Ronsard's *Discours des misères de ce temps* and Aubigné's *Les Tragiques* are such radically different works written from such radically different perspectives, the first being an immediate Catholic response written and published in the heat of the moment in 1562, the second a Protestant epic elaborated much later and over a long period of time between 1577 and the publication dates of 1616 and 1623.

Just as remarkable, perhaps, is the way each of these two works deals with fundamental problems inherent in their common undertaking—those of representing and interpreting a single historical moment, and of forging some fictional perspective from which to view the always elusive present. In the following pages I would like to consider how Ronsard and Aubigné present and solve these problems of temporal perspective spatially, both through images of space and within

YFS 80, *Baroque Topographies,* ed. Timothy Hampton, © 1991 by Yale University.

the actual space of their poems. As I hope to suggest, *Les Tragiques* constitute a direct response to the *Discours* in this important respect. By reading it as such, we may begin to perceive more clearly the profound unity of this great "baroque" work, as well as the nature and meaning of its formal structure and double plot.

Before 1562 Ronsard's poetry radiated a supreme confidence in the future, founded on the conviction that history had entered its final, definitive stage. Now that the dark "Middle Ages" separating enlightened Modernity from radiant Antiquity were over and gone, civilization could resume its course as if the barbarian invasions had never occurred. And the accomplishments of the present—those humanist accomplishments that revived and rivaled those of Antiquity—seemed destined to live on forever in a kind of infinite moment of classical stasis.

We sense this attitude clearly in the "Ode à Michel de L'Hospital" (1552), which traces the history of poetry from the first prophetic utterances to the writing of the ode itself, and in the "Hymne de la Justice" (1555), which traces the history of justice from the beginning of the Golden Age in the reign of Saturn to the beginning of a new Golden Age in the reign of Henri II. Both poems follow the basic scheme of a return to original purity and perfection after an intervening period of corruption and chaos. And both end abruptly in the present with untroubled, infinite vistas on the future. The Muses, like Astraea, have returned to France after their long, "medieval" exile, this time to stay for good. The new culture of the present, like the poems through which Ronsard gives it expression, is to be *aere perennius*, more lasting than bronze.[1]

This naïve confidence in the permanence of the new Golden Age was shattered forever with the massacre at Vassy on 1 March 1562. The *Discours*, written within weeks of that event, expresses with unprecedented urgency Ronsard's new-found, shocked awareness that the present is in fact an extremely precarious moment and that another descent into postclassical chaos may already be imminent.

The stated purpose of the *Discours* is to exhort the queen mother,

1. The edition of Ronsard used throughout these pages is Pierre de Ronsard, *Oeuvres complètes*, ed. Paul Laumonier (completed by I. Silver and R. Lebègue), 20 vols., STFM (Paris: Hachette-Droz-Didier, 1914–75). Works referred to here are: "Ode à Michel de L'Hospital" (vol. 3, 118–63), "Hymne de la justice" (vol. 8, 47–72), "Discours des misères de ce temps" (vol. 11, 19–32), "Continuation du discours des misères de ce temps" (vol. 11, 35–60), and "Remonstrance au peuple de France" (vol. 11, 65–106).

All translations from French and Latin into English are mine.

Catherine of Medici, to save the French ship of state, which is at this
very moment ("en ce temps") so battered by seditious winds that it is in
imminent danger of sinking (43–50). The queen must do this not only
by seizing the helm with a firm hand (48–50) but by imposing her
authority (54 and 210) in such a way as to quell the storm itself (51–54
and 197–212). Framed by this exhortation to act (25–54 and 197–
212)—which is itself framed by parallel passages concerned with
God's providential role in history (1–24 and 213–36)—the main body
of the poem fulfills the promise of its title by discoursing at length on
the "misères de ce temps." Ronsard does not describe these miseries in
any detail, of course, because his intended readers are firsthand witnesses and participants in the events of 1562. His purpose is rather to
impress upon his contemporaries the momentousness of the moment.
This he does in several ways—once within each of the two separate
parts of the poem, and yet again in the structure of the poem as a whole.

The first half of the framed poem represents the present moment as
a historical focal point on which all eyes, past and future, are fixed. All
the kings and generals of past history are horrified to look from beyond
the grave upon the present and see how we are destroying with our own
hands the realm they defended with their blood and bequeathed to us
as a rich inheritance (54–86):

> Ha que diront là bas soubs les tombes poudreuses
> De tant de vaillans Roys les ames genereuses!
> . . . .
> Que diront tant de Ducs, et tant d'hommes guerriers
> Qui sont morts d'une playe au combat les premiers,
> Et pour France ont souffert tant de labeurs extremes,
> La voyant aujourd'huy destruite par nous mesmes?
>
> [55–64]
>
> Oh! what will the noble souls of all those valiant
> kings say, down there below their dusty tombs? . . .
> What will all those generals and warriors say, who died
> first in battle and suffered so many hardships for
> France, seeing her today destroyed by us?

Similarly, all future generations will look back with horror on the
"history of our time" and see how we have brought down the scepter of
France (115–26):

> De quel front, de quel oeil, ô siecles inconstans!
> Pourront-ils regarder l'histoire de ce temps!

> En lisant que l'honneur, et le sceptre de France
> Qui depuis si long age avoit pris accroissance,
> Par une Opinion nourrice des combats,
> Comme une grande roche, est bronché contre bas.
>
> [121–26]

With what countenance, with what eyes, ô mutable age, will they look
on the history of this time, when they read that the honor and the
scepter of France, which had grown ever greater over the ages, was
brought tumbling down like an enormous rock by an Opinion, mother
of strife.

Only we of the present—we who are living under the fixed gaze of
all past and future generations at the very focal point of all history—do
not see ourselves (87–114):

> C'est grand cas que nos yeux sont si plains d'une nue,
> Qu'ils ne cognoissent pas nostre perte avenue.
>
> [87–88]

Our eyes are so befogged that they cannot see that our ruin is at hand.

This blindness is all the more scandalous because ancient signs and
prophecies (95–106) and recent climatic irregularities (107–14) had
predicted that the year 1562—"l'an soixante et deux" (97)—would
bring calamity to the French. All in vain, for even now that the foretold
disaster has befallen us, we "see without seeing":

> Nous sommes accablés d'ignorance si forte,
> Et liés d'un sommeil si paresseux, de sorte
> Que nostre esprit ne sent le malheur qui nous poingt,
> Et voyans nostre mal nous ne le voyons point.
>
> [91–94]

We are weighed down by such ignorance, immobilized by such sloth,
that we do not feel the pricks of our own misfortune, and seeing our ills
we do not see them at all.

The year 1562, represented at the center of this panoramic review of
past, present, and future observers of France, is both the central point
and the blind spot of history, known to all times except to itself.

The first part of the poem ends as Ronsard, having deplored our
blindness and exhorted today's historians to record the "monstrous
history of our time" for future readers to behold (115–20), appears
ready to reveal the history of our own calamity to us. But here at the

midpoint of the poem a curious thing happens. Rather than proceeding as promised in the historical mode to narrate the events of 1562, Ronsard shifts abruptly to a poetical, fictional mode to narrate the origin and cause of these events.

The second half of the poem begins with a mythological narrative transposed directly from Virgil's famous allegory of "Fama" ["Rumor"] in Book IV of the *Aeneid* (4.173–97). To punish mortals for their presumptuous curiosity about divine things (127–30 and 153–54), Jupiter sent them a terrible monster called "Opinion," which confused the minds of theologians with contradictory passages of Scripture and then proceeded to set France at war with herself, arming brother against brother, wife against husband in a bloody free-for-all over faith (127–66). The meaning of the allegory is obvious and predictable: our civil war, like the heresy over which it is being fought, results from the presumptuous arrogation of authority by unauthorized individuals. But the use of Virgilian allegory to express this idea is itself highly significant. It bestows upon the events of the present a literally epic magnitude.[2]

When Ronsard goes on to evoke at last the pandemic lawlessness and iniquity unleashed in France by Opinion (155–96), he does so not as a chronicler of our times but once again in a poetical mode, in terms borrowed this time from Ovid's famous description of the Iron Age in Book I of the *Metamorphoses* (1.128–50; cf., especially *D* 159–66 and *M* 1.142–48, *D* 175–78 and *M* 1.129–31, *D* 182–84 and *M* 149–50). Contrary to his intimations in the "Hymne de Justice" of a definitive return of Astraea and the Golden Age, Ronsard here laments, following Ovid, that

> Au ciel est revollée, et Justice, et Raison,
> Et en leur place helas! regne le brigandage,
> La force, les cousteaux, le sang et le carnage.
> [182–84; cf., *Metamorphoses* 1.129–31 and 149–50]

---

2. These intimations of an epic dimension are reinforced by two extended "Homeric" similes, one placed at the end of the "epic" half of the framed poem (191–96), the other immediately after it at the beginning of the concluding frame (199–212).

Ronsard took up the allegory of Opinion again the following year in the *Remonstrance au peuple de France,* treating the figure somewhat differently. Here Opinion pronounces a fine prosopopeia to her "son" Luther and sows the seeds of war by slipping a serpent into the folds of Luther's robe. Her words and gestures imitate exactly those by which Allecto starts the war for Latium in Book VII of the *Aeneid* (cf., *Remonstrance* 235–356 and *Aeneid* 7.341–434).

> Back to heaven Justice and Reason have flown, and in their place, alas!
> reign pillage, violence, knives, blood, and slaughter.

The Golden Age so recently restored by humanism may already have
degenerated irreparably into Iron once again. Indeed the only difference between the first Iron Age and the new one is that the classical
notion of filial piety, which Ovid linked to Astraea-justice, is replaced
by a monarchist's notion of authority, which Ronsard links to justice
and reason. Thus the famous tag "Victa iacet pietas" ["piety lies vanquished"] in Ovid (1.149) becomes "Morte est l'autorité" ["authority is
dead"] in Ronsard (175).

It is on this grim note—"Ainsi la France court en armes di-
visée, / Depuis que la *raison* n'est plus *autorisée*" (195–96; my emphasis) [Thus France runs headlong, divided and armed, since reason is
no longer subject to authority].—that the second half of the framed
poem ends, allowing Ronsard to return to the frame by exhorting
Catherine of Medici once again to end discord in France by exerting her
"authority" (209–12).

The two parallel parts of Ronsard's poem buttress and give urgency
to its framing call to action by pointing to the crucial importance of
"this time" in a number of mutually reinforcing ways. The first part
shows us that the present is a focal point of history and indeed a kind of
pivot on which the entire history of France will eventually be seen to
have turned. The second part intimates that the events of today are
literally epic events, similar in nature and equal in magnitude to those
narrated in the *Aeneid* and the *Metamorphoses,* and suggests intertex-
tually through Ovid that they may even mark the beginning of a new
Iron Age. But most significantly, perhaps, the two parts of the poem
work together to imitate, spatially, what each one separately suggests,
for the whole poem hinges at the center, highlighting by its central
disjunction between history and epic the pivotal moment, the critical
blind spot of history, that is now.

Rather than filling the gap at the center with a full account of the
events of 1562, the poem contains, and even constitutes, a powerful
monition that those events, which we see without seeing, are in fact a
kind of fulcrum, and that we in 1562 are perched on a razor's edge,
teetering on the brink of the abyss. Whether our newly regained Gold-
en Age of arts, letters, and laws is to continue, or whether we are to be
plunged once again into an Iron Age of gothic darkness, depends on
God, on the Queen, and on us . . . *now.*

Agrippa d'Aubigné grew up obsessed with Ronsard. His earliest datable work, "Vers faits à seiz' ans" [Lines written at age sixteen], is a short poem in the style of Ronsard expressing unabashed envy for Ronsard's poetic gifts and reputation; his youthful collection of love poems, Le Printemps [Spring], written when he was about twenty, explicitly rivals Ronsard's Amours and Odes and is inspired, according to the poems themselves, by the niece of Ronsard's Cassandre; and his letters written in old age contain proud recollections of distant meetings with the great master.[3]

Yet by religion, politics, and temperament, Aubigné was Ronsard's opposite, and this opposition made his relation to the master extremely complex. As a born Huguenot and civil warrior he was condemned in advance by the author of the Discours, and undoubtedly shared his coreligionists' well-documented sentiment that the Discours and its sequels remained, even years after their first publication, extremely powerful and effective—and therefore satanically pernicious—pieces of rhetoric. But as a brilliant poet and longtime emulator of Ronsard, Aubigné, unlike most of his coreligionists, was able to respond in kind.

To a far greater degree than is commonly realized, Les Tragiques are Aubigné's direct Protestant response to the polemical poems of his Catholic mentor and idol, Ronsard. A crucial aspect of this response is the way Aubigné adopts and transforms Ronsard's unique representation of 1562 and of the historical present. Aubigné, in effect, appropriates Ronsard's poem, adopting and elaborating the strategy of the Discours in such a way as to reveal both Ronsard's errors of interpretation and the true meaning of 1562.[4]

Of course, Aubigné's perspective on 1562 differs from Ronsard's not only ideologically but temporally, for having been born the year Ronsard published his first Amours (1552) Aubigné was only ten in the critical year of the Discours. By the time he began writing Les Tra-

3. Aubigné is quoted throughout these pages in the Pléiade edition of the Oeuvres, ed. Henri Weber, Jacques Bailbé, and Marguerite Soulié (Paris: Gallimard, 1969). For Aubigné's references to Ronsard alluded to here, see, in this edition, "Vers faits à seiz' ans" (319); Le Printemps: L'Hécatombe à Diane, 5 (249); and "Lettres touchant quelques poincts de diverses sciences," 11 (860). See also in the same edition, Le Printemps: Odes, 13 (303); Les Tragiques, "Aux lecteurs" (5–6); and Méditations sur les pseaumes, "Préface, l'autheur au lecteur" (494).

4. Les Tragiques respond directly and in detail to Ronsard's other polemical poems of 1562–63 as well, most notably to the Continuation du discours, written later in 1562 (cf., e.g., Les Tragiques 2.19–20 and Continuation 5–6, and below, note 7). But such considerations lie well beyond the scope of the present study.

giques the even more memorable year of the Saint Bartholomew's day massacre, 1572, was already a date in the historical past. Nevertheless, *Les Tragiques* deliberately maintain the pivotal importance attributed by Ronsard to the year 1562.

The principal plot of *Les Tragiques*, narrated in Books III, IV, and V, takes place entirely within the last moments before the outbreak of civil war in 1562. Moved by the complaints of Justice, Piety, Peace, and all the angels, by the arrival in droves of the souls of martyred Huguenots, and by the prayers of those still living (3.33–122), God decides to visit earth and see with his own eyes how a corrupt system of justice is condemning and executing his elect (Books III and IV). Returning to heaven, wroth at what he has seen but assured of the steadfastness unto death of his "witnesses," he allows Satan to put the faithful to an even greater test by granting them success in arms, thus tempting them to put their faith in princes and in their own resources rather than in God alone (Book V). The three central books of *Les Tragiques* thus narrate at length, in an epic mode and from a divine perspective, the precise historical turning point whose pivotal nature and epic dimension Ronsard's poem had only hinted at.

Les Tragiques maintain Ronsard's scheme of representation as well, portraying both the pivotal year of history (1562) and the new historical present (1577) in a way imitated directly from the *Discours*, but recasting the scheme so as to give it an entirely different meaning. This recasting takes place twice, on two separate levels: once within Book I for the representation of "this time," and again in the articulation of the epic as a whole for the representation of 1562.

In Book I ("Misères"), Aubigné in effect rewrites the *Discours des misères de ce temps* from the perspective of 1577, describing at great length what Ronsard had only hinted at. Or rather, he explodes the *Discours* by cramming into the empty space at the center a thousand lines of energetic description, replacing Ronsard's pivotal, punctual blind spot with gruesome scenes witnessed over the fifteen years that have elapsed since 1562.[5] It is as though Aubigné had answered Ronsard's call near the midpoint of the *Discours:*

> O toy historien, qui d'ancre non menteuse
> Escrits de nostre temps l'histoire monstrueuse,

---

5. Aubigné goes out of his way to establish the present of Misères" as being exactly fifteen years after the crucial date of 1562. He states in the prose introduction (4) that *Les Tragiques* were begun during the wars of 1577 ("aux guerres de septante et sept"), and

Raconte à nos enfans tout ce malheur fatal,
Afin qu'en te lisant ils pleurent nostre mal.

[115–18]

O historian, you who write with unadulterated ink the monstrous
history of our time, tell our children the whole story of this baneful
disaster so that reading you, they will weep for our woe.

Yet as he does this, Aubigné repeats the articulation of Ronsard's
poem exactly, for at the midpoint of the book the poet concludes his
lurid account of the historical present to take up a new question:

Voila le front hideux de nos calamitez,
La vengeance des cieux justement despitez.
Comme par force l'oeil se destourne à ces choses,
Retournons les esprits pour en toucher les causes.

[1.679–82][6]

This is the hideous face of our calamity, the vengeance of a justly angry
heaven. Despite itself the eye turns away from these things. Let us
therefore direct our thoughts elsewhere to consider their causes.

Thus exactly like the *Discours,* "Misères" hinges at the center, dividing into two equal sections, the first of which is devoted to the cata-
strophic present, the second to the causes of our present miseries. Each
section, moreover, contains a direct response to its corresponding part
in Ronsard.

The first half of "Misères" is organized in a manner vaguely reminiscent of Ronsard's play of historical perspectives in the first half of
the *Discours:* purely symbolic representations of France (1.97–190 and
1.609–78) frame a "general discours," or survey of all estates and
classes of French people from royalty to urban bourgeoisie to rural

---

insists in two separate passages of Book I that the miseries of "today" (1.437, 581, 1097,
1121) have now lasted for "fifteen years" (1.267–69 and 1.1042–44).

The datable scenes described in Book I do in fact tend to fall within this fifteen-year
period: the "tragic story" witnessed by the poet at Montmoreau during the third war
(1569: 1.367–436), the aftermath of the battle of Montcontour (1569: 1.463–94),
Aubigné's duel (1572: 1.1067–78), the death of the Cardinal de Lorraine (1574: 1.1005),
etc. Only the gruesome case of maternal cannibalism (1.495–562) is generally identified
by commentators as having taken place much later, at the siege of Paris (1590). But such
acts were also attested during the siege of Sancerre, which occurred in 1573.

6. The first two lines quoted here are repeated almost verbatim at the end of the long
section introduced here, near the end of the book (1.1207–08). The effect of this echo is to
make the articulation of the main body of "Misères" into two separate sections even
more apparent.

peasantry and back to royalty (1.191–366 and 1.563–608), which is interrupted at the center by a description of man-made famine (1.437–94) flanked by two unforgettable scenes of individual suffering wrought by starvation (1.367–436 and 1.495–562). At the focal point of this symmetrical construct, and in the blank place left at the focus of Ronsard's fixed gaze of past and future history, Aubigné lodges the most specific, concrete representations of "misères" imaginable, portraits of starving, dying mothers who either are devoured by death (1.414–27 and 1.435–36) or devour their own children (1.549–60)— images that reflect the frame's general, symbolic image of France as an afflicted mother devoured by her children (cf., 1.97–98 and 1.423–24).[7] Thus Aubigné focuses on the present moment as Ronsard had done but in a far more vivid way, moving from the abstract and general to the concrete and particular as his gaze hones in from the periphery to the center of the passage.

Correspondences between the second half of "Misères" and the second half of the *Discours* are more specific and direct. Exactly like Ronsard, Aubigné shifts abruptly here from a historical to an allegorical mode as he turns from "misères" to "causes." Exactly like Ronsard, he narrates a myth of sin and divine punishment. The two narrations are exactly parallel, moreover, but small differences between them are crucial. In place of Ronsard's pagan, Virgilian allegory of Jupiter and Opinion, we find a biblical, prophetic allegory about an Old Testament-style God and the "new scourge" he visited on a rebellious nation. To punish France for its pride, superstition, and worship of idols (i.e., its obstinate catholicism), God sent the French two murderous spirits formed of the "excrements of hell," distilled into two baleful "new comets," and then incarnated in two vicious bodies to wreak even more havoc on France than the comets that bring plague, famine, and war. These infernal spirits are none other than Catherine of Medici and her henchman-lover, Charles the Cardinal of Lorraine.

In the place of Ronsard's epic Opinion, in other words, Aubigné substitutes the dedicatee of Ronsard's *Discours*.[8] What Ronsard had

7. Aubigné's symbolic image of France as a "mere affligee" (97) is itself borrowed in part from Ronsard's *Continuation du discours*, which ends with the allegorical description of France as a "poor woman stricken with death" and a "mother of so many kings" (319–34 and following). Aubigné thus gives a potent, concrete reality to what for Ronsard had been merely a symbolic, literary device.

8. The Cardinal of Lorraine does not figure in Ronsard's polemical poems, but was the dedicatee and hero of the *Hymne de la Justice* to which Aubigné also responded in *Les Tragiques*, most notably in Book III ("La Chambre dorée").

thought was the remedy for the crisis of 1562 proves in retrospect to have been precisely what made 1562 everything Ronsard feared it might be. Catherine *did* intervene at the critical pivot of French history as Ronsard had exhorted her to do—not as a vicar of God, but rather as the chosen instrument of God's wrath against the French, the scourge that God will throw into the fire once it has served its purpose (1.802–04). Instead of saving the French from one another she decimated the nobility of France, not only in war but even in time of peace, thanks to her Machiavellian invention of the duel and the Italian "point of honor" (1.1045–66). Instead of quelling civil discord by reconciling the two sides she deliberately played both sides against each other so that she might reign supreme in the middle (1.755–62 and 1.771–82). The result of her intervention has been not a return to Ronsard's threatened Golden Age but fifteen years of Iron Age hell, clearly signaled as such at the midpoint of the book through an adaptation of the same Ovidian lines on the flight of Astraea that had served Ronsard in petitioning Catherine's intervention at the end of the *Discours* (1.692–95; cf., *Metamorphoses* 1.149–50 and *Discours* 175–78 and 182–84).

Poor Ronsard got his history wrong. His solution to the crisis of 1562 is precisely what precipitated the crisis in the first place; his defender of the new Golden Age was the providential agent of the new Iron Age. By intervening, Catherine merely fulfilled the implications of the scheme Ronsard had invented to exhort her to intervene.

Having adapted Ronsard's scheme of temporal representation to the new present of 1577 in "Misères" to reveal the historical errors of the *Discours,* Aubigné recasts that same scheme once again on the much larger scale of the whole epic, this time to reveal the true meaning of Ronsard's present of 1562. It is a remarkable if insufficiently considered fact that this long historical epic hinges, like the *Discours,* at its precise midpoint, and that the point around which it turns is the pivotal date of the *Discours,* 1562.

The central Book IV of *Les Tragiques* ("Feux") is a martyrological sampler designed to avoid invidious human distinctions among God's elect by including random, representative martyrdoms of every sex, estate, and age (4.19–22 and 4.1285–1318). Indeed, the book follows no apparent temporal, sociological, or logical sequence as it wanders from country to country, nationality to nationality in its desultory survey of religious sadism and fortitude. Yet despite this deliberate principle of evenhanded randomness, the book cleaves neatly into two distinct sections of exactly equal length (710 lines each), and draws attention to the division by means of corresponding introductions placed at the beginning of each half:

> Voici marcher de rang par la porte doree,
> L'enseigne d'Israel dans le ciel arboree,
> Les vainqueurs de Sion . . .

[4.1–3]

Behold, marching arrayed in columns through the golden gate, the victors of Zion, bearing high the banner of Israel.

> Tels furent de ce siecle en Sion les agneaux,
> Armez de la priere et non point des couteaux:
> Voici un autre temps, quand des pleurs et des larmes
> Israël irrité courut aux justes armes.

[4.711–14]

Such were the lambs of this age in Zion, armed with prayer, not with knives. Behold now another time, when an angry Israel left weeping and tears to rush to righteous arms.

The division is highlighted even further by the fact that the midpoint is preceded and followed by strictly parallel martyrs' speeches whose common theme is the necessity of choosing between two mutually exclusive alternatives of belief or action (cf., especially 4.699–706 and 4.751–58). Similar parallels between corresponding passages extend outward from the center through every book of *Les Tragiques*, thus infusing the entire epic with a large-scale symmetry around its central, pivotal point.

As the transition between the two halves of the book and the epic make plain, the "other time" introduced at the midpoint is one in which "Israel" (i.e., the Protestant elect) resorted to "just arms," so that the irons of war ("fers") replaced the fires of martyrdom ("feux") as the principal means of defending the true faith (4.714–15). The pivot around which "Feux" and *Les Tragiques* turn is thus clearly designated as the precise moment at which the civil wars began. And indeed the dozens of martyrdoms mentioned in random order in the first half of the book all took place before 1562; those few mentioned in the second half all took place after 1562.[9] *Les Tragiques*, like the *Discours*, thus

9. The latest martyrdom mentioned in the first half is that of Anne du Bourg on 23 December 1559 (4.543–602). The earliest mentioned in the second half are those of Richard de Gastine and his father and uncle on 30 June 1569 (4.719–996).

hinges around the crisis of 1562. Aubigné has given literally epic proportions to Ronsard's representation of a single, critical moment on which all history turns.

But for Aubigné, the pivotal crisis is no longer an unrepresentable blind spot between a known past and an unknown future. The passage of fifteen years and divine illumination allow Aubigné to see clearly and interpret in perspective what Ronsard himself could only "see without seeing," from within. Contrary to what Ronsard's spatial representation of a historical turning point poised between history and epic suggested, 1562 was not a crossroads at which free human action could determine the future course of French history. By situating the same historical turning point midway between "Misères" and "Jugement," between "Princes" and "Vengeances," Aubigné suggests that 1562 was, on the contrary, a predetermined moment in a much larger, symmetrical, divinely ordered scheme, a turning point fixed from the beginning between the suffering of the just and the triumph of the wicked in this world and the eschatological vindication of the persecuted and retribution of the persecutors in the next. No human intervention could have saved France in 1562, least of all Catherine of Medici, for 1562 was the year that Catherine of Medici, acting not as a free agent but as an instrument in the hands of a providential God, was destined from the beginning to draw up the lines between the sheep and the goats, in preparation for Christ's final, definitive judgment.

The space of Aubigné's poem and the space of Ronsard's poem highlight the same critical moment at the center, but by the arrangement of parts around the center, Aubigné succeeds in making the pivotal moment of 1562 mean precisely the opposite of what it had meant in the *Discours*.

It is not only hindsight and the constantly reiterated claim to divine inspiration that affords Aubigné the advantage of his perspective on 1562. Throughout the poem he develops the fiction that what allows him to perceive the true nature, place, and meaning of both 1562 and the contemporaneous present is less a temporal remove from his subject than a spatial remove. Taking his cue once again directly from Ronsard, Aubigné establishes two privileged places far from the scene of contemporary events from which he is able to view them clearly.

Adapting in his turn Ovid's famous lines on the Iron Age at the pivotal midpoint of "Misères," Aubigné states: "Au ciel estoit bannie en pleurant la justice, / L'Eglise au sec desert, la verité apres." (1.694–

95) [To heaven was banished Justice in tears, The Church to the arid desert, followed by Truth].

These lines are far more significant than they might first appear, for the dispersion they describe is scrupulously maintained throughout the entire epic. Strictly parallel passages in Books II and III, in particular, elaborate at length on the banishment of Truth to the desert (2.162–82) and the banishment of Justice to heaven (3.33–54). More important, the dispersion described here forms the basis for the entire secondary plot of *Les Tragiques*, according to which the poet himself follows Truth, the Church, and Justice to their respective places of exile outside France, and from these privileged vantage points looks back upon the Iron Age of our time to see them and describe them, for the first time, as they truly are.

In Book II ("Princes"), before revealing the revolting truth about France's royal house and about the three degenerate sons of Catherine of Medici in particular, Aubigné clearly sets forth the circumstances that allow him to do so (2.1–193). For many years abject "fear" (2.27–37) had prevented him from speaking the "truth" (2.22, 23, 25, 32, 45, 156, 162) about a court where vice is concealed and maintained by the flattering lies of poets and courtisans (2.85–161; see also 2:819–62). But recently he overcame this fear (2.38–58) when, banished to the desert from the court, he came upon Truth in her exile, "banished, wounded and mutilated . . . in the desert" (2.162–63). Swooning at the sight of her, he found the courage at last to present her whole to his readers, and then to die (2.162–93). "La voici" [here she is], he exclaims triumphantly from his desert exile, just before launching into the most appalling description of the royal court imaginable (2.173).

At the end of the book (2.1099–1486), Aubigné completes this indirect autobiographical narrative with the allegorical fable of an ingenuous young man, presumably himself many years earlier, confused and perplexed by his first experiences in a vicious court. Fortune and Virtue appear to him in a vision, the first promising him wealth and prestige at court, the second true honor won through a life of hardship in the abode of Necessity. Virtue presumably wins the debate, for Aubigné, now far from the court, ends the book with dire warnings of damnation for all who remain there. Virtue's victory was not immediate, however, for in Book VI ("Vengeances") the poet tells us once again that for many years "fear" and reverence for kings at court kept him silent about the "truth," and that only recently he has found the "courage" to wage war against "stinking Nineva" by revealing how God has always punished the powerful persecutors of his elect (6.99–140, especially, 119–24).

This much of the secondary plot is revealed proleptically in the verse Preface that precedes the epic. Here the anonymous poet of *Les Tragiques* claims to have written his work in voluntary exile (3, 12, 85), in the desert (168, 169; cf., 30, 104–05, 343), where he found both Truth, the "daughter of heaven," and the Church (115–44, 163–68, 187–92). The entire preface is in fact predicated on a systematic opposition between the "logis de la verité" ["abode of truth"] (120) in the desert and the "logis de la peur" [abode of fear] (112) in the fastuous courts of the Valois kings. The poet could not have exposed the real truth about the miseries of France and their causes unless he had fled the craven courts of princes, from which fear had banished Truth, to join Truth and the Church in exile in the desert (cf., 97–132 and 337–54). Only there, exiled with the Church and working in direct collaboration with Truth herself (157–68), could the poet write and publish a work that reveals the truth and "heaven's secrets" (362). And indeed the title page of the original edition of *Les Tragiques* identifies its place of publication as the "dezert" and its author as "L.B.D.D.," "Le Bouc Du Désert" ["The Desert Goat"], thus confirming in advance the part of the secondary plot narrated in Books II and VI.

The second privileged vantage point from which *Les Tragiques* could be written was heaven. Taking up once again the pivotal passage of "Misères"—"Au ciel estoit bannie en pleurant la justice / L'Eglise au sec desert, la verité apres" (1.694–95)—Aubigné begins Book III ("La Chambre dorée") by narrating the arrival of Justice, now a sweating, panting fugitive from earth, at the celestial Palace of God (3.33–54). Exactly like "banished" Truth, "fugitive" Justice arrives "wounded and mutilated" to her place of exile (3.34–35 and 45–46; cf., 2.162–63). And exactly as the poet had presented Truth to his readers, Justice presents herself, in the third person, to God: "La voici" (3.45; cf., 2.173).

This arrival is the event that sets in motion the principal plot of *Les Tragiques* (see above, p. 20). But near the end of this long central narration Aubigné takes up once again the thread of his secondary plot to narrate the circumstances that have allowed him to know and to write what he has written. At the conclusion of the section of Book V ("Fers") devoted to the Saint Bartholomew's day massacre, the poet relates his own experience in the days following August 24 1572. For seven hours his body lay wounded and senseless at Talcy while his spirit, like Saul-Paul's on the road to Damascus, ascended to heaven where it beheld celestial "tableaux" and astral signs that revolve around the axis of the universe and represent all past, present, and future episodes in the Wars of Religion, from 1 March and 19 December 1562 (the massacre of Vassy [5.545–84] and the battle of Dreux [5.363–80]) to 1666 (Last Judgment [5.1413–16]).[10] Having seen from the perspective of God and his angels the whole panoramic history of the civil wars from beginning to end, Aubigné's spirit may rejoin his body, not only to continue the fight but, like John on Patmos, to write what he has seen in a book of revelation (5.1417–26; cf., Rev 1.9–11 and 22.6–12).

This visit is what allows Aubigné to reveal "heaven's high secrets" (5.1200, 1246, 1424), not only by narrating the principal plot of God's providential role in the events of 1562 and prophecying the events of the future but, more important, by interpreting all past, present, and future calamities in the context of the larger scheme of history and of divine justice. For by ascending in the spirit to heaven the poet did not simply accede to a divine vantage point from which to view the injustices perpetrated here below. He actually visited the place of exile where Justice herself, that other daughter of God banished from the Iron Age world, now resides in person, and from which she will not return again until the Last Day, when Christ the just judge will come again to apportion Justice to God's creatures, once and for all (cf., 3.821–84 and 7.661–1218).

And thus it is that we have *Les Tragiques*. Aubigné knows the vices of princes because he, like Ronsard, spent many years at court and saw with his own eyes its secret sins. But Ronsard could not tell what he knew because he remained at court, writing in and for that abode of fear from which Truth had been banished. Aubigné, on the contrary, fled to the desert where he found Truth in her exile and can now, with her assistance, write in a book what he has seen. Similarly, Aubigné

10 It is interesting to contrast this section of "Fers" with the first half of the *Discours*. Whereas the present in Ronsard is represented as the blind spot of history and the focal point of all past and future gazes, the everadvancing present in Aubigné is represented as the precise point in the vault of heaven, the zenith, at which rising astral signs are replaced by fully comprehensible paintings. And whereas Ronsard's contemporaries are blind to themselves and to their situation, Aubigné's dead coreligionists arrive in heaven to see their own deaths clearly and freshly represented (see, e.g., 5.301–06, 691–704 and 831–36). Thanks to the tableaux, the martyred and massacred are entirely present unto themselves, and know themselves and their present perfectly.

knows the horrors of civil war because he spent years on the battlefield and experienced its tragedies firsthand. But even if Ronsard had seen what Aubigné has seen, he could not have known where justice lay in the crimes of the present because he remained in a world literally abandoned by Justice. Aubigné can interpret what he has seen of the miseries of our time because he once left this Iron Age world of misery and injustice to find Justice herself exiled in God's own tribunal, his celestial "palais de justice."

In short, if the view from the desert is what allows Aubigné to observe and represent the *Truth* about the present "misères" and their causes, the view from heaven is what allows him to perceive and represent the place, the meaning, and the *Justice* of those same "misères" within the larger scheme of divine justice.

In its spatial organization, then, *Les Tragiques* mimic the *Discours* in such a way as to make 1562 signify precisely the opposite of what it had signified for Ronsard. And in its representation of space it authorizes its view of history by using Ronsard's own intimations of a new Iron Age to show that Ronsard was a prisoner not only of his time but of his place as well. He was quite literally in the wrong place at the wrong time, and therefore could either not know or not tell what Aubigné has revealed in the space of his own book.

Paradoxically, it is precisely because Ronsard was right in both his spatial representation of time and in his intimations of a new Iron Age in 1562 that Aubigné could transform Ronsard's blind spot of history into an epiphanic illumination, and precisely because Ronsard's Catholic faction was so overwhelmingly victorious in 1577 and subsequent years that Aubigné could transform the worst Protestant tragedies into a Protestant triumph. For by narrating a decentered poet's own exile and defeat in terms of the diaspora of Truth, Church, and Justice, *Les Tragiques* created both the textual space and the spatial paralax by which alone sixteenth-century Frenchmen might apprehend not only the meaning of 1562 but the place of their own present in history.

GISÈLE MATHIEU-CASTELLANI

The Poetics of Place: The Space of the Emblem (Sponde)

Etymology notwithstanding, there are no places in the commonplace, unless in those nowhere-places whose strictly codified description always takes on the value of a sign or a signal.[1] One thinks of the fine analyses of Curtius, and in particular those of the *locus amoenus*,[2] which plainly demonstrate how in antiquity and the Middle Ages the literary landscape copied not the real but an *already written copy* of the real: this is still true at least into the sixteenth and seventeenth centuries. If the places evoked in Renaissance poetry are quite different from those of baroque literature, which transforms the landscape by opening it up to the desolate, the funereal, the sinister, the macabre,[3] this in no way means that the poetics of place emerge from the rhetorical models conserved by each tradition of tone and genre, but only that the tradition of the commonplace modifies itself in the baroque, and annexes other traditions (notably that of the Italian *Disperata*). The baroque landscapes of an Aubigné or a Sponde, of a La Ceppède or a Chassignet, like the "libertine" landscape of Théophile, Saint-Amant

---

1. The value of a sign, since every object which is codified by the tradition of the commonplace receives a stable meaning, which must be deciphered without any "remainder"; the value of a signal, since each genre or subgenre has at its disposal a certain number of topoi which are sufficient to inscribe the text in one or another subgenre of the *Disperata*, etc.

2. E. R. Curtius, *La Littérature européenne et le Moyen Age latin* (Paris: Presses Universitaires de France, 1956), 226–47, passim.

3. On the natural backdrop and modifications of landscape, see my article "Orientations baroques", in *Les Thèmes amoureux dans la poésie française (1570–1600)* (Paris: Klincksieck, 1975), 349–97.

YFS 80, *Baroque Topographies,* ed. Timothy Hampton, © 1991 by Yale University.

or Tristan,[4] while perhaps seeming at first less "natural" than the Vendôme landscape of Ronsard or the Anjou setting of Du Bellay, simply say more explicitly that their components obey cultural codes; but neither group aims to photograph a "real" which would not be legible and intelligible.

Moreover the fact that a description of places obeys a topography, as that of people or characters obeys a prosopography or that of epochs a chronography, does not theoretically rule out the possibility of the concert of codes being exploded or realigned at the whim of the imaginary. Topography no more hinders the emergence of signifying networks than does any other commonplace tradition, and while particular utterances may remain relatively stable on a given cultural ground, their production bears the mark of singularity. In other words, without underestimating the weight of the tradition of commonplaces or the norms of rhetoric, one must consider, for every work, for every text, the poetics of place. And notably the "place" of the setting, its mode of construction, its structural situation, its function. The very notion of a *setting* must be questioned: is it no more than *ornatus*? a simple bonus of pleasure? or else a masked rhetorical figure?[5] a clue to be deciphered? And what if it were also the trace of an imaginary which projects its own fantasies as it evokes those nowhere-places, those places not shown on any map, any itinerary, where the relation of the subject to the world and to others is expressed?

REPRESENTING/SIGNIFYING

This possibility, one may object, is excluded for "old" (prenineteenth-century) poetry where all representation is oriented toward meaning, where in particular the representation of place always has the status of a deictic indication. Indeed.

All representation oscillates between presence and absence: "figure porte absence et présence" says Pascal. *To represent* is to put before the eyes, to allow to be seen, to put on a scene or a spectacle (and baroque art, moved by a theatrical sense of ostentation, is an effect of

4. See Odette de Mourgue's fine book *O Muse fuyante proie: essai sur la poésie de La Fontaine* (Paris: Corti, 1962), 13–36.
5. The enumeration of places and components of places, in Petrarch as in Ronsard, constitutes a figure of *amplificato*. The backdrop is a figure of metaphor in one place, elsewhere an allegory, still elsewhere a metonymy. The rhetorical status of place merits a separate study.

visualization), but it is also to stand in for an absent person or an absence; like the death mask which in funerary processions represented the deceased, like the heir taking the place of the deceased testator, that which represents always occupies the place of the dead. Doesn't representation always act upon signs, stand-ins, substitutes? It pretends to re-present (present all over again, present afresh) what can only be absent. Like those flowers of the poet, not found in any bouquet; like the body, rebelling against the status of sign; the "natural" landscape is never there where it is represented, in those words, in those letters which restore only a simulacrum, a fiction of it. The whole question would then be to know how—or rather why—the landscape of Ronsard *seems* "real" to the reader and "felt" by the speaker, while the baroque landscape is from the first perceived as "allegorical." Could it be that the rhetoric of one is more effective than that of the other? That one more skillfully combines the details, the slight "reality effects" which legitimate the description and present themselves as evidence of something seen/felt, while the other advertises signs as signs? Could it be that one lets us see, while the other lets us understand?

The case of Sponde is exemplary in this regard. Here in fact is writing (prose in the superb *Meditations sur les Psaumes*, verse in *Les Amours* and *l'Essay de quelques poesmes chrestiens*)[6] which shows off the emblematic status of representation: places or characters, animal, vegetable or mineral, they all "signify," like the beasts of medieval Bestiaries, all are emblems, designating a concept or a notion. The Emblem, whose success was affirmed everywhere in Europe after the publication in 1531 of the *Emblematum liber* of Alciati, imposed its ordered mode of composition: an inscription-motto or "device" fixing the referent (a notion or concept, a critical statement, or a sententious saying), an image-icon of variable rhetorical status (allegory, metaphor, symbol, or metonymy), and a versified gloss shedding light on the action of the players in the scene and their relation to the "title." Among these three little units correlated by the artifice of a *like,* the relations between text and "depiction" are hierarchised: the image is the *body,* the "words" are the *soul* of a composition which resorts to

6. We have A. Boase, the discoverer of Sponde, to thank for the edition of Sponde's *Oeuvres Littéraires* (Geneva: Droz, 1978). Unfortunately the texts were not established with all the necessary rigor, especially the *Amours,* which appeared posthumously at the end of the sixteenth and the beginning of the seventeenth centuries in collective "recueils."

the figural only in order to be more effective; the verses themselves are only an auxiliary to the process of communication, delighting the ear so as to touch the heart. At least, that is the intention! Working by metonymy, the emblem[7] designates synecdochally a notion or a concept: featured in the tripartite composition, it pretends to let us see something visible, while it lets us read something intelligible. There is nothing more abstract than the emblem, despite appearances. Unlike allegory, which metamorphoses a notion into a character—Jealousy, Death, Youth—the emblem transforms a character into an idea.[8] Dido-suicide or Phoenix-immortality.

Outside the emblem-books, composition of the emblematic type functions as a system of representation which establishes a model for discourse.[9] Thus the structure of Sponde's sonnets on love or death[10] belongs to this type of organization: an image (which is what the other parts are compared to), an inscription—a theme from the commonplace tradition—and a versified gloss. Here the "image" which fulfills the function of an *exemplum*, even if it borrows its codes from various intertexts, the Bible or legends, mythology or history, is always emblematic: the dominant attribute (so determined by the doxa) of any object, whether natural—animal, vegetable, mineral—or cultural—a mythic hero, a legendary city, an event or hero whose memory survives in chronicles—is to be deciphered in these poems as the sign of another "reality"—a reality of a notional or conceptual kind. Here Actaeon "signifies" *mutilation* and *tearing*, the Giants scaling the Heavens *hybris*, Rome or Carthage *the will to power*, Alexander or Caesar *ambition*, etc. Everything, down to the landscape, combines its natural signs (flowers faded by the sun's heat, snow melting in the spring, torrents drying up in the summer, waves breaking on the frothy river-bank) with the manifestations which affect it (storms and rain, wind and tempests, excessive heat or drought) so as to compose a tableau whose codes are fully readable, a metaphor of the microcosm.

It seems then that the poetics of place in Sponde's work can be reduced to rhetoric: there is not a single object in this dazzling land-

7. I have chosen to capitalize the word when it designates a form (bi-, tri-, or quadripartite composition), as opposed to the figure (of metonymy).

8. See Paul Zumthor, *Essai de poétique médiévale* (Paris: Seuil, 1972), 122–23.

9. For these emblematic compositions (in anatomical plates, for example), I refer the reader to my book *Emblèmes de la Mort* (Paris: Nizet, 1988).

10. In *L'Essay de quelques poemes chrestiens*, the *Stances de la Mort* are followed by the *Sonnets sur le mesme subject*, called here for convenience "Sonnets de la Mort."

scape which does not have the status of an *exemplum* in the service of persuasion, there is not a single feature which does not constitute a sign and cry out to be deciphered; landscape appears to be a protocol for reading the (mental) world—not allegorical, but emblematic. The visible as entirely readable, the readable as thoroughly intelligible. The place-*locus*, whether *amoenus* or other, would thus be nothing but a place-*topos*. The position of the demonstrator would be that of a director arranging his actors on a platform to catch the innocent spectator in the trap of fiction, as a victim of the referential illusion.

And yet if the reader says, before these scenes staged by persuasive rhetoric: "Yes, I know but still," if, beyond programmed signification (which finds its ultimate form in the stiffness of an ineffectual maxim), meaning continues to circulate, irreducible to the discourse of the gloss, if this letter-landscape breaks free by challenging the *sententia*, this is probably because the weight of the tradition of commonplaces and the artifice of sententious rhetoric are not enough to prevent the emergence of another speech, which constructs, next to or against the *exemplum*-landscape, an exemplary landscape, an interior landscape which is represented by rhythm. Let us turn to the last sonnet of the *Amours*:

> Les vents grondaient en l'air, les plus sombres nuages
> Nous dérobaient le jour pêle-mêle entassés
> Les abimes d'enfer étaient au ciel poussés
> La mer s'enflait des monts, et le monde d'orages:
>
> Quand je vis qu'un oiseau délaissant nos rivages
> S'envole au beau milieu de ses flots courroucés
> Y pose de son nid les fétus ramassés
> Et rapaise soudain ses écumeuses rages.
>
> L'amour m'en fit autant, et comme un Alcion
> L'autre jour se logea dedans ma passion
> Et combla de bonheur mon âme infortunée
>
> Après le trouble, en fin, il me donna la paix
> Mais le calme de mer n'est qu'une fois l'année
> Et celui de mon âme y sera pour jamais.[11]

11. The text given here differs slightly from that used by Boase. I have kept the reading offered in the collective *Recueils* which I have consulted (published by Raphaël du Petit Val: a copy at Aix dated 1599, with a 1597 privilege, an undated copy at Versailles in a factitious *recueil*, and a copy in Paris dated 1604): "des monts" in verse 4 instead of "de monts," and a different punctuation. The spelling has been modernized.

The winds rumbled in the air, the darkest clouds,
Heaped up pell-mell, were stealing the day from us,
The depths of Hell were pressed to the sky,
The sea was swollen with mountains and the world with storms,

When I saw that a bird, deserting our shores,
Flies to the very center of the angry waves,
Sets there the bundled straw of his nest,
And suddenly calms the foaming fury.

Love did as much to me, and like a Halcyon,
The other day took up residence in my passion
And filled my unfortunate soul with happiness.

After the agitation, finally, he gave me peace,
But the sea is calmed only once a year,
And my soul will be calm forever.

FROM MIMESIS TO SEMIOSIS

The sonnet's structure is modeled on emblematic composition: the
quatrains (Q) stand for the image-picture, the tercets (T) stand for the
gloss, while the "device" is included in the text: "après le trouble, la
paix" [after agitation, peace]. The organization of the lines, their contours clearly delineated by syntax, copies the explicit figure of sim-
ilarity (autant, comme) from the sonnet's conventional division into
two blocks (Q,T). By means of comparison, two objects belonging to
two distinct paradigms, the bird, love, are placed in a position of equivalence, the description of one serving as a model for the evocation of
the other, based on a dominant attribute which founds the analogy.
The relation of A (the bird) to B (the sea) is presented as similar to the
relation of A' (love) to B' (the soul). At the very last moment, a "correc-
tion" seems to bring an internal criticism to bear on these re-
semblances (Mais . . .), ruining the edifice of the comme.
    This descriptive operation is clearly that of the Emblem, selecting
the indirect path of analogy, and presenting a commonplace scene of
everyday life as the metaphor of another scene. The postulate common
to both compositions remains that of the correspondences between
microcosm and macrocosm, mirrors of each other in the symbolic
tradition. Two parallel sequences are thus put on a plane of semantic
equivalence; one (T) has the status of the thing compared, the other (Q)
what it is compared to; they have the same superficial narrative struc-

ture, producing two mirrored stories, one written in meteorological code, the other in metaphorical code, "a symbolic" rewriting based on the "remains" of mimesis (*se logea, trouble, paix*) [it took up residence, agitation, peace].

Structure itself produces effects: the descriptive operation metamorphoses the object "love" into an object from the natural world, subject to the cycle of seasons and meteorological accidents—all in spite of the final denial opposing the sea and the soul on one point. The first description, reread in light of the second, displays its emblematic character: no longer the mimesis of a natural event, seen only once, as the preterite indicated, by a privileged spectator, but a whole made up of coherent signs to be deciphered like so many clues. The anomaly— the curious change which comes over the temporal system in Q2: Quand je *vis* qu'un oiseau . . . / *S'envole* . . . / Y *pose* . . . / Et *rapaise* . . . [*When I saw that a bird* . . . / *Flies* . . . / *sets therein* / *and calms*]—signals that we are "leaving" the "historical" account in order to enter into the commentary, that the "witnessed" scene is atemporal. As in the Emblem and all the "peintures savantes" monumentalized by Père Menestrier in his *Philosophie des Images* in the seventeenth century, representation here is undertaken only in order to signify: the supposed *visible* or *seen* is of the order of the intelligible, the thing seen is (only) a sign, the "real" metaphor of the mental world. What seemed to depend on mimesis, the naked imitation of nature, belongs to semiosis, an inquiry into signs, which is ensnared from the start since they are pre-interpreted. Although the initial sequence has the status of an account accredited as a personal history, all the sources of information in the pseudoaccount reveal their functioning as clues: so many signs recounting another story. An allegorical tale, hiding beneath the *littera* (a meteorological phenomenon "explained" by mythology, the calm of the sea when the halcyons build their nests once a year) the *sententia*. At the same time description is invaded by metaphor, the landscape is anthropomorphized as soon as the properties of humanity's "own little world" are transferred to its elements: *gronder, s'enfler, enrager, se courroucer* [scolding, swelling, fury, anger]. It becomes a mental landscape.

Moreover the quatrains themselves have the status of a rhetorical figure: a vast antonomasia, the periphrastic equivalent of a still-hidden name, Alcion, which encodes the description. The tercets, then, play the role of the gloss, first of all by producing this name: it was a question not of *a* bird, but of *the* bird, an emblem-bird which is a signifier like the animal of the Bestiaries, the idea-bird, the peace-bird. Next, by producing in their turn a tale which is also a pseudotale, since the narrative covering (*l'autre jour* . . . , *après, enfin*) [the other day . . . after . . . finally] is only the mask of a definition, the equivalent of a maxim: *love is* (or *is only*) . . . the alternation of turmoil and peace. The double status of each sequence, story/definition, is modeled on the Emblem's statement, always programming a double reading. A masked discourse? To be sure, but still otherwise.

FROM SEMIOSIS TO MIMESIS

So here is a text which does the opposite of what it *says* it is doing, pretending to describe a landscape in order to describe the state of a wretched soul. But which also does the opposite of what it *thinks* it is doing; is the landscape the metaphor of the soul? It appears rather that the soul is the metaphor of the landscape. The thing-compared-to becomes the thing-compared, and the tormented soul sketches a landscape of conflict and discord. Whereas the scenery is anthropomorphized in the quatrains, the mental world is naturalized in the tercets, becomes a natural landscape ruled by the cycle of the seasons. The equivalency is inadequate if the need is to express a peace attained forever, as the gloss asserts, yet it is perfectly adequate if it is a matter of declaring the incessant alternation of turmoil and calm. But more than anything else, beneath the sententious discourse can be heard another muted voice which murmurs something quite different. Against semiosis, a representation oriented toward meaning, stands mimesis, the mimesis of the internal rhythms of fleshly existence, no longer significant but signifying.

The dynamic scheme which sustains and undermines representation produces two opposing forces, one of swelling, the other of rupture, both equally violent, and equally aggressive.[12] This swelling/rupture scheme supports at the same time the infrastructure of the sonnet and the imaginary which unfolds in it. Whether it is the quatrains "describing" the natural world caught at a decisive moment, or the tercets "describing" the world of passion, also in crisis, the same scene is being played out: a suddenly interrupted violence, a surge all at

---

12. See my articles "L'Emblème et le corps. Anatomie d'un paysage," in *Littérature* 78, *Anatomie de l'Emblème*, special issue 1990, and "La Mort-paysage," in *Le Paysage de la Renaissance* (Freiburg: University of Freiburg Press, 1988), 249–55.

once broken off, a vertical upward thrust suspended or arrested in an instant, as in the eighth "Sonnet de la Mort":

> Voulez-vous voir ce trait qui si roide s'élance
>> Dedans l'air qu'il poursuit au partir de la main?
>> Il monte, il monte, il pend, mais hélas! tout soudain
>> Il retombe, il retombe, et perd sa violence. . . .

> Do you wish to see this arrow which, so stiff, flies off
>> Into the very air that, leaving the hand, it pursues?
>> It rises, it rises, it hangs, but, alas, suddenly
>> It falls back, falls back, and loses its violence. . . .

A violence which, brutally broken off by the irruption of a contrary violence, continues to threaten the fragile equilibrium, to trouble the precarious peace; for in the world of Sponde, if rupture follows inflation, another inflation soon answers the rupture:

> Mille flots, mille écueils, font tête à votre route,
>> Vous rompez à travers, mais à la fin sans doute
>> Vous serez le butin des écueils, et des flots.
>
> [Sonnet V de la Mort]

> A thousand waves, a thousand reefs, obstruct your path,
> You break through them, but in the end, to be sure,
> You will be the booty of the reefs, and of the waves.

Sponde's imaginary privileges those decisive instants, when violence yields or may yield, but when turmoil and agitation are about to be reborn, those moments of suspense in an unstable balance between two opposing forces. And this dynamic is in keeping with elementary physics. . . .

We are here far beyond the emblem and its system of commonplaces. That system offered visible matter in order to give access to the intelligible; the mimesis of internal rhythm—from the surge which sweeps up a body swollen with ardor, to the fall back to earth which shows its heaviness—transforms the perceptible, the felt. It is from the body and the images which it elaborates, at the intersection of anatomy and fantasy, of the organic and the libidinal, images of weight and lightness, interior and exterior, movement and stability, that the "landscape" is born, and this landscape is no longer written by cultural codes, but by rhythms. The body triumphs over the emblem; the emblem imposed a single meaning, while the body organizes a signifying process.

Under the contours clearly outlined by syntactical ribs and logical joints, a kind of second syntax is set in unseen motion, a second logic, produced by the phonic and rhythmic networks. Opposites from the semantic point of view, since Q1 represents disturbance and swelling, Q2 soothing and rupture, the quatrains are united by the signifying system like two mirrors. Bolted together by the A rhyme of suspensive final consonants (*nuages/orages/rivages/rages*), enclosing in this frame the B rhyme of conclusive final vowels (*entassés/poussés/courroucés/ramassés*), they place in a position of semantic equivalence words which are grammatically identical, nouns for the A rhyme, past participles for the B rhyme. All fall under the same paradigm, of violence, turmoil, perturbing activity. The landscape of swelling is also sketched in them: the bird's energetic and effective activity corresponds to the violence of the tempest. Two homophonic chains dominate the network:

—The muted/voiced consonants V/F: *v*ent-en*f*er-en*f*lait-*v*is-ri*v*ages-S'en*v*ole-*f*lots-*f*étus

—The vibrating R present in the rhyme beginning with line 4, o*r*ages/ *r*ivages/cou*rr*oucés/*r*amassés/*r*ages, and scattered in the two verses, g*r*ondaient-l'ai*r*-somb*r*es-dé*r*obaient-jou*r*-enfe*r*-me*r*-apaise. . . .

R, the "littera canina," the letter of aggressivity,[13] combines with phonemes of angry expulsion, V and F, while the rhythms mime a rolling and coiling which makes the poem pitch like a boat caught in the swell. It matters little then that the explicit discourse of Q2 describes the return of peace: here there is nothing but tempest and fury.

As opposed to the block of the quatrains, a territory of violence, the tercets "represent" the fall back to earth, the landscape of rupture. And this fall is dominated by the nasal consonant M, the liquid L, and the open vowel A. A chain is formed: *L'AMOUR-ALCION-MON AME-CALME-MER*. The phonic identification produces a semantic dynamization: it opens the two semantic fields *mer/amour* to each other, and pushes *ALcion* and *cALme* toward synonymy. The phonic/rhythmic network

13. Cf., Bembo: "La R aspera ma di generoso spirito" in *Della volgar Lingua*, and Geoffroy Tory in *Champ fleury*. "When dogs are challenging each other, before they bite each other, it seems as if they are pronouncing the letter R, owing to which the Persian poet . . . calls it *Littera canina*, the canine letter." There is a stunning V/F sequence in Aubigné's *Tragiques*, Book VII "Jugement," 1.223 and ff.: "Vous qui persécutez par *f*er mon héritage, / Vos *f*lancs ressentisseront le prix de *v*otre ou*v*rage, / Car je *v*ous *f*rapperai d' épais aveuglements, / Des playes de l' Egypte et de *f*orcènements . . . / Vos *f*illes se *v*endront, à *v*os yeux impuissants / On les *v*iolera: leurs e*f*frois languissants / De *v*os bras en*f*errés n' auront point d'assistance. / Vos *v*alets *v*ous *v*endront . . ."

generates a predicative relation between two objects which are distant from each other in the real world, but close in the world of the text: the sea, the soul.

The explicit discourse of the gloss evokes a durable calm, and takes care to distinguish the sea from the soul; the subterranean discourse opposes two "states" in constant conflict, swelling/rupture, whose struggle can never end, a permanent dispute and discord between Eros, the force of life and efflorescence, and Thanatos, the force of return to an inanimate state. Thus governed by these antagonistic violences, the landscape is a psychosite where death drive and life drive are simultaneously at work; every object in it is the site of an indecisive combat, pitting an energy which seeks to reproduce life and becomes exalted in an activity of inflation, expansion, and swelling, against a force which tends to return to the inorganic. Tumescence/detumescence. . . .

Thus emblematic representation, composing allegorical scenery in which the *littera* serves as guide to the *sententia*, banishing all the realistic effects of mimesis from a place which presents itself as symbolic (belonging not to the individual symbol but to the traditional symbolic order, positing an analogical relation between microcosm and macrocosm, mirrors of each other), should not mask what is produced, beside it and against it, by the work of writing and the signifying organization of the text. On the one hand there lies the space of the emblem, closely circumscribed by the gloss, caught between two layers of texts, a space closed in on itself, the place of a sententious discourse where the only voice heard is that of the *doxa*, stuck in the promise of constancy. On the other side there lies the space of the body, shot through with thematic and pulsating forces which recompose in all its violence and instability the landscape of conflict and internal discord. A place where Eros and Thanatos confront each other, in a battle constantly renewed.

—Translated by Katherine Lydon

JACQUELINE LICHTENSTEIN

What Is the Subject of
La Place Royale?

Moi seul

—J. J. Rousseau. *Les Confessions*

Mesurons le rayon de notre sphère et restons au centre comme
l'insecte au milieu de sa toile.

—J. J. Rousseau. *Emile*

Printed in 1637, the year in which the whole of Paris talked of nothing but Corneille and rushed to applaud the heroic love of Rodrigue and Chimène, *La Place Royale* was first performed in 1633 or 1634. The title succeeded in surprising some spectators and there were even those malicious wits who made fun of it, such as this lampoonist who wrote at the height of the *Querelle du Cid*: "Il a fait voir une *Mélite*, une *Galerie du Palais* et *La Place Royale*, ce qui nous faisait espérer qu'il annoncerait bientôt le *Cimetière de Saint Jean*, *La Samaritaine* et *La Place aux Veaux*" [he has given us a *Mélite*, a *Galerie du Palais* and a *Place Royale* which led us to hope that we would soon get a *Cimetière de Saint Jean*, a *Samaritaine* and a *Place aux Veaux*]. Even today, the finest Corneille scholars continue to view the title which Corneille gave to this comedy as, if not unfortunate, then at least ill-chosen, and in any case, lacking any strong connection to the subject of the play. André Stegmann, in the essay which accompanies *La Place Royale* in the *Corneille* published by Seuil, writes: "le titre rend mal compte du sujet et, comme pour *La Galerie du Palais*, n'est qu'un panneau publicitaire" [the title gives a poor account of the subject and as for *La Galerie du Palais*, is really no more than a 'bill-board']. Now it seems to me that, on the contrary, the title gives a perfectly good account of the subject and that, far from treating it as a mere "billboard," we should take it seriously, examine its signification and investigate the indications it gives us concerning the meaning of the comedy. For the

YFS 80, *Baroque Topographies,* ed. Timothy Hampton, © 1991 by Yale University.

title, *La Place Royale,* clearly identifies what is at stake in this play which itself occupies a unique "place" in Corneille's oeuvre, a strategic place at the crossroads of tragedy and comedy.

In his *Discours de L'Utilité et des Parties du Poème Dramatique,* Corneille writes that, unlike comedy, tragedy "veut donner des malheurs plus grands que la perte d'une maîtresse" [gives rise to fears greater than those occasioned by the loss of a mistress]. He adds that: "sa dignité demande quelque grand intérêt d'Etat ou quelque passion plus noble et plus mâle que l'amour" [its dignity demands some great political interest or some passion nobler and more masculine than love].[1] If one accepts these criteria, that is to say, if one adopts a Cornelian perspective on this play, then *La Place Royale* could almost be considered a tragedy. The passion which dominates the hero is indeed "une passion plus noble et plus mâle que l'amour"; that of liberty; Alidor fears a misfortune which is indubitably greater than the "loss of a mistress": slavery. But Alidor's battle against tyranny is not fought in the political arena and it does not involve any mortal danger. It affects only the individual without concerning city or state. To be a tragedy, this play lacks only "quelque grand intérêt d'état," ultimately, all that is lacking is that Alidor is not a king.

"LA SCÈNE EST À PARIS DANS LA PLACE ROYALE" [THE SCENE IS PARIS IN THE PLACE ROYALE].

La Place Royale refers first to a geographical site: the current *Place des Vosges.* This square which received both its name and its monumental appearance from Henri IV had been created as a place to take walks, with its arcades in which numerous boutiques soon opened. So the scene is Paris. Now in the eyes of seventeenth-century readers and spectators, Paris was not just any town but a marvelous city boasting the most splendid monuments and the most beautiful young women, a city in which the real blended with the imaginary and which seemed to be straight out of a novel. In *Le Menteur,* Dorante, who has just arrived from the provinces, and who has previously only encountered the

---

1. Pierre Corneille: *Discours de l'utilité et des parties du poème dramatique,* cited from André Stegmann's edition of Corneille's *Oeuvres complètes* (Paris: Editions du Seuil, 1963), 824. All citations from Corneille will be taken from this edition. When Corneille reedited his complete works in 1660 each of the three volumes begins with one of his three discourses on dramatic poetry (the *Discours de l'utilité et des parties du poème dramatique,* the *Discours des trois unités* and the *Discours de la tragédie*).

marvelous in books, cries out at the sight of all these splendors: "Paris semble à mes yeux un pays de roman" (Paris to me seems like a fairy tale country).[2] Paris is not a town, but a land whose geography the provincial must learn. To cite La Bruyère: "la ville est partagée en diverses sociétés qui sont comme autant de petites républiques qui ont leurs lois, leurs usages, leur jargon et leurs mots pour rire" [the town is divided into different societies like so many little republics, which have their own laws, their customs, their jargon and their jokes]. Anyone who is uninitiated in the mysterious rules organizing these societies immediately feels like "un étranger" [a foreigner] as La Bruyère puts it: "Il se trouve là comme dans un pays lointain dont il ne connaît ni les routes, ni la langue, ni les moeurs, ni la coutume" [He feels as he would when in a distant country of whose roads, language, morals and customs he is ignorant].[3]

Paris is a land in which paths are marked out by the exchange of glances, organized by words, identified by means of a gesture or a smile, a land whose geography is social and which demands of its inhabitants a very precise knowledge and one that is all the more difficult to acquire since it cannot be learned from books, the knowledge of signs. Every Parisian is a surveyor when it comes to signs: a person who moves in a symbolic universe in which he knows how to measure distances, how to calculate the slightest difference in levels, a world which no one can penetrate without first knowing the unwritten rules of language and taste. For in this land, any mistake counts as an error incurring social and moral exclusion. Dorante in *Le Menteur* finds himself constantly repeating this painful experience. For example, when his valet Cliton tells him that the beautiful Lucrèce "loge à la place" [lives in *la Place*] he naively asks him: "quelle place?" [which place?], Cliton replies "*Royale,*" astonished that his master should be ignorant of the rule which requires that one say "*la Place*" and not "*la Place Royale.*" Dorante will soon come to understand that such errors are egregious, not only because they reveal his provincial origins, but because they constitute an obstacle to the achievement of his romantic goals. A man who says "*la Place Royale*" can never attract women who talk of living in "*la place,*" for the town's social geography is reduplicated in its romantic geography.

If Paris is a marvelous city it is in part because women hold sway

2. *Polyeuctus, The Liar and Nicomedes,* trans. John Cairncross (London: Penguin Classics, 1980), 160.
3. La Bruyère, *Les Caractères,* "De la ville."

there. In 1656, the Abbé de Pure writes that "La plus grande douceur de notre France est celle de la liberté des femmes. Et elle est si grande dans tout le royaume que les maris y sont presque sans pouvoir et que les femmes y sont souveraines" [The greatest charm of our France lies in the liberty of its women. It is so great that throughout the kingdom, husbands are almost powerless while their wives hold sovereign sway].[4] And since Paris is at the center of this kingdom, it is there that this sovereignty expresses itself with the greatest evidence and the most freedom. In this "marvelous land," women lord it over men who are their subjects. In the heart of the cities as in the hearts of men, women have their place—the *whole* place, and exercise a power which, at the time, was unanimously described as being "absolute." Now this term must be, demands to be, understood in its fully political sense. The absolutism of feminine power corresponds to a political model of domination of which history offers numerous examples and which is not the absolute of monarchic power but that of tyranny. In seventeenth-century discourse, the woman's place is not that of the king, but rather that of the tyrant.[5]

Restoring the categories and divisions inherited from antiquity, seventeenth-century political thought makes a distinction between two forms of absolutism: an illegitimate form that rests on the use of constraint and to which the other submits as a result of the exercise of force and not of his own free will, and a legitimate form which demands that power be founded on something other than force and implies an assent based on the recognition of a right. The former case is that of the despot or tyrant, the latter that of the true absolute monarch. Fundamental to the seventeenth century, the question of absolutism and its legitimacy is at the heart of the political enquiry which Corneille pursues in all his tragedies. Firmly established in *Horace* and then in *Cinna*, the distinction between legitimate and usurped power, between the absolute monarch and the tyrant, appears in all his plays as a distinction at once necessary and precariously fragile, constantly threatened by despotic forces rendered all the more dangerous by the fact that they believe themselves to be acting in the name of freedom.

4. Abbé Michel de Pure, *La Prétieuse ou le mystère des ruelles* (Paris: De Lyune, 1636).

5. We are aware that this terminology of slavery, tyranny and empire belongs to the vocabulary of preciosity. But the frequency of these metaphors in the amorous discourse of the seventeenth century discloses the close links established by the period between the spheres of politics and love. In this study we have chosen deliberately to ignore the metaphorical status of these terms in order to consider their literal meanings.

But why should the power exercised by women necessarily be of a despotic or tyrannical nature? Pascal's analysis provides a philosophical answer to this question which is essentially political—even when it is raised, as it is here, in the domestic realm. This is because the opposition between the king and the tyrant which appears in many of the *Pensées* has, for Pascal, a paradigmatic value; it demarcates a force field in which the political encounters the moral and the metaphysical. Pascal writes that "La Tyrannie consiste au désir de domination, universel et hors de son ordre" [Tyranny consists in the desire to dominate everything regardless of order].[6] Now not all desires to dominate are tyrannical, a desire becomes tyrannical when it attempts to extend its dominion to areas in which it has no right to exercise any power, however slight, when it seeks to dominate everywhere, in other words, to reign even in domains where it is not master. Tyranny begins where power parts company with mastery and where domination is no longer justifiable but cannot be contradicted. If it is legitimate for beauty to demand to be loved, strength to be feared, and science respected, it is on the contrary, wholly illegitimate for beauty to demand respect, science to demand fear, and strength to demand love. Any desire for domination which extends beyond its own order immediately becomes tyrannical because it uses its mastery in one area to exercise power in another, thus circumventing any possibility of control, controversy, critique or limitation. Here it becomes necessary to read in its entirety the remarkable *pensée* on tyranny:

> La tyrannie consiste au désir de domination, universel et hors de son ordre.
>
> Diverses chambres de forts, de beaux, de bons esprits, de pieux, dont chacun règne chez soi, non ailleurs; et quelquefois ils se rencontrent, et le fort et le beau se battent, sottement, à qui sera le maître l'un de l'autre; car leur maîtrise est de divers genre. Ils ne s'entendent pas, et leur faute est de vouloir régner partout. Rien ne le peut, non pas même la force; elle ne fait rien au royaume des savants; elle n'est maitresse que des actions extérieures.
>
> *Tyrannie*—. . . Ainsi ces discours sont faux et tyranniques. "Je suis beau, donc on doit me craindre. Je suis fort, donc on doit m'aimer. Je suis . . ."
>
> La tyrannie est de vouloir avoir par une voie ce qu'on ne peut avoir

---

6. *Pascal's Pensées*, trans. Martin Turnell (New York: Harper and Brothers, 1962). This is #332 in the Brunschvicg edition (Paris: Hachette, 1909). Hereafter cited in the text.

que par une autre. On rend différents devoirs aux différents mérites:
devoir d'amour à l'agrément; devoir de crainte à la force; devoir de
créance à la science.

On doit rendre ces devoirs là, on est injuste de les refuser et injuste
d'en demander d'autres. Et c'est de même être faux et tyrannique de
dire: "il n'est pas fort, donc je ne l'estimerai pas; il n'est pas habile, donc
je ne le craindrai pas."

Tyranny consists in the desire to dominate everything regardless of
order.

In the various departments for men of strength, beauty, sense and
piety, each man is master in his own house but nowhere else. Sometimes they meet, and the strong and the handsome contend for mastery,
but this is idiotic because their mastery is of different kinds. They do
not understand each other, and their mistake lies in wanting to rule
everywhere. Nothing can do that, not even strength: it is of no effect in
the learned world and only governs external actions.—So these arguments are false. . . .

Tyranny. Tyranny is wanting to have by one means what can only be
had by another. We pay different dues to different kinds of merit; we
must love charm, fear strength, believe in knowledge.

These dues must be paid. It is wrong to refuse them and wrong to
demand any others, so these arguments are false and tyrannical: 'I am
handsome therefore you must fear me, I am strong therefore you must
love me, I am . . .' In the same way it is false and tyrannical to say 'He is
not strong, so I will not respect him. He is not clever, so I will not fear
him.' [Pascal #332]

Nero's tyranny does not manifest itself in his desire to dominate
Rome but in his desire to dominate poetry, in the use of his imperial
crown to gain recognition as the greatest Roman poet. His fault, as
Pascal writes, is "vouloir régner partout" [to want to reign everywhere],
while justice requires that "chacun règne chez soi" [each person be
master in his own domain]. This is the point of the opposition which
Pascal establishes between the King and the Tyrant. If the tyrant is the
person who dominates beyond the bounds of his own order, the king,
by contrast, is the legitimate sovereign who "is master in his own
domain" and only dominates within the bounds of his own order. That
is why Pascal can write at the same time in two different places that "la
force est la reine du monde" [power . . . is mistress of the world] but "la
force en est le tyran" (Pascal #303, 311), [force is its tyrant]. It is entirely legitimate for force, in its empirical reality, in its brute existence,
its brutal form, to dominate within its own order, that of relations

governed by force, but this very force becomes tyrannical when it seeks to dominate the mind or the heart. If force must be obeyed, it cannot legitimately demand to be loved.

If we follow Pascal's analysis, we inevitably come to the conclusion that, of all desires, there is one which is of necessity tyrannical: the desire of love. This is because love destroys the boundaries which separate the different orders. It penetrates the heart in order to gain a hold over reason, it uses sensual pleasure to obscure the truth, it dominates by means of pleasure and attraction. In his *Opuscules*, Pascal writes that pleasure is "cette voie basse, indigne et étrangère" [this motive for belief . . . superficial, undignified and strange][7] which brings us to assent to opinions without first consulting the understanding, a power which prevents reason from exercising its legitimate sovereignty, for, he adds, "nous ne croyons presque que ce qui nous plaît" [we in fact scarcely believe but what pleases us]. (Pullen, 316). Pleasure is the privileged instrument of tyranny since it permits the desire for domination to take other paths, to infiltrate secretly by oblique paths, to leave its own territory and become universal. It is the means employed by all desire for domination in attaining its expansionist ends. "Eloquence qui persuade par douceur, non par empire, en tyran, non en roi" (Brunschwicq #15) [Eloquence which persuades by its appeal rather than its authority, as a tyrant, and not as a king], writes Pascal. How could love, which always persuades by appeal not be tyrannical? "L'amour est un tyran qui n'épargne personne" [Love is a tyrant who spares no one], says Elvire in *Le Cid*. If the power exercised by women is always tyrannical, it is quite simply because they always rule by means of attraction and pleasure. If in love there is no master who is not a tyrannical master, if love necessarily entails a transgression of all limits, if love is indeed the one desire which does not have, which refuses to have its own order, acting rather as a universal principle of disorder ready to invade all other domains, then women, who are masters in the order (or disorder) of love, are always tyrannical masters. Love does not content itself with a partial domination, it attacks the core of the subject and empties out its substance in order to make place for an image; it attacks the core of the subject and deprives it of its essence and then installs an image in its place.

Such is the drama of Alidor and the source of his despair: he is in

7. "Reflections on Geometry and the Art of Persuading," in *The Essential Pascal*, trans. G. F. Pullen (New York: New American Library, 1966), 315. Hereafter cited in the text.

thrall to the tyranny of love, he no longer belongs to himself, he is dispossessed of himself and is no longer master of his own domain: he has been enchanted, ravished by Angélique, and ever since, her image has occupied him completely.[8] From the very start of the play he laments his fate to Cléandre when he meets him in the *Place Royale:*

Cléandre: Mais voir de ce côté ta démarche avancée,
            Montre bien qu'Angélique est fort dans ta pensée.
Alidor: Hélas! C'est mon malheur: son objet trop charmant,
            Quoi que je puisse faire, y règne absolument.

[Act I, v, 181–84]

Cléandre: But to see you walking in these parts
            Shows that Angelique is very much in your mind.
Alidor: Alas! That is my misery: her too beautiful image,
            Rules there absolutely, no matter what I do.

Alidor will have to use all his ingenuity to deliver himself from this tyrant who has taken the place of his 'I', to free himself from this passion which keeps him subjugated to a woman and prevents him from being his own master. *La Place Royale* is first and foremost the story of someone who wants to regain possession of himself, to expel the other from the place that it occupies in him and to become once more the sole occupant of himself, to rule over himself alone. By the end of the play, Alidor has achieved this goal, but it is at the price of the greatest solitude. In becoming master of himself he becomes a king, but a very solitary monarch who rules only himself.

La Place Royale: this title does indeed refer to a space, but this space is not merely geographical. It is also, and perhaps primarily, a political space and a philosophical space, a politicophilosophical space: that of the subject. The *Place Royale* is the place of the subject, or more precisely, the place in which the subject discovers himself as master. For Corneille, as for Descartes, the subject is always defined in terms of mastery. But for Corneille, mastery in its philosophical sense is indissociable from mastery in its political sense. A master is, first and foremost, a person who has put an end to the tyranny of the other.

We can now understand why love constitutes the greatest obstacle to mastery. In love, the individual is subject, not to himself, but to another. "Je veux la liberté dans le milieu des fers" (Act I, iv, 204) [Though in chains, I want my freedom], exclaims Alidor. His revolt

8. Seventeenth-century usage always gives the double sense of pleasure and kidnapping to the terms "ravish" and "ravishment."

against the sweet tyranny of Angélique is expressed in the language of the purest stoicism, it is the cry of a desperate will which knows itself powerless to fight against its tyrant. Alidor has no illusions: he knows that the image of Angélique encloses him in a prison far more terrible than any cell or dungeon, for his captivity deprives him of the possibility of even an interior freedom. Confronted with Angélique's beauty, the battle is lost before it has begun:

> **Alidor:** Mes pensers ne sauraient m'entretenir que d'elle,
> Je sens de ses regards mes plaisirs se borner;
> Mes pas d'autre côté ne sauraient se tourner,
> Et de tous mes soucis la liberté bannie
> Me soumet en esclave à trop de tyrannie.
>
> > [Act 1, iv, 214ff.]

> **Alidor:** My thoughts can only make me think of her,
> I feel that her look is the limit of my pleasure,
> My steps can turn nowhere else,
> And liberty, banished from my cares,
> Subjects me as a slave to too much tyranny.

Love is a form of tyranny because it does not content itself with the domination of the body, but subjugates even the least thought and affects the very will of the slave so that it becomes a slave's will: to paraphrase Rousseau, the will of someone in chains who loses everything, including the desire to release himself from his chains. Women possess the secret which permits them to oppress the individual both permanently and absolutely, this "great secret" which, as Spinoza will say, has as its result that men "fight for their slavery as though it were their salvation".[9] Indeed, it suffices to read Spinoza to recognize that the "great secret" of the political is also that of love, the great secret of the politics of women:

> He has another under his authority, who holds him bound, or has taken from him arms and means of defence or escape, or inspired him with fear, or so attached him to himself by past favour, that the man obliged would rather please his benefactor than himself, and live after his mind than after his own. He that has another under authority in the first or second of these ways, holds but his body, not his mind. But in the third or fourth way he has made dependent on himself as well the mind

---

9. Benedict de Spinoza, *Traité des autorités théologique et politique,* preface to the Pléiade edition (Paris: Gallimard, 1954), 609.

as the body of the other; yet only as long as the fear or hope lasts, for upon the removal of the feeling the other is left independent.[10]

Through love, women exercise a power of the third or fourth kind; the cords with which they bind the lover are infinitely more robust than all the bonds used in restraining the prisoner's body for they are "des cordes d'imagination" (Brunchvicg #304) [bonds forged by the imagination], as Pascal puts it in *Les Pensées*. It is these bonds that Alidor seeks to untie in order to regain his freedom:

> **Alidor:** Je n'ai que trop langui sous de si rudes gènes:
> A tel prix que ce soit il faut rompre mes chaines.
>
> [Act 1, iv, 221]

> **Alidor:** I have languished too long in her rough bonds:
> I must break my chains at any cost.

Alidor does not want to give up love, but he wants love without the tyranny which unfailingly accompanies it. He wants to be able to love without feeling bound, to remain free amidst his chains, to reconcile pleasure and freedom:

> **Alidor:** Il ne faut pas servir d'objet qui nous possède,
> Il ne faut point nourrir d'amour qui ne nous cède:
> Je le hais s'il me force et quand j'aime je veux
> Que de ma volonté dépendent tous mes voeux,
> Que mon feu m'obéisse au lieu de me contraindre,
> Que je puisse à mon gré l'enflammer et l'éteindre,
> Et toujours en état de disposer de moi,
> Donner quand il me plaît et retirer ma foi.
>
> [Act 1, iv, 205ff.]

> **Alidor:** I must serve no object that possesses me,
> I must cherish no love that does not obey:
> If it forces me, I hate it, and when I love I want
> All my wishes to depend on my will alone,
> And my flame to obey me instead of constraining me,
> To fan it or extinguish it at my will,
> And, always in control of myself,
> To give and retake my trust as I please.

Alidor's discourse corresponds perfectly to the love ethic of the libertine, the man who refuses to become attached to any one object so that he can maintain the distance necessary to control the unstable

10. Spinoza, *A Theologico-Political Treatise and a Political Treatise*, trans. with an introduction by R. H. M. Elwes (New York: Dover Publications, Inc., 1951), 295.

and dangerous universe of emotions and representations, the lover who will never abdicate his position as master, as foundational subject free to pledge and to withdraw his faith as he pleases. Now this ethic is also Corneille's, if we are to judge by the dedicatory epistle of 1637 in which he writes to his addressee:

> C'est de vous que j'ai appris que l'amour d'un honnête homme doit être toujours volontaire, qu'on ne doit jamais aimer en un point qu'on ne puisse n'aimer pas; que si on en vient jusque là, c'est une tyrannie dont il faut secouer le joug; et qu'enfin la personne aimée nous a beaucoup plus d'obligation de notre amour, alors qu'elle est toujours l'effet de notre choix et de son mérite, que quand elle vient d'une inclination aveugle et forcée.[11]

> From you I learned that an honest man's love must always be a voluntary love, that one must never love to such an extreme that one cannot not love; that if one reaches such an extreme, love becomes a tyranny whose yoke must be shaken off; and that, finally, the person we love owes us much more for our love when it is brought on by our choice and her worth, than when it comes from a forced and blind obligation.

Although the *Examen* of 1660 somewhat tempers the remarks that succeeded in shocking the readers of the first edition, in which Alidor is qualified not as an *"honnête homme,"* but as an "esprit extravagant" [an extravagant person], Corneille does not in fact abandon the ethical signification attached to this character from the outset. Moreover, Alidor's "extravagance" is clearly that of the libertine since his spirit, as he writes, "se trouve incommodé d'un amour qui l'attache trop" [finds itself indisposed by a love that binds it too tightly].

How can one avoid an attachment which is too vehement and which impinges on the freedom of the subject? How can one take pleasure in love without suffering its tyranny? *La Place Royale*, formulates not one, but two answers to this question. The first is that of Phylis and it is put forward at the start of the play. Phylis's brother, Doraste is in love with Angélique, but the latter loves Alidor, and refuses to let Phylis, who is defending her brother's interests, convince her:

> **Angélique:** Vois tu, j'aime Alidor, et c'est assez te dire.
> Le reste des mortels pourrait offrir mes voeux,
> Je suis aveugle, sourde, insensible pour eux.
> [Act 1, i, 34ff.]

---

11. See Stegmann's edition, 150.

Angélique: Don't you see, I love Alidor, and to say that is enough.
Other mortals might offer me their vows,
But to them I am blind, deaf and insensitive.

To Phylis, this attitude seems ridiculous and unreasonable, and she explains to her friend the reasons for her disagreement:

Phylis: Dans l'obstination où je te vois réduite,
J'admire ton amour et ris de ta conduite.
Fasse état qui voudra de ta fidélité,
Je ne me pique pas de cette vanité
Et exemple d'autrui m'a trop fait reconnaître
Qu'au lieu d'un serviteur c'est accepter un maître.

[Act 1, i, 45ff.]

Phylis: I admire your love and laugh at your behavior,
In this stubbornness to which you are reduced.
Let anyone who likes make a big deal of your faithfulness,
It is a vanity that means nothing to me,
And the examples of others have made me see
That you are accepting not a servant, but a master.

For Phylis, the only way to avoid an overpowering attachment which subjugates you to another person's tyranny is to become attached to all and sundry, to cultivate many lovers. If the result of an exclusive love is a rapid fall into the deepest dependency, then it suffices to love everyone to escape submission to a single object and to keep your freedom:

Phylis: Quand on n'en souffre qu'un, qu'on ne pense qu'à lui,
Tous les autres entretiens nous donnent de l'ennui;
. . . .
Pour moi, j'aime un chacun et sans rien négliger
Le premier qui m'en conte a de quoi m'engager:
Ainsi tout contribue à ma bonne fortune;
Tout le monde me plaît et rien ne m'importune.
De mille que je rends l'un de l'autre jaloux,
Mon coeur n'est pas à un et se promet à tous.

[Act 1, i, 50ff.]

Phylis: When you have only one lover, and you think only of him,
Anyone else bores you,
. . . .
As for me, I love them all, without exception.
The first one to come along can attract me;

Thus everything contributes to my good fortune,
Everyone pleases me and nothing puts me out.
I make a thousand of them jealous of each other,
My heart is promised to all, but belongs to none.

To protect herself against the tyranny of a single person, Phylis demands the love of many; in order not to give herself to someone, she claims the right to accept whomever she chooses. To the problem posed above, that is, of how to take pleasure in love without suffering its tyranny, Phylis presents a clear solution: the solution of Don-Juanism which is founded on the obvious conclusion that love ceases to be tyrannical when the subject prevents anyone but himself from occupying the place of the unique, in other words, the place of the tyrant. Corneille's Phylis gives voice to exactly the same arguments as Molière's Don Juan, and Sganarelle's portrait of this "grand seigneur méchant homme" [wicked nobleman] who loves "all" women and would like to possess them all right up to their maidservants and their lap dogs, would need only minor modifications according to *la bien-séance* and the social allocation of roles to fit this female character who, in order to protect herself better, advocates sharing the lover and cooly confesses to her friend that "Je puis avec joie accepter tous maris" (Act I, i, 80) [I could willingly accept all husbands].

Phylis may well elect to love everyone so as not to depend on any one person, but this option is not available to Alidor since he has already accepted a master, or rather a mistress. He could adopt Phylis's axioms, but unfortunately, he would be unable to apply them. The Other, that is to say, the tyrant, is there, has already taken possession of his heart, and keeps him from living by the rules he has set himself. The lines in which he expounds to his friend his own maxims culminate in a terrible avowal of impotence. "*Je veux* la liberté dans le milieu des fers, / *Il ne faut point* servir d'objet qui nous possède, / *Il ne faut point* nourrir d'amour qui ne nous cède, / . . . . *Je veux* / Que de ma volonté dépendent tous mes voeux." [Though in chains, I want my freedom, I must serve no object that possesses me, I must cherish no love that does not obey. . . . I want all my wishes to depend on my will alone]. This series of imperatives is followed by a terrible admission: "pour vivre de la sorte Angélique est trop belle" (Act I, iv, 213) [I cannot live by this for Angélique is too fair].

If Phylis has discovered the means of forestalling tyranny by not giving herself a tyrant, Alidor fights a battle whose degree of difficulty is entirely different: not only because in his case it is no longer a question of resisting, but of conquering a tyranny to which he is already subject, even as he knows himself incapable of fighting against his tyrant. The moral precepts of Descartes would be of no use to him. If, as Descartes writes, it is better to want to change one's desires than the order of the world, in certain cases, the order of the world prevents one from changing one's desires. In this extremity, the only option is to escape the world order, not by breaking away from it, but by diverting it from oneself. Angélique is one of these cases. Alidor's misfortune is to love a woman who is "trop belle" [too fair]. Here it is the very being of the other which foils all the efforts of the self. In the words of that model libertine, the Chevalier de Méré, one must always be wary of too stunning a beauty because "elle occupe trop et qu'on ne veut pas être trop longtemps ébloui" [It occupies one too thoroughly, and one does not want to remain bedazzled for too long].[12] To stay free, it is not enough to want one's liberty and to alter the nature of one's own desires; one must also give up certain love objects, exclude any that are too enticing, and avoid women who are too fair and who exercise too much control over sight and mind.

Alidor's response to the question: how can one take pleasure in love without suffering its tyranny? differs significantly from that of Phylis. While Phylis wants to take whatever is available and to encourage all those whom she pleases, Alidor wants to give only what he chooses and to serve only as it pleases him. Whereas Phylis, to protect herself, has chosen to please everyone, Alidor, to protect himself, must displease someone: "Puisqu'elle me plaît trop, il me faut lui déplaire" (Act I, iv, 246) [Since she pleases me too much, I must displease her].

The different responses of Phylis and Alidor correspond perfectly to the seventeenth-century conception of the allocation of roles in the domain of love. The difference between these two approaches derives from an allotment which, very simply, comes down to sexual difference. In love, it is the object who is the master, that is to say, who occupies the position of subject; it is woman who lays down the law.

From this perspective, Scene vii of Act II is particularly significant. Cléandre, Alidor's friend and Phylis's lover, refuses to suffer any longer the consequences of his mistress's inconstancy. He no longer cares to share her with others, and has therefore decided to give up his place since she will not allow him to occupy it exclusively. Phylis is as-

12. Antoine Gombauld, Chevalier de Méré, *Des Agrémens.*

tonished to see him pass by without addressing her, and he responds: "Il me faut bien passer, puisque la place est prise" [Since the place is taken I must pass (it) by]. Phylis finds this reason to be "de mauvaise mise" (a weak argument), and tells him so:

> Phylis: D'un million d'amants je puis flatter les voeux
> Et je n'aurais pas l'esprit d'en entretenir deux?
> Sortez de cette erreur, et souffrant ce partage
> Ne faites pas ici l'entendu davantage.

> Phylis: I can flatter the vows of a million lovers
> Yet I haven't the spirit to speak to two?
> You're mistaken; accept the situation
> And stop being a nuisance.

Unfortunately, Cléandre has already decided that he will not countenance it anymore. Like Alceste, he wants to be singled out, and however strong someone's interest in him, he will refuse an advantage unless it is offered to him alone:

> Cléandre: Encore que votre ardeur à la mienne réponde,
> Je ne veux plus d'un bien commun à tout le monde.

> Cléandre: Even though your passion responds to mine,
> I want no more of something that everyone
> can have.

And if Cléandre's anger strangely resembles Alceste's, Phylis, in her response, uses words that Célimène could have spoken:

> Phylis: Mais mille aussi bien faits ne sont pas mieux traités
> Et ne murmurent point contre mes volontés.
>   Est-ce à moi, s'il vous plaît, de vivre à votre mode?
> Votre amour, en ce cas, serait fort incommode;
> Loin de la recevoir, vous me feriez la loi:
> Qui m'aime de la sorte, il s'aime et non pas moi.

> Phylis: But a thousand men, as handsome as you, are treated no
>   better,
> Yet they never complain against my wishes.
> Is it my duty, if you please, to live as you say?
> In such a situation your love, would be quite unpleasant;
> Instead of receiving my law, you would impose yours:
> Whoever loves me in this way, loves himself and not me.

In love, it is not the man who imposes the "mode" (fashion); it is not up to him to make the law it is not the person who loves who dictates the law but rather he, or rather, *she* who is loved.

If such is the tyrannical law of love, man can never cease being enslaved unless his tyrant frees him from his slavery. Alidor has understood this. He could have his freedom if he only would give up his love. But, being a man, he lacks this option, it is a privilege exclusive to women. A man cannot stop loving an object which is too lovable, he can only stop acting as a lover. This is the origin of Alidor's peculiar idea of giving Angélique to someone else. Although this idea obviously reflects a mind which, if not perverse, is at least, "extravagant," it nevertheless demonstrates that Alidor has no illusions about his own power. Knowing himself to be entirely subjugated to the law of the other, he realizes that his only chance lies in turning this subjugation into the means of his liberation. He does not expect to win his freedom by an act of revolt, but rather by an act of allegiance, as a freedom returned rather than a freedom won. His independence will be the result of his obedience, of a final and ultimate act of obedience: he waits for woman to impose freedom on him in the same way that she imposed slavery: by a look. When Angélique stops loving him, when she turns her gaze on another, he will at last be able to take possession of himself again. He will be a free man, unhappy no doubt, but also at peace.

> **Alidor:** Dis mieux que pour rentrer dans mon indifférence
> Je perdrai mon amour avec mon espérance,
> Et qu'y trouvent alors sujet d'aversion,
> Ma liberté naîtra de ma punition
>
> [Act I, iv, 257 ff.]

> **Alidor:** Say rather, that by returning to my indifference,
> I shall love both my love and my hope,
> And that, finding thus no more cause for hatred,
> My freedom will be born of my punishment.

When at the end of the play, Angélique, wounded by the lies and the betrayals to which she has fallen victim as a result of Alidor's stratagems, decides to retire to a convent, Alidor is delighted by this decision which favors his designs. In leaving, she restores to him a liberty which would have been constantly imperiled by her "trop belle" presence:

Alidor: J'avais beau la trahir, une secrète amorce
   Rallumait dans mon coeur l'amour par la pitié:
   Mes feux en recevaient une nouvelle force
   Et toujours leur ardeur en croissait de moitié.

           [Act V, viii, ll. 1494ff.]

Alidor: Though I betrayed her, a secret trap
   Revived, through pity, love in my heart:
   My flame took on a new force
   And its ardor increased ceaselessly.

Angélique, whom he planned to give to Cléandre, has herself re-
leased him from his chains. She has freed him from his enslavement
and put an end to his torment in a way that he could never have hoped
for: not by showing an interest in someone else—which could not have
failed to arouse his jealousy—but by giving herself to God:

Alidor: Ravi qu'aucun n'en ait ce que j'ai pu prétendre,
   Puisqu'elle dit au monde un éternel adieu,
   Comme je la donnais sans cesse à Cléandre,
   Je verrai sans regret qu'elle se donne à Dieu.

Alidor: Happy that none other had what I wanted,
   Since she says an eternal farewell to the world,
   And since I gave her ceaselessly to Cléandre,
   I don't mind her giving herself to God.

Alidor has attained his goal and can proclaim his victory:

Alidor: Je suis libre à présent qu'elle est désabusée,
   . . . .
   Je cesse d'espérer et commence de vivre;
   Je vis dorénavant, puisque je vis à moi;
   Et quelques doux assauts qu'un autre objet me livre,
   C'est de moi seulement que je prendrai la loi.

           [Act V, viii, ll. 1500ff.]

Alidor: Now that she is disappointed, I am free,
   . . . .
   I stop hoping and start living;
   Henceforth, I live, for I am my own;
   And despite the attacks others may launch against me,
   I subscribe only to my own law.

Alidor has finally become a subject, a free, independent subject who obeys only the laws he gives himself. The 'I' no longer has a tyrant, and can dominate its own order, that is to say, be master of its own domain. His 'I' no longer belongs to another person, or more precisely, to another woman; it is its own. Alidor can now say that "Je vis dorénavant, puisque je vis à moi".

To live for oneself, to be one's own person: this, for Corneille, is the *place royale* of the subject, the place of mastery where the subject rules as a king. And this act of appropriation or reappropriation, which permits the individual to occupy the center of a sphere whose circumference he himself traces, carries out a circular movement of temporality that also encloses the subject. If the subject is always defined by a place, it is because, first of all, for classical thought, every subject presupposes a place, a spatial determination in which he cannot maintain himself unless all forms of temporal change are excluded. The individual can only be the subject of a place—that is, of a fixed point. He can never be the subject of time, since time, as every writer of so-called Baroque literature notes, is a perpetual change that carries away everything in a ceaseless movement of metamorphosis. As Pascal says in his *Opuscules*, "le présent est le seul temps qui est véritablement à nous" [the present is the only time that truly belongs to us].[13] This is why Alidor begins living at the very moment he stops hoping. Given back to himself, he lives in the present, that is to say, in the only time that permits the individual to say, "I live for myself."

Thus Alidor lives. He has freed his self from the Other who had taken up residence in it and occupied its place. But does he truly occupy this place that he has freed? Does this place that he has emptied not remain an empty place? If *La Place Royale* ends with the victory chant of a freedom that has at last been restored, this freedom remains a freedom without content, what Descartes would call a liberty of indifference. Hence the rather sad tone of the last scene which Corneille wrote in the form of a regular poem in which the quatrains follow each other in a monotonous, melancholy rhythm. Its tone is not what one might expect from a hymn to freedom, having neither the accentuation nor the gusto of an epic poem. At the end of *La Place*

---

13. Blaise Pascal, letter to Mlle de Roannez of December 1656. This theme is taken up and developed at length in a *Pensée* #172 of the Brunschvicg edition which begins "Nous ne tenons jamais au temps présent." This same *Pensée* ends with a point that will be taken up by Rousseau, most particularly in the *Emile:* "Ainsi nous ne vivons jamais, mais nous espérons de vivre; et nous disposant toujours à être heureux, il est inévitable que nous ne le soyons jamais."

Royale, the subject has situated itself, but this place still lacks a subject worthy of filling it. Even if Alidor can enjoy the contentment of at last being his own master and obeying only himself, his 'I' is still not that of a king. For his freedom has not been won, but rather granted to him by a sovereign power, what is more, as a punishment. He possesses the negative freedom of the freed slave, of someone who is no longer subjugated to a master, rather than the positive freedom of the person who imposes himself as his own master and the master of others.

For Corneille, as is known, no one is master of himself if he is not at the same time master of others. Corneille assigns to the subject a double foundation, philosophical and political, needing to reign over two domains at one time. If every subject is a master, then accession to mastery implies both a philosophical victory over the self and a political victory over the other. The royal status of the subject is inscribed in a relation which is doubly specular, reflexive and reflective, of cognition and recognition. The movement which marks the emergence of the subject in Descartes, is, in Corneille, just the first stage in a constitution which is complete only after the acquisition of a political status. However, this first stage is logically necessary in ensuring that the power which is the object of the second stage is entirely legitimate. Auguste can only become an absolute monarch when he has triumphed over himself. To rule as a tyrant, it suffices to be master of the world, but only he who can say "I am master of myself as well as of the universe" philosophically merits the glorious title of king. Both philosophical and political subject, master in all senses of the word, of himself and of others, the character of Auguste represents the fullest expression of the Cornelian subject-king. With *Cinna,* the Cornelian conception of the subject comes to its fullest realization; for the first and only time, the *place royale* of the subject is identical to the place of the royal subject.

This is not Alidor's place but it is almost that of Rodrigue after his victory against the Moors. By subjugating the enemy, Rodrigue obtains the right to be recognized as subject for both his military prowess and his courage. This recognition receives immediate expression in a name change: having become his own origin, author and founder of himself, he will bear his own name, El Cid, in other words, a name which is proper to him alone.[14] After this it does not matter if he marries

14. Like Louis XIV, who will give up being called Louis XIV, that is, the fourteenth in a line, to take on the title of Louis the Great, a proper name, unique to him, which affirms the incomparable character of the absolute monarch. On this question of Louis's incom-

Chimène. Rodrigue no longer risks anything by being a slave where love is concerned because he has won his glorious titles in the political arena. Always an object subjugated to the tyranny of women who are sole rulers in the domain of love, man only becomes a subject in the philosophical sense of the term when he changes domain, when he gives up once and for all the desire to dominate in an order which is not his own in order to dominate in the order proper to him. Thus the apparently strong 'I' of Alidor is philosophically uncertain because he dreams of victory on the field of his own defeat, rather than fighting his battle elsewhere. Sexual difference in Corneille corresponds to what Pascal would call a difference of order. Although the desire to dominate is equal in both sexes, man and woman dominate in different orders and in different ways. For a man, this political desire cannot triumph and achieve its ends unless it changes stages and becomes desire for politics.[15]

La Place Royale. This title refers to the place of a subject which, in *La Place Royale* is still embryonic, a place which Rodrigue, Auguste, Polyeucte, Pompée and others will come to occupy; Alidor seems to remain transfixed on the edge of this place which he has nevertheless constructed and which Corneille delineates here because of his predicament.

In this sense, it is correct to affirm, as has often been said, *La Place Royale* occupies a key position in Corneille's oeuvre. It represents the first stage of the movement which culminates in the achievement of mastery, the preliminary moment of the subjective and individual freedom in which the subject, by turning in on itself, is born to itself. Even before *Cinna* and *Polyeucte*, *La Place Royale* describes this first moment as a moment which is always painful because it consists in the immense and difficult attempt to tear oneself away from the other, to detach oneself from the other or the other from oneself. The theater of Corneille here offers the dramatization of a thought which is at the center of the philosophy of Descartes: that is, that the emergence of the subject necessarily traverses the painful experience of solitude by which the subject learns to belong to itself, in other words, to rely on itself alone. On the path which leads to the encounter with itself,

---

parability, see the work of Louis Marin, most specifically, *Le Portrait du roi* (Paris: Minuit, 1981).

15. This is why the man who is most a subject in the theater of Corneille is Auguste, the absolute monarch, the King of whom all others are subjects.

the subject advances, to quote Descartes's admirable formulation, "comme un homme qui marche seul et dans les ténèbres" [like a man who walks alone and in darkness]. It is only when he has passed the test of the greatest solitude that Auguste can finally be born to himself, become an absolute subject, a true monarch. In the long monologue of Act IV, scene ii, he addresses himself thus: "Rentre en toi-même Octave et cesse de te plaindre" [Come to your senses Octavius and pity not yourself].[16] He will address Cinna in the same way at the end of Act V: "Apprends à te connaître et descends en toi-même" (Cinna, V, i, l. 1517) [Turn your eyes inwards. Learn to know yourself]. And this sentence is no mere injunction. It establishes Auguste's superiority as incontestable and shows Cinna his place. Cinna is not a master because he has not gone through the first stage, he has not withdrawn into himself, and does not know himself. And were he now to follow Auguste's advice, he would still not become one, for a master is a subject who does not need anyone else to tell him what to do. Alidor, by contrast, has gone through at least the first stage, for he says at the end of the play: "C'est de moi seulement que je prendrai la loi." [I shall obey only the law I give myself].

But he cannot go any further. Alidor continues to project his freedom into the future whereas Auguste enunciates his in the present. He does not say: "I will be," but "I am." If La Place Royale is a comedy which ends on a rather melancholy note, it is because the itinerary of the subject does not progress beyond its first stage. At the end of the play, Alidor finds himself in the solipsistic and solitary position of the Cartesian subject. He can finally appear to himself as a free subject and experience satisfaction when he contemplates himself in the mirror, but his image illuminates no one except himself. It exists for him alone. He is visible only to himself. He experiences a metaphysical liberty which is the object of a purely narcissistic pleasure. He cannot know the glory which accompanies freedom when it is heroic in nature.

Now this heroic freedom which defines the subject-king, is not for Corneille the exclusive privilege of the king: it is also the privilege of the artist.

La Place Royale, this title which designates a geographical place, a philosophical place and a political place also designates the place which Corneille assigns to the poet. This title of a play corresponds

---

16. *Cinna*, act IV, ii, l. 1130. In *The Cid, Cinna, the Theatrical Illusion*, trans. John Cairncross (London: Penguin Books, 1975), 167. Hereafter cited in the text.

very closely to the place which Corneille, as the author of the play, claims for himself. Alidor and Auguste, these two complementary figures of Corneille's theater, these two characters who represent the double face, negative in comedy, and positive in tragedy, of a single subject in its pursuit of mastery and freedom, are also two figures by which the poet represents himself. In the dedicatory epistle to *La Place Royale,* Corneille recognized the affinity between himself and his character. However, Alidor's maxims do not merely reflect his views on love, they also express an ethics which, in his case also correspond to an aesthetics. For Corneille, the poet's freedom obeys the same rules as those which protect the lover's freedom. "Il ne faut point servir d'objet qui nous possède" [I must serve no object that possesses me], says Alidor. "Je veux . . . / Que mon feu m'obéisse au lieu de me contraindre, / Que je puisse à mon gré l'enflammer et l'éteindre." [I want . . . / my flame to obey me instead of constraining me / To fan or extinguish it at my will]. Corneille, in the dedicatory epistle writes: "On ne doit jamais aimer en un point qu'on ne puisse n'aimer pas . . . si on en vient jusque là, c'est une tyrannie dont il faut secouer le joug." [One must never love to such an extreme that one cannot not love . . . . If one reaches such an extreme, love becomes a tyranny that must be shaken off.]

These maxims about love strangely resemble those which Corneille prescribes for the writer. They take up the very terms which he uses in the preface to *Clitandre* to expound the principles of his poetic art:

> J'estimerai avoir en quelque façon approché ce que demande Horace au poète qu'il instruit, quand il veut qu'il possède tellement ses sujets, qu'il en demeure toujours le maître, et les asservisse à soi-même, sans se laisser emporter par eux. [Stegmann's edition, 53]

> I presume to have in some way drawn near to what Horace requires of the poet he teaches, when he wants him to possess his subjects, to become their master and subject them to him, without him becoming carried away by them.

The poet's demand for freedom is analogous to the lover's, and could be expressed in the same terms which Alidor employs to speak of the fires of love.[17] The writer too wants his art to obey rather than to

17. This analogy between the maxims of love and the rules of poetic creation is part of a long tradition that goes back to Plato—a tradition to which the notion of "genius" will give new twists. Corneille here picks up the well-known theme of "poetic furor" and gives it his own orientation.

constrain him. The poet's accession to mastery also involves a fight against tyranny: the tyranny of rules. Alidor seeks to free love of the tyranny which all too often accompanies it: Corneille pursues the same ends. He wants to love the rules but refuses to be tyrannized by them. At the height of the *Querelle du Cid*, at the very moment when he is attacked from all sides, he writes this in the dedicatory epistle of *La Suivante:* "J'aime à suivre des règles, mais loin de me rendre leur esclave, je les élargis et les ressère selon le besoin qu'en a mon sujet." (Stegmann, 127) [I love to follow rules, but, far from becoming their slave, I expand and reduce them according to the needs of my subject].

But the poet does not merely demand the freedom of an Alidor, he also wants that of an Auguste, freedom in its heroic form which, as we have seen, consists in a double mastery of self and other. In speaking of himself, Corneille employs the very terms which in his plays, and most notably in *Cinna*, qualify the hero. It is doubtless in *L'Excuse à Ariste*, which appeared in 1637, at the very height of the *Querelle du Cid*, that this heroic conception of the poet is most clearly expressed. The *Excuse* is addressed to a certain Ariste who has asked for a text which he can set to music, and to whom Corneille explains the reasons for his refusal. From the very beginning of the poem, Corneille opposes to the request of the said Ariste the poet's incapacity to subjugate his art to the exigencies of a composer of songs:

> Son feu ne peut agir quand il faut qu'il s'applique
> Sur les fantasques airs d'un rêveur de musique,
> Et que, pour donner lieu de paraître à sa voix,
> De sa bizarre quinte il se fasse des lois;
> Qu'il ait sur chaque ton ses rimes ajustées,
> Sur chaque tremblement ses syllabes comptées,
> Et qu'une froide pointe à la fin d'un couplet
> En dépit de Phoebus donne à l'art un soufflet.

> His flame cannot move when it must be applied
> To the imaginary airs of a musical dreamer,
> And in order for his voice to come forth,
> He must make laws out of the strange fifth tone,
> He must have his rhymes arranged to each note,
> His syllables counted for each modulation,
> And, at the end of a couplet, a chilly point
> Must, regardless of Apollo, slap art in the face.

Corneille invokes the liberty of the poet, employing the same political metaphors as those used in the discourse of love when he invokes the absolute freedom of the poet:

> Enfin cette prison déplaît à son génie,
> Il ne peut rendre hommage à cette tyrannie,
> Il ne se leurre point d'animer de beaux chants,
> Et veut pour se produire avoir la clef des champs.

> After all, this prison displeases his genius,
> He cannot honor such a tyranny,
> He does not let himself be sidetracked in making
> Pretty songs, and longs to express himself, for
> The key to the open country.

However, Corneille is not satisfied by this negative freedom of a subject whose will refuses to obey any law other than the one it gives itself. Having first spoken like an Alidor, the poet now addresses himself to Ariste with the proud majesty of a new Auguste. The passage to this second form of freedom, its positive or heroic form, is marked by the sudden change in the grammatical subject of the verse. In contrast to the preceding lines, Corneille no longer speaks of himself in the third person: he now says *Je:*

> Nous parlons de nous-mêmes avec toute franchise,
> La fausse humilité ne met plus en crédit.
> *Je sais ce que je vaux, et crois ce qu'on m'en dit.*
> . . . .

> Je satisfais ensemble peuple et courtisans,
> Et mes vers en tous lieux sont mes seuls partisans,
> Par leur seule beauté ma plume est estimée,
> Je ne dois qu'à moi seul toute ma renommée.
>   [Emphasis mine]

> We speak frankly of ourselves,
> False modesty gains us nothing.
> I know my worth and believe what I am told of it.
> . . . .

> I satisfy both the people and the courtiers,
> And my verses are my only supporters,
> For their beauty is my pen respected,
> I owe my fame to myself alone.

The passage from the "il" to the "je" in the progression of the poem corresponds very closely to what we have characterised as the second stage of the royal constitution of the subject, the stage of true mastery in which the subject, no longer content with ruling itself, comes to rule over the other as well. The sudden appearance of the "Je" marks a rupture in the poem, denotes the moment in which Corneille possesses himself as subject in the fullest sense of the word. And this inaugural moment of a subject, which finally enunciates itself in a foundational "I" indicating that it has become its own origin, coincides with a double affirmation of the self, both private and public, subjective and objective. It is the moment in which the subject knows its worth, and in which the worth of the subject is recognized: "Je sais ce que je vaux et crois ce qu'on m'en dit." [I know my worth and believe what I am told of it].

The "I" marks the emergence of the unique and absolute I of an individual who is both a meritorious and a glorious subject, a subject authorized to believe what is said of him precisely because he needn't believe it to know it. With the self-possessed assurance of extraordinary pride, Corneille attributes to the poet—to himself—a mastery greater and more noble than that of a king. In the case of a king, merit follows glory, and legitimizes it *après-coup*. Auguste is master of the world before becoming master of himself. Auguste's clemency, which marks the birth of a new reign, is not his first victory, but, as he himself expresses it, his "dernière victoire" [final victory]. The words uttered by Auguste in the last scene of *Cinna* are very close to those used by Corneille to praise the sublime generosity of Louis XIV. The poem which he addresses *Au Roi, sur la paix de 1678*, to celebrate the Treaty of Nimègue by which France had decided to return the greater part of the occupied provinces, begins with an "it was not enough" that articulates in the most explicit way not only the inadequacies of glory when it is not accompanied by merit, but also, in the case of the king, the fact that merit is posterior to glory.

> Ce n'était pas assez, grand Roi, que la victoire
> A te suivre en tous lieux mît sa plus haute gloire;
> Il fallait pour fermer ces grands événements,
> Que la paix se tînt prête à tes commandements.

> It was not enough, great King, that Victory
> Set its highest glory in following you everywhere;
> To bring these great events to an end Peace itself
> Bowed to your commandments.

It was not enough for Louis to conquer, he had to complete his conquests, to seal them [fermer], as Corneille suggestively phrases it, by a final victory, the same as the victory of August. He had to show himself to be generous, as Corneille puts it a few lines later, to "complete" the peace "as a master and enforce it as a king." And having described all the effects of this eminently royal act, Corneille concludes with a phrase that could have served as the inscription on Auguste's monument: "Vainqueur de toutes parts, tu t'es vaincu toi-même" [Conqueror of all, you then conquered yourself].

The greatness of kings consists in becoming worthy of the name they bear, in becoming what they are, in deserving their glory, in giving their history a foundation that assures, after the fact, its ontological dignity. "Je le suis, je veux l'être" [I am, I wish to be] says Auguste. The temporality of beings corresponds to what, in Cartesian terms, could be called the order of analysis—an order whose historical unfolding is the inverse of chronological order in which that which is chronologically first is revealed last. The order of analysis is an order of consciousness whose reflexive moment ends with the discovery of what grounds it. The temporality of the artist, by contrast, corresponds to the ontological order of the real, to the very movement of the production of things. The artist's order is not the order of analysis, but the order of synthesis, since it is the order of creation.

For the artist, origin coincides with beginning. He becomes what he wants to be. The artist gives himself a name and depends only on his works, that is, on his merit. Corneille gives lofty expression to this in the *Excuse à Ariste:* "Je ne dois qu'à moi seul toute ma renommée" [I owe all my fame to myself alone].

The place which Corneille assigns himself is neither that of Auguste nor that of Louis XIV: it is quite simply the place of God. He defines the poet as an absolute subject who reigns amid his own glory, and dispenses this glory to all those whom he deigns to touch with his grace. Sole author of his own fame, the poet is also the unique source of the glory of others. First and foremost among these are kings whose power only becomes effective by means of the images employed to represent it. Whatever their merits or their deeds, kings do not owe their renown to themselves alone, but to the genius of the artist who builds monuments in their honor. In 1667, Corneille addresses to Louis XIV a *Remerciement* for the pension of 2,000 *livres* which he has just been awarded as "premier poète dramatique du monde" [the world's foremost dramatic poet]. In this poem, Corneille distinguishes, in the most explicit manner, three phases of the constitution of the royal power: a past, a present, and a future. To a 'now' in which Louis XIV holds the reins of state and governs alone, he opposes a 'before' in

which the king was not yet his own master since his genius remained
dependent on that of the great Mazarin:

> Jusque-là toutefois tout n'était pas à toi,
> Et quelques doux effets qu'eut produit ta victoire
> Les conseils du grand Jules avaient part à ta gloire.

> Until then, however, everything was not yours,
> And, no matter what the sweet results of your victory,
> The counsel of the great Jules shared in your glory.

It is only "now" that he reigns alone that the king is his own and can
say, like Alidor, "I live, for I am my own / . . . / I subscribe only to my
own law." But according to Corneille, whose organization of the different moments of temporality is strikingly Augustinian in distribution,
this 'now' which illuminates the past and gives it, retrospectively, the
status of an antecedent moment, can only come to completion in a
future. And this future, this moment which has not yet come into
existence but which the present requires for its own fulfillment, is the
time of art, for the artist alone can constitute the actual present as a
'now', as an absolute present:

> Maintenant qu'on te voit en digne potentat
> Réunir en ta main les rênes de l'état,
> Que tu gouvernes seul, et que par ta prudence
> Tu rappelles des rois l'auguste indépendance,
> *Il est temps* que d'un air plus élevé;
> Je peigne en ta personne un monarque achevé;
> Que j'en fasse un modèle aux rois qu'on verra naître
> Et qu'en toi pour régner je leur présente un maître.
>
> [Stegmann, 884]

> Now that, as a worthy ruler, we see you
> Hold in your hand the reins of the state,
> Which you govern alone, and now that you recall,
> Through your prudence, the august freedom of kings,
> It is time that, with higher aim,
> I paint you as a complete monarch;
> That I make of you a model for the kings who will
> Be born, and that I offer you as master to those
> Who will one day reign.

It is the poet who transforms the king into a "model" for eternity, who
gives his existence the value of an archetype, who represents him as an

absolute point of reference to which all subsequent history must refer. It is to the poet—and to him alone—that the king owes the right to be considered as he would like to be considered; that is, as an origin. If the king should protect poets, it is in the name of a well-understood self-interest, since poets give to him the one thing he lacks in order to be an absolute subject, the one thing he cannot give himself if he is to be himself. The poets constitute the king as an origin. The great king, writes Corneille in his "Remerciement," who is "the perfect image of the King of Kings," thus needs the artist to paint the image and make it adored. "Je rendrai de ton nom l'univers idolâtre" [I will make the universe idolize your name], he writes before adding: "Mais pour ce grand chef-d'oeuvre il faut un grand théâtre" [but this great masterpiece demands a great theater].

Thus no greatness, not even royal greatness, can equal that of the poet, for he alone can offer the scepter of glory, and he alone holds in his hands the keys that open the doors of eternity. Corneille makes this very explicit in a poem addressed to a certain Marquise de B.A.T: "Sur le départ de Madame la Marquise de B.A.T"

> Car vous aimez la gloire, et vous savez qu'un roi
> Ne vous peut jamais en assurer tant que moi.
> Il est plus en ma main qu'en celle d'un monarque
> De vous faire égaler l'amante de Pétrarque,
> Et mieux que tous les rois je puis faire douter
> De sa Laure ou de vous qui le doit emporter.
>
> [Stegmann, 881]

> For you love glory, and you know that not even a king
> Can assure you as much of it as I can.
> It is more in my hand than in the hand of a monarch
> To make you the equal of Petrarch's beloved,
> And better than any king I can raise the question
> Of whether you or Laura should win the prize.

The theater alone occupies the only truly royal place, and Corneille is its king.

Corneille could thus not have found a better title for his play. In *La Place Royale*, Alidor's 'I' triumphs in effect after witnessing the success of a dramatic fiction of which he is at once author, director, and leading actor. In order to become a subject, to live at last, to belong to himself, Alidor stages a play with a very complicated plot: he deceives everyone, organizes a false kidnapping (although it fails), acts out a comedy. In order to win his freedom, he constructs a drama in which he himself takes charge of both the production and the direction of the actors, and which culminates in the victory of his 'I'. In imagining a story, creating a setting, inventing its various episodes, changing the cast and moving people around to suit the plot, Alidor is staging theater, and it is thanks to this theater that he can accede to mastery. His self, the position of subject that he holds at the close of the play, is the very real effect of a dramatic fiction, the happy end of a comedy that he has invented. In the last scene of *La Place Royale*, when all of the other protagonists have left him, he remains alone, like a king at the center of his own theater. Alidor's final sentence before the curtain falls ends with the word "God"—God, the last word of the play, the only rival to whom Alidor is willing to give Angélique without regret, is also the only Other against whom the artist can be measured, and the artist's only rival.

As Corneille indicates at the start of *La Place Royale*, the scene is Paris. And this scene is set in a theater.

—Translated by Madeleine Dobie

JOHN D. LYONS

Unseen Space and Theatrical Narrative: The "Récit de Cinna"

Theatricality and the baroque are widely recognized as intertwined both inside and outside of the dramatic playhouse. During the baroque period urban space was transformed into a setting.[1] Jean Rousset formulated this relationship concisely: "there is no baroque church without a façade; one could more easily imagine a baroque façade without a church."[2] The façade, in Rousset's account, plays a role analogous to a stage set: an outside without an inside, or with an inside that is left to the imagination of the viewer. In this way the viewer is invited to assume responsibility for giving meaning to the façade by an imaginative act of completion or extension.

The theatrical concept of "unity of place," which was given fervent theoretical support toward the end of the reign of Louis XIII, is inextricably linked to the phenomenon of the façade with its division between the seen and the unseen. So often mentioned in discussions of the drama of Corneille and Racine, the unity of place is rarely appreciated as a constructive concept. Instead it is sometimes associated with the faintly ridiculous image of Academicians keeping score in the battles of the unities. Yet the increasing theoretical insistence on strict limitation of the space presented on stage had important consequences, some of which are more liberating and creative than restrictive and inhibiting.

The "unity" of place is a way of expressing the binary quality of baroque space as Deleuze has described it: "the world with only two

1. G. Carlo Argan, *The Europe of the Capitals: 1600–1700* (Geneva: Skira, 1964).
2. Jean Rousset, *La littérature de l'âge baroque en France. Circé et le paon* (Paris: José Corti, 1965), 168.

YFS 80, *Baroque Topographies,* ed. Timothy Hampton, © 1991 by Yale University.

floors, separated by the fold which reverberates on each side according to a different system, this is the baroque contribution par excellence. It expresses . . . the transformation of the cosmos into *mundus*."[3] The enclosure of space in seventeenth-century theatre proceeds from a porous, loosely structured stage setting, to a rigorous dualism. The multiple simultaneous sets of the early seventeenth century were re-placed towards midcentury by a single visible location. Characters could no longer walk from one part of a city, for instance, to another part by crossing from one area of the stage to another. From many spatial divisions the theatre is reduced to two, offstage and onstage, made even more strictly binary by the absence of a stage curtain.[4] The onstage thus entirely and permanently coincided with the visible and the offstage with the invisible. One consequence of the unity of place is to put into the hands of playwrights an instrument for framing the visible action of the play, giving them a boundary beyond which the spectator will never see, like Rousset's façade without a church. Only through verbal accounts of dramatic characters can this invisible space be created for us.

One way of conceiving the offstage world is to picture it as the reality which is filtered to us through the stage. This is the view of Leo Spitzer, in his classic article "The 'Récit de Théramène'," which analy-ses in fine detail the account of Hippolyte's death given by the young hero's mentor in *Phèdre*. Through "intermediate persons who lend us their eyes," we learn what has happened in the great region of unseen space which surrounds the theatre of the seventeenth century.[5] Spitzer, however, in showing how Racine's style moderates the horror of the attack of the monster, may have been excessively reluctant to confront the possibility that what is monstrous is not the creature from the sea but the unseen space which is evoked by dramatic nar-rative or *récit* itself. This unseen space, the offstage or *hors scène*, is generated by the practices of seventeenth-century theatre in such a way that it is idle to try to decide which came first, the imposition of the "unity of place" which gives practical motivation to have charac-ters tell each other (and the audience) what has happened elsewhere or rather the preference for verbal account over physical enactment of

3. Gilles Deleuze, *Le Pli. Leibniz et le baroque* (Paris: Minuit, 1988), 41.
4. Jacques Scherer, *La Dramaturgie classique en France* (Paris: Nizet, 1950 [rpt. 1968]), 175–95. Hereafter cited in the text.
5. Leo Spitzer "The 'Récit de Théramène'," in *Linguistics and Literary History* (Princeton: Princeton University Press, 1948 [rpt. 1967], 107.

certain events.[6] The theatre of Corneille, Racine, and their contemporaries in France pays at least apparent homage to the increasing theoretical demands for a single concrete place within which all visible action would take place. Jacques Scherer has shown, however, that playwrights seldom really met the goals set forth by such theorists as d'Aubignac (*La Dramaturgie classique*, 194). It may be of more importance to turn this perspective around and to ask not about the space that is presented onstage but rather about the vaster and more mysterious space which theatrical practice keeps us from seeing.

There is something terrifying about this absent space. In Racine's tragedy, as Barthes has shown, the offstage is identified so closely with death that the order to leave the stage is equivalent to the command to die.[7] In all seventeenth-century theatre after the 1630s the offstage is where all violence, mortal illness, and physical sexuality occurs. It is also, as La Mesnardière wrote in 1639, where acts too dangerous for the actors to perform were relegated to the imagination of the spectators. This practical observation can lead to an important theoretical one. What happens offstage does not, in concrete terms, happen at all.

This is a crucial quality of offstage space which Spitzer's expression and our submission to the fictions of the theatre prevent us from seeing: offstage space is **imaginary** in a way that onstage space is not. Théramène and other characters who give a *récit* are not shielding us from "crude reality" but giving us instead the illusion of an elsewhere. If there is reality to this "elsewhere" it is not beyond the words of the speaker but only in those words. Narrative has a paradoxical status in drama because it speaks *of* space but not *in* space, that is, narrative does not use space as its primary medium or signifier (as do dance and mime) but in first instance as its signified or content. Yet the purely discursive accounts of what happens in the imagined unseen space invoke spatial categories in such a way as to make the spatial signified a spatial signifier.[8] Where things are reported to be, with which other

6. Thomas Pavel formulates this preference by the question, "How otherwise grasp the effect of *Horace*, a play in which the characters never stop telling on stage events that have just happened a few seconds before behind the stage, except by seeing here the triumph of verbalization over *mimésis*?" "Espaces raciniens," (*Communications* 47, 1988) 181.

7. Roland Barthes, *Sur Racine* (Paris: Le Seuil, collection "Pierres vives," 1963), 17ff.

8. Thus fitting Barthes's definition of connotation, in which a primary signified becomes a signifier (*Eléments de sémiologie* [1964; rpt. with *Le Degré zéro de l'écriture*, Paris: Editions Gonthier, 1969], 163–68).

things they are juxtaposed or from which they are separated—these features or accounts of offstage space give spatial categories active meaning even though the "space" in question does not exist.[9]

The distinction between offstage and onstage space coincides largely with the Platonic distinction between diegesis (or report) and mimesis (or enactment). The stage is the space of enactment and the offstage is the space of reported events. Our access to offstage space lies through what characters tell us in onstage narratives. In French theatre after *Le Cid,* characters do not usually retell what has already happened onstage in full sight of the public, but instead narrate what the spectators have not seen (Scherer, 232–33). Therefore verbal reports in practice are associated with the unseen, the absent in space, and removal in time. What is spoken about in dramatic narrative is generally an event from the past or a plan for the future. Our view of the offstage is, in a sense, lateral. Blocked by the scenery straight in front of us, we cannot look through to know what is happening *right now* somewhere else. Instead we know, or think we know, what has happened or what will happen. In the midst of the full presence and within the present time of the stage scene, reports of the unseen world are pockets of foreign time, bearers of absence. What is reported as being absent occurs in a place, the offstage, which has both literal and figurative functions. We pretend to believe (and thus somehow really do believe) that characters literally go somewhere when they leave the stage and return from somewhere (other than their dressing room) when they return. Yet we also know that the category "offstage" marks all that is said of it with a different relationship to reality. What can happen offstage does not happen onstage, just as what can happen figuratively cannot always happen literally. When a poet declares a sexual love for a rose, his words are assigned to a different category from mania or fetishism. Likewise the appearance of Théramène's monster offstage is not only technically more feasible but differently understood (less ridiculous, more freely associated with the dark forces of human hate, more purely "symbolical") than if Racine had made of *Phèdre* a "pièce à

9. The imaginative investment of the spectator in what is hidden or left unrepresented has been discussed with regard to D'Aubignac's theories of drama by Timothy Murray in his recent *Theatrical Legitimation* (New York: Oxford University Press, 1987), 166–217. See also Harriet Stone, *Royal DisClosure: Problematics of Representation in French Classical Tragedy* (Birmingham: Summa Publications, 1987) and Stone's forthcoming publications on the role of the subject in classical representation.

machines" with a visible monster. Dramatic narrative therefore is the mode of existence of the offstage and thus the discourse of the invisible, the "elsewhere."

The division of dramatic space into seen and unseen and the considerable increase in the amount of space that remains unseen (through greater stress on representing a single place) take on particular importance in a period during which space was controlled by a centralizing political power which used space in significant ways, that is, as a way to convey meaning.[10] Several aspects of the culture of the baroque are especially pertinent to the tragic *récit:* the dominance of public space, the belief in spatial continuity, and the relationship of the thematics of illusion with distance and exteriority.

The baroque has been described as differing from mannerism in its struggle for concentration, unity, overwhelming centralizing power, all aspects which affect the perception and representation of space. The dominance of public spectacle over intimacy, of centralizing urban plan over individual enterprise mark many of the architectural and even horticultural creations of the seventeenth century. In works as different as Saint-Amant's "Contemplateur," Descartes's *Discours de la méthode,* and Lafayette's *La Princesse de Clèves,* the central figures are shown resisting the temptations of public space for retreat in the exceptional private space, while these texts at the same time display considerable doubt about the possibility of achieving such a retreat. Against this centrifugal movement, the comedies of the early Corneille with their use of settings in the public square reflect the attractiveness and importance of public space.

A second aspect of the baroque aesthestic with important consequences for the theatre is the long-emerging belief in spatial continuity and homogeneity as requirements of correct representation.[11] This entails the study of perspectivist drawing and optics and prevents the assumption that any aspect of space within visual range can be left unaccounted for. Even "empty" space must figure into perspective, and

10. The *Discours de la méthode* is probably the most revealing document of this political control of space because its information is apparently offhand or lateral and thus expresses the extent to which the control of space was already taken for granted by its author. See Jean-Joseph Goux, "Descartes et la perspective" *L'Esprit Créateur* 25, 1 (Spring 1985): 10–20.

11. Erwin Panofsky's concise formulation of the goal of spatial representation at the end of the Renaissance is the production of "an entirely rational space, that is, infinite, continuous, and homogeneous," *La Perspective comme forme symbolique* (Paris: Minuit, 1975), 41.

the size of objects does not depend solely on their importance but on their location in the spatial grid. In this system the fact that some part of the space may be blocked from sight is not sufficient to permit the assumption that it is different from the space we see. Yet baroque architecture and sculpture plays on this Renaissance conviction that space is continuous and homogeneous by presenting paradoxical cases in which the theoretically true spatial relationships are represented through illusionistic means. Stairways, windows, vents, and curtains allow us to believe that there is space similar to what we see just outside of our visual field. But this "unseen space" is frequently not at all similar to the visible space with which it seems to be connected. A divorce arises between intellection and perception in which the representation of the unseen becomes a major aesthetic as well as epistemological effort. This importance of the baroque unseen has been expressed in widely diverse idioms. Wylie Sypher, for instance, writes, "Thus the 'secret' of baroque space is not its infinity; rather this illusion of infinity is due to a special access to 'farther' space that occurs whenever we seem to break through, or pass beyond, hugely defined boundaries . . ."[12] Michel Foucault speaks of the "uncertain corridors" of Velasquez's "Las Meninas," a painting which exhibits the power of "that invisible and hidden space," an unseen space in which we must believe in order to assure the coherence of what we do see.[13]

Thirdly, despite the importance of firm belief in a farther space beyond our sight, external space is frequently associated with illusion and the fantastic, not only the illusion of the visual artistry or distortion which points towards such space—like the "fake windows for symmetry" which Pascal ridicules in his *Pensées*—but also the illusions of uncontrolled imagination which populate that space. The New World plays that role in Montaigne's *Essays*. The discovery of a space which is connected to ours through measurable extension and rationally accessible through our means of transportation, permitted illusions and fantasies concerning what existed in that space to multiply through the tenuous and intermittent links of travel narrative. In the seventeenth century, Montaigne's diligent reader Descartes formulated more rigorously the nature of extension. No longer interested in the reports of travelers, Descartes thought himself free to determine

12. Wylie Sypher, *Four Stages of Renaissance Style* (Garden City: Doubleday, 1955), 213.

13. Michel Foucault, *Les Mots et les choses* (Paris: Gallimard, "Bibliothèque des sciences humaines" collection, 1966), 26.

through his reason alone what must exist in space even if he dis-
believed the reports of his own senses. Yet however much Descartes
attempts in the *Discours* and the *Méditations* to provide an account of
the world prior to invoking his potentially misleading sense percep-
tions, the rationally defined extension-space is frequently populated
with visions or specters.[14] Still later in the seventeenth century, in one
of the most powerfully erotic passages of French literature, the
princess of Clèves believes she sees her lover, the duke of Nemours, in
the shadowy space outside the illuminated room in which she reclines
in revery. Though Nemours was really there, the heroine's imagination
might very well have projected this vision, and this potential figment
of her daydream is located, significantly, in the area that is beyond the
defined space in which she felt herself to be protected and alone.

Unity and dominance of public space, continuity of seen and unseen space, and, despite the belief in spatial continuity, the paradoxical
ascription of illusion to the unseen space—this closely related set of
spatial values confers special significance on dramatic *récit* in seventeenth-century theatre. Our access to the offstage is through the words
of characters and especially through dramatic narrative, the *récits*
made by characters onstage. These narratives serve as the threshold to
the offstage space, which is of a radically different nature from the
space of the stage. The stage is a real and public place. There, a character is exposed to the gaze of the assembled spectators who all become
mutually supporting witnesses to what happens. Chimène's apartment in *Le Cid* is private space, it is private space invaded by the gaze of
the (fictively) unseen public. With certain noteworthy exceptions—
most especially Corneille's *Illusion comique*—what happens onstage
"really" happens within the fiction of French classical theatre. Dream-
visions do not appear to the spectators, who can only obtain knowledge
of the unreal through the deranged actions and gestures of a character
in prey to delusions, seeing his actions and hearing his words in response to those imaginary beings, which do not become visible to the
spectator (e.g., Eraste's attack of madness in *Mélite*). The narrative of
the offstage world has a much more tenuous claim to our belief than
what is acted out before us, for such narratives depend either on the

14. See my "*Camera obscura:* Image and Imagination in Descartes's *Méditations,*"
in *Convergences: Rhetoric and Poetic in Seventeenth-Century France. Essays for Hugh
M. Davidson,* ed. D. L. Rubin and Mary B. McKinley (Columbus: Ohio State University
Press, 1989), 171–90.

words of a single individual or on the often conflicting accounts of several characters.

The monster from the sea in *Phèdre* can be treated as a metonym for the double space from which it comes: first from the sea and then from the offstage, both spaces that remain unseen, as does the monster itself. The kind of monstrosity that inhabits the offstage varies from tragedy to tragedy and from author to author, but is rarely free of some taint. In Racine's theatre narratives usually bring accounts of human or divine crime and excess, from Néron's monstrous voyeurism in *Britannicus* to the sacrilege of *Athalie*. In Corneille's theatre, the *récit* tends to be impure in an even more radical way, by pretending to be an account of truth when it is illusion and self-deception. The information of Cornelian *récits* is *usually false or misleading*, making the offstage the place of error and fantasy, not because error occurs offstage but instead because this invisible space is figuratively the location into which the narrators project their interpretations or obsessions. The *récit* of Dorante in *Le Menteur* (II, 5) conjures up in words a nonexistent bedroom in which the hero claims to have had an amorous adventure with a lady who later turns out not to exist. In *Horace* the misleading narrative of Julie (III, 6) describes the defeat of Rome at the hands of the Curiaces, a defeat which, of course, later seems not to have happened when Valère arrives with the "correct" account of the battle (IV, 2). Likewise in *Théodore*, the first narrative (by Paulin in IV, 3) of the heroïne's violent subjection to repeated rape turns out to be false when Didyme arrives on stage with a later version, itself difficult to verify (IV, 5). *Héraclius* ends virtually in an aporia when conflicting *récits* by the same narrator (Léontine) undermine the credibility of all evidence from outside the closed, onstage space.

As both figurative and imaginary space, the offstage structures the onstage characters. This is the corollary to the fact that the narrating characters structure our view of the offstage space. Just as Descartes in the *Méditations* finds his mind inhabited by chimeras which seem to be "outside" him but, as he convinces himself, are generated by his imagination, so also the "elsewhere" of the dramatic narrative is the character of the narrating *persona*. By reminding ourselves of the physically nonexistent nature of the offstage space, we can perceive the fact that what we hear in the *récit* is what the character believes, wishes, or fabricates—not what *is*. Far from being the "crude reality" which, in Spitzer's description, is filtered by the narrative, the content of the *récit* gives the image of the recesses of the character who presents the narrative. At times this process advances to the point of undermining all credibility of the character, of isolating him with his private account, his private "elsewhere," within the public world of the stage.

Cinna's narrative of his conspiracy in the first act of *Cinna* is one of the most interestingly problematic of baroque *récits*. It shows how the constant regression of the character's imagination into the always-just-beyond in the offstage space can finally result in undermining the character's reality onstage. We thus find ourselves entertaining the possibility that illusion has spilled from off to onstage. At the same time Cinna's account of his recent meeting with the conspirators raises questions about the improper mixing of public and private space as factors which lead to political as well as theatrical disorder. Corneille himself was both proud of this narrative and sensitive to its disturbance of the unity of space. In the *Examen* (1660) of *Cinna*, Corneille praised its diversity of figure as well as its appropriateness for both speaker and onstage listener. Yet he noted,

> In fact there is here a doubling of specific locations. Half the play takes place in Emilie's apartment, and the other half in Auguste's chamber. I would have been ridiculous if I had shown that Emperor deliberating with Maxime and Cinna as to whether or not he would give up the imperial power exactly *in the same place where Cinna had told Emilie about the conspiracy formed against Auguste.*[15]

The need to distinguish spaces according to what happens in them, as if each act imprinted itself on the place, seems to be stronger in Corneille than in other playwrights (cf., Racine's practice in *Britannicus*). Corneille's expression of the fear of contamination points toward the strong attachment of the baroque for distinctions between public and private space. Moreover, as will appear shortly, Cinna's own account reveals his own simultaneous fear of the breakdown in the public/private distinction and his own characteristic inability to maintain a distance between these two domains.

Let us consider for a moment the mimesis/diegesis (or enactment/reporting) opposition mentioned above. Gérard Genette, who has most contributed to the revival in theoretical interest of these concepts, adopts the Platonic terminology, in which mimesis refers to the quotation of character's direct speech and diegesis the report of a

15. Pierre Corneille, *Oeuvres complètes*, ed. André Stegmann (Paris: Le Seuil, "Intégrale" collection, 1963), 269.

character's words in the words of a narrator: "Poetry and fiction fall into three classes. First, that which employs representation only, tragedy and comedy. . . . Secondly, that in which the poet speaks in his own person; the best example is lyric poetry. Thirdly, that which employs both methods, epic and various other kinds of poetry."[16] Separating mimesis from diegesis would seem to be a very easy, even mechanical task, one that could be accomplished by drawing up a formal description of the markers of reporting (e.g., greater frequency of past tenses, transformation of first- and third-person pronouns, etc.) and of direct speech. Of course, this "simple" task is, in practice, almost impossible, but next to it there is an even more complex activity: the description of the *effect* of these two opposed modes. Genette, in his "Discours du récit" proposes a description of the effect of the mimesis/diegesis opposition by studying it under the heading of narrative "mode"—that is, the greater or lesser amount of information conveyed and hence, in figurative terms, the greater or lesser distance of the narrated events from the narrative audience: "the 'pure narrative' [le 'récit pur'] will be considered more *distant* than 'imitation' " (184).

Although tragedy and comedy are the classic examples of enactment (mimesis) for Plato and Aristotle, these forms contain reporting, the *récit* made by a character, from Valère in *Horace* to Théramène in *Phèdre*. But how, exactly, can we tell the difference between enactment and reporting? In the "mixed" forms mentioned by the ancients and familiar to us, the contrast between the "voice of the poet" and the "voice of the character" allows us to perceive the point where one stops and the other starts. In a work that is all enactment, it is harder to recognize enactment, or mimesis, for what it is. Theorists, including Genette, take for granted the existence of a framing device which permits us to differentiate an "act" from an "enactment"—though we have all heard of the fabled spectator who could not refrain from jumping on stage to bring help to the hero or heroine. We assume that the institution of the theatre itself, with its varying architectonics (stage, curtain at times, amphitheatre) will signal to us that there is a difference between the actor and the character. Another way to describe this is to say that enactment as a mode transfers the distancing mechanism outside the enacted utterance itself, especially through location codes. Reporting, on the other hand, contains within itself the features

16. Plato, *The Republic*, trans. H. D. P. Lee (Baltimore: Penguin Books, 1955), 133. See also Gérard Genette, "Discours du récit," in *Figures III* (Paris: Le Seuil, 1972), 184–88 and his *Introduction à l'architexte* (Paris: Le Seuil, 1979).

required to permit its recognition. For example, if a speaker were to begin by saying, "I must report that . . ." the utterance would be recognized as a speech-act called "reporting," but whether or not this report took place as an enactment could only be determined by other evidence. Thus mimesis and diegesis are not symmetrical nor are they mutually exclusive modes. Enactment distinguishes between the actor and the role (or the "poet" and the "character" whose words are quoted), while report distinguishes between present and nonpresent in both temporal and spatial senses.[17] Thus both enactment and report draw a boundary which the audience is expected to recognize, but those boundaries are drawn in different ways.[18] In the case of *récit* in the theatre an actor is performing the role of a character, who becomes the narrator of an event that is supposed to have happened, usually offstage.

Cinna's narrative in act I, scene 3 of Corneille's Roman tragedy of that title is a traditional set-piece, characterized not simply by its use of reporting verbs but by its monologic form, its length (104 verses, nearly 6% of the text of *Cinna*), and its reference to offstage space. The term narrative, however, may be misleading, for Cinna's *récit* complicates the relationship between enactment and report. An actor performing the role of Cinna (mimesis 1) tells (diegesis 1) of an assembly in which Cinna told (diegesis 2) of Augustus's evil role in the civil wars. At certain points in his telling (diegesis 1) the character Cinna enacts (mimesis 2) his earlier oration. He abandons the role of the private speaker to embody the energetic public orator—or rather one role encloses the other, so that Cinna is speaking to his lover Emilie as if he were still before the assembly. The second level (diegesis 2, mimesis 2) are those utterances which are rooted in the offstage scene: the account

---

17. Nina C. Ekstein notes, "diegetic presentation of offstage or past events often takes the form of a récit," *Dramatic Narrative: Racine's Récits* (New York: Peter Lang, 1986) 12.

18. Both boundaries are drawn at the same time in certain canonical texts of the "mixed" category, that is principally, epic. Odysseus's narrative to the Phaiakians (*Odyssey*, books 9–12) is mimetic—the poet or general narrator does not simply report what Odysseus said but reproduces his own words and thus verbally enacts the role of Odysseus for four continuous books without interruption from the "poet" (by this token, thus all homodiegetic metadiegetic narratives are both mimetic and diegetic). Similar situations can arise in texts that belong to the purely dramatic category. It is an odd aspect of the history of poetics that the concept of mixture should apply only to mixing in one direction but not to the other. If the narrator speaks as a character, the mode is mixed. But if the character speaks as narrator, we are still in a purely mimetic (dramatic) mode.

Cinna gives his coconspirators, whether summarized (reported) (what Genette calls "narrativisé" or "raconté") [*Discours du récit*, 191], or reproduced (enacted). Both of these second-level utterances involve a doubling of Cinna. In one case Cinna is talking about Cinna and in the other Cinna is playing for Emilie the role that Cinna had in the conspirator's assembly. One can interpret Corneille's text as authorizing a still deeper embedding of enactment, if one assumes that Cinna's earlier rhetorical display was already a role, a contrivance of the fickle Cinna to appear more politically committed and motivated more purely than we find him to be later.

During Cinna's report to Emilie it is hard at times to tell whether he is merely talking to Emilie or whether he is enacting his previous speech. At several points in the *récit*, distancing words—markers of reporting—help remind the public that Cinna is telling Emilie of something done elsewhere: "J'ajoute à ces tableaux . . . ," "Je les peins dans le meurtre . . ." [I add to these pictures . . . , I paint them in the act of murder . . .]. At times Cinna is merely being "himself," Cinna, in the present and in the presence of Emilie; at other times he is being the Cinna of the recent past, as he was before the conspirators. There is a split in Cinna, which can be called the mimetic split or mimetic distance. It is similar to what Bullough called many years ago the "aesthetic distance."[19] The aesthetic distance refers to the audience's ability to distance itself from the events on stage in order to prevent interruption of the drama by spectators perceiving the drama as immediate, "real" event. Cinna's split between himself *now* and himself *then* is in some sense "within" the character, but it is usually marked by gestures, changes in voice, effects of rhythm. This permits the audience to assume such a distance in regard to the speeches Cinna reenacts. We can say to ourselves, "he's not really saying that; he's only quoting what he said earlier." Played in certain ways, however, Cinna can appear to be plunged into a vivid memory of his recent success, not only acting it, but reliving it. When this happens, Cinna becomes— before our eyes—two persons: the lover Cinna who frames the appearance of the brilliant orator Cinna. Such dramatization confirms our earlier claim that enactment transfers its markers outside of the enacted utterance, for the *contrast* in Cinna's way of speaking would

19. Edward Bullough, "Psychical Distance," *British Journal of Psychology* V, part 2: (June, 1912), 85–118.

permit us to recognize when he is speaking as lover directly to Emilie and when he is reproducing for Emilie the speech and behavior of Cinna the orator.

Why should Cinna put on this performance? Why should his performance, that is his enactment or mimesis, be the performance of a report? Or rather than ask why Cinna should do it, we should ask why Corneille would use this mixture of enactment and report at this point in his play. *Récit*, a character's report, serves several functions in classical tragedy. It permits concision in presenting the subject (in the formalist sense of *sujet*) by allowing elements of the *sujet* to be incorporated in summary rather than acted out. It thus facilitates "unity of time"; it permits the play to convey events which, for technical or material reasons, could not be presented on the stages of the seventeenth century (e.g., naval battles);[20] it allows the play to be limited in its place (*unité de lieu*); finally, it allows the play to convey events which cannot be staged for reasons of ideology, that is, for reasons of decorum or *bienséance*.[21] Of all of these functions, the "*récit* de Cinna" in its primary level as diegesis 1 seems to serve only one: maintaining the unity of place. The thematic importance of this limitation of space represented in *Cinna* will appear later. There is, however, an effect of *récit* which does not fit any of the above strictly theatrical functions. Cinna's *récit* reports that which by its nature cannot be seen and must remain always just beyond our sight. Theatrical report, as the mode of distance, absence, and temporal disjunction, flickers in this scene as an unstable mixture with dramatic enactment. Let us consider more carefully the several instances of enactment and report mentioned above.

One of these instances can be dismissed right off as too general to need detailed comment in relation to seventeenth-century theatre. Mimetic level 1 is simply the fact that an actor is playing a role in a play.

20. This category is described by La Mesnardière as "*Spectacles full of danger*, those which it is very difficult to produce on stage without putting the theatre people in danger: like the death of Lycas thrown into the sea by Hercules, Phaëton's fall, Hyppolitus's dismemberment," *La Poëtique* (Paris: Sommaville, 1639), 202.

21. This category is described by La Mesnardière as "*Horrible Spectacles*, those which show us detestable acts, which make us shudder with horror at the sight of their cruelty; for example, the parricides of Medea and Tantalus . . ." (*La Poëtique*, 202). It is worth recalling that for La Mesnardière some spectacles of death and wounding are highly appropriate for stage presentation. These *Spectacles genereux* include such moments as when "glorious Cato tears out his guts so as not to see the dying Republic expire" (203). These "beautiful homicides . . . having nothing odious which might offend our sight" should not be banished from the stage (206).

However, mimetic level 2 and the two levels of diegesis are all worth looking at closely. Diegetic level 1 consists of Cinna's direct report to Emilie of the conspiratorial assembly and his role in it. This report contains within it another report, the report of Auguste's activities, which Cinna had delivered in different words to the conspirators. One of the principal themes of diegetic level 1 is the *reaction* of the conspirators. Cinna has already insisted on this in his eight-verse initial report (lines 145–52) on how the other members of his political group displayed their willingness to proceed. In beginning the long monologue Cinna directs Emilie's attention to the invisible scene of these eager faces,

> Plût aux dieux que vous-même eussiez vu de quel zèle
> Cette troupe entreprend une action si belle!
> Au seul nom de César, d'Auguste, et d'empereur,
> Vous eussiez vu leurs yeux s'enflammer de fureur . . .
>
> [Ll. 157–59]

Would to God that you had seen for yourself with what zeal that company undertakes such a beautiful act! At the mere names Caesar, Augustus, and emperor, you would have seen their eyes blaze with furor . . .

The *reaction* to the internal report (diegesis 2) intensifies the effect of this report by an effect of contagion, which could be called—if it were not an additional source of confusion—mimetic. The Girardian mimesis of desire and admiration functions fully in this group effect through which the conspirators excite one another towards violence.[22] Here, however, by reporting the incendiary effect of his words on the invisible conspirators, by attempting to get Emilie to *picture* this reaction, Cinna is pointing towards the source of that reaction, Cinna himself, and to create an imitative admiration for himself.

Right from the beginning the report uses visual terms as if to make immediately present what is absent, but by being purely imaginary the reported scene transcends both the limitations of the stage and the limitations of the supposed original scene itself. Diegetic level 1 enfolds diegesis 2, the content of Cinna's oration. For example,

> Je leur fais des tableaux de ces tristes batailles
> Où Rome par ses mains déchirait ses entrailles,

22. This effect is studied at length by René Girard both in *Mensonge romantique et vérité romanesque* (Paris: Grasset, 1961) and in *La Violence et le sacré* (Paris: Grasset, 1972).

Où l'aigle abattait l'aigle, et de chaque côté
Nos légions s'armaient contre leur liberté

[Ll. 177–80]

I make them pictures of those sad battles, in which Rome with her
hands tore her innards, where the eagle struck down the eagle, and on
each side our legions took up arms against their own freedom

not only includes the account of Cinna's own verbal action with the
conspirators, but also contains portions of his account of the civil war.
This account is diegesis 2, the offstage *récit* delivered with full or-
atorical emphasis. Like the report to Emilie, this oration heavily emphasizes visual terms to create *pictures* of the civil war. Cinna insists
on how his audience was meant to decode visually the information he
gives them: "Je leur fais des tableaux . . ." (l. 177), "j'ai dépeint les
morts" [I depicted the dead] (l. 206), "un crayon imparfait" [an un-
finished sketch] (l. 204). This vision of Rome, doubly framed by its two
audiences, Emilie and the conspirators, gives a vision of civil space
colored in blood red and black. Civil space is not what we would
consider "realistic" presentation of space, but rather is a selection of
places and details in function of their political and emotional significance. This space is traversed neither in chronological order (that is, in
following the sequence of the events of the wars), nor in contiguity
(from one point to another neighboring point in the material world).
Instead the ideology of Rome provides the map. First a general view
("Rome entière noyée au sang de ses enfants" [all Rome drowned in the
blood of her children] l. 196) and then partial views distinguishing the
social organization of Rome as it affects space: "Les uns assassinés
dans les places publiques, / Les autres dans le sein de leurs dieux domestiques" [Some murdered in public places, others in the midst of the
gods of their home] (ll. 197–98). This public/private distinction has
implicit echoes in the following verses. The wicked man (*le méchant*)
is a broad social and presumably public menace whose repeated crimes
threaten everyone, while the mariticide threatens the most private
family space within which husbands are considered safe ("Le mari par
sa femme en son lit égorgé" [The husband's throat cut by his wife in his
bed] l. 200). The subsequent verses link the private and public spaces in
an abnormal way, sadly characteristic of civil strife: "Le fils tout dé-
gouttant du meurtre de son père, / Et sa tête à la main demandant son
salaire" [The son drenched in his father's blood brings his head for
payment] (l. 201–02). The "private" parricide ceases to fill domestic

space and moves into the public view as decapitation and dismemberment become part of the market place and the severed head becomes a commodity with a price.

In the context of classical theatre, the concentrated power of the *récit* takes on a special value. As tragedy is more concentrated than history, so Cinna's *récit* is more concentrated than what we can see on stage.[23] Cinna's *récit* is not concerned with the mechanics of entrances and exits, with the introduction of characters to the audience in a timely manner, or with the respect of the unities. Freed from the necessary transitional and technical details which make some moments on stage seem "filling" the *récit* can select whatever it needs for spatial semiotics—that is, the use of events or objects which purportedly occupy space to bear significance. This significance can include unrestrained emotional impact, cause-effect linkages, a classification of social values, etc.

These verbal *tableaux* do not have to link the significant places— the assassinations in public squares (l. 192) and the husband killed in bed (l. 200)—by including the in-between spaces required by the perspectivist system. In this way the verbal account is able to use space without being subject to the centralizing control of spatial uniformity imposed on the plastic arts and on the theatre as an art of space. Yet in escaping the homogeneity imposed on visual space, the offstage space relegates itself to the status of the place of distortion, error, madness, and crime. The offstage is somehow continuous with our visual space, yet different from it in regard to the laws which govern it.

With Cinna's *récit* the glance backward towards the civil war is succeeded by the view forward to a scene which has not happened and will never happen, the assassination of Auguste. This scene is also topological; it assigns particular values to spaces. Cinna quotes himself as saying,

> Demain au Capitole il fait un sacrifice;
> Qu'il en soit la victime, et faisons en ces lieux
> Justice à tout le monde, à la face des dieux.
>
> [Ll. 232–33]

Tomorrow on the Capitol he makes a sacrifice; let him be the victim; let us do justice in this place for everyone, before the gods.

---

23. This concentration can be inferred from looking at Aristotle's comments on the greater seriousness and more universal quality of poetry than history (*Poetics*, chapter 9) and from his remarks on the necessity of unity in plot (chapter 8).

The rhyme *lieux* is not a mere *cheville* or filler to accompany *dieux*. The two words go together and refer back to the horror of citizens murdered "dans le sein de leurs dieux domestiques" (l. 198). Gods dwell in places and the Capitol as a *lieu* offers the hierarchical culmination of civil religion, where all the preceding deaths can be avenged by a single gesture.

The sacrifice in the Capitol is also a changing of places. It links the innermost unseen space of the *récit* to the outermost level of the performance of Corneille's *Cinna*, for a kind of miming is being planned for the offstage. Auguste and the animal victim change places. This change of places appears in the metonym, "je veux pour signal que cette même main / Lui donne, au *lieu* d'encens, d'un poignard dans le sein" [As signal I want this very hand to give him, in *place* of incense, a dagger in the chest] (ll. 235–36). Auguste becomes the victim while Cinna becomes the officiator. Oddly, the spectacle of Auguste's blood is meant to manifest publicly the blood that is in Cinna's veins: "Ainsi d'un coup mortel la victime frappée / Fera voir si je suis du sang du grand Pompée" [Thus the victim, stricken with a fatal blow, will show that I am of the blood of the great Pompey] (ll. 238–39). The logic that presides over the use of *récit* in the tragedy here reaches its apogee. *Récit* is used to show the unshowable, to bring to the spectator something that cannot be put on stage, something that is beyond the limits of enactment/mimesis. Even within Cinna's *récit* this offstage remains *off* as being too interior to be seen, since it is the essence of Cinna, the life-fluid which links him to his ancestors. Cinna plans to prove his blood by shedding Auguste's. This seems to be the kernel around which the whole *récit* is organized and by which it is generated. Cinna's drive to show—in fact, to show off—what stuff he is made of, places him in a peculiar relationship to the offstage. He desperately wants to make visible something that would destroy him if it should be displayed. He therefore adopts the detour through a ritual substitution. However this substitution must itself always remain out of sight, for its visualization would destroy the play *as theatre*, within the conventions of the mid–seventeenth century. Both Cinna as character and Cinna's planned demonstration of the quality of his blood depend on constant reference to this never visible space.

Let us consider again the split that exists in both enactment and report. In both cases there is some kind of substitution taking place, and for enactment the ritual sacrifice on the Capitol is a perfect model. Auguste will offer an animal sacrifice in place of a human one, a gesture that is enactment because it substitutes the gesture for the "reality" of human sacrifice.[24] Cinna's plan to offer Auguste in place of this normal victim displaces this existing displacement. Auguste, in this forward-looking part of the *récit*, is a substitute both for the intended victim, for the dead of the civil war, and for Cinna himself (as future victim of Auguste once the conspiracy is known). Cinna becomes the officiator in place of Auguste. Sacrifice is therefore both a reenactment of past violence to atone for that violence and an enactment which preempts acts that might otherwise occur. As spectators of *Cinna* we have come to know that this offstage scene will never occur, that Cinna will not upset Auguste's enactment. However, this failed mimetic violence at the heart of Cinna's *récit* shows the triumph of report over enactment in the role of Cinna. Cinna can only report enactment and can only enact reporting.

As an illusory window onto the world offstage, Cinna's narrative is reminiscent of the architectural illusions of its day. This *récit* is only a window into Cinna's illusions, projected offstage and built on a still deeper regression into the unseen. Like Théramène's account of Hippolyte's death, with its seashore just beyond our sight and its never seen deep sea, Cinna's story has both a kind of stage (the altar) and the unseen deeper space (the interior of Cinna's body, itself referring further back to his ancestry). The belief in a continuity of space permitting access to this other place in which Cinna's valor can be attested is both crucial to his existence as a character and an illusion. Offstage and elsewhere Cinna is a hero and the son of heroes. Onstage, in the public world of Auguste, Cinna is a traitor and the son of traitors. By breaking down the boundary between report and enactment, this first appearance of Cinna on the stage in *Cinna* shows him to be possessed by an illusion that empties the stage, creating a kind of hole in the visible realm. In some ways it is as if Racine's monster had managed to crawl from the shore all the way to the palace in Trézène. A "word-creature" who is two-dimensional has come to the stage and enacted what he did offstage, which itself was a report from still further offstage. This enacted report makes a spectacle of Cinna's emptiness through the gesture to a constantly slipping reference further out of our sight.

Cinna's *récit* is the first of many in the play, including Euphorbe's false account of Maxime's death (IV, 1), Fulvie's alarming account of

24. This logic of substitution is made clearer in Corneille's *Horace*, when king Tulle recalls the murder of Remus by Romulus, grants Horace his life, and then states the necessity of a propitiatory sacrifice (other than Horace).

Cinna's arrest (IV, 4), and Maxime's narrative of previous deceptions (a *récit* that, by preterition, disdains to make "des récits superflus," l. 1684). This very first *récit* by Cinna is echoed by Auguste's narrative in the first scene of Act V, when Auguste gives an account of Cinna's life story, including the planned assassination. Auguste's narrative can be seen as counteracting Cinna's control of the offstage. First, Auguste corroborates that the earlier narrative does reflect what Cinna did really plan offstage. Secondly, by subsuming this private account in the greater imperial view of the world, Auguste "corrects" the view of history presented by his opponents. Yet despite the emperor's momentary triumph as narrator of the offstage world, both Auguste and Cinna suffer from the divorce between their onstage expressions of power and their lack of control of what is happening offstage. Just as Auguste is savoring his triumph over Cinna and Emilie, a triumph due to his apparent mastery of information, Maxime arrives (V, 3) to show that Auguste is still mistaken about what has happened. The fragility of the connection between the characters onstage and the offstage world by which they are controlled thus cuts through the whole of the play and all of the characters. By proposing still another and final *récit*, Corneille ends on a tentative note of closure, but in keeping with his problematizing of the relationship between what we see and what we do not see, Livie's *récit* is a prophetic *deus ex machina*, a narrative which claims to bridge the gap by referring to higher sources of information:

> Oyez ce que les dieux vous font savoir par moi;
> De votre heureux destin c'est l'immuable loi.
> Après cette action vous n'avez rien à craindre . . .
> [Ll. 1755–57]

Listen to what the gods tell you through me; it is the unchanging law of your destiny. After this act you have nothing to fear . . .

The belief in the continuity of onstage and offstage appears here as an act of faith, like Auguste's act of will in declaring himself the master of the universe.[25] Such an assertion of belief resembles very strongly

25. Deleuze writes of a baroque phenomenon analogous to the mystery of the connection between offstage and onstage in describing the way baroque architects introduce sunlight indirectly into a room in such a way that the viewer does not "know" where the light is coming from, because it penetrates openings "invisible to the inhabitant" (*Le Pli*, 39). What is the invisible source of illumination that motivates Auguste? The history of criticism of *Cinna* demonstrates that readers do not agree on the source and motivation of Auguste's final decision.

the Cartesian decision to assert selective belief and disbelief of the evidence of his senses. Descartes, like Auguste, had pretty much come to the end of his tether when he had to try to make a final decision about assigning things a place within himself or outside of himself. Descartes begins by pretending that they are a projection of himself: "As for thoughts that I had of several other things outside of myself, such as sky, earth, light, warmth and a thousand others, I was not troubled to know whence they came, because, not finding in them anything that made them seem superior to me, I could believe that, if they were true, they were projections of my nature . . ."[26] Later, however, Descartes, finally has recourse to God to reassure himself that what he thinks he sees must "have some basis in truth; for it would not be possible that God, who is all perfect and all true, would have placed them in us otherwise" (153). Likewise to reassure Auguste, Livie must appeal to the divine when all other sources of information about what has or will happen outside of the immediate visible world of the stage have repeatedly failed.

The concept of illusion which runs through so much of the baroque seems to require that a space be maintained for the uncertain. What is onstage cannot be doubted; therefore not only must the offstage exist, but rules for preventing the collapse of the offstage into the onstage must be observed. The unity of place, which often seems to be a hallmark of something "classical" about seventeenth-century theatre, can thus be appreciated in a different light, as the foundation of the invisible. If only one place can be seen, the multiplicity of unseen places is protected from our eyes and made available to language. On the other hand, if the French stage moved freely through all space, other devices would have to be created to guarantee the realm of the imaginary. Unity of place is closely related to the exploration of the distinction between public and private space. Because the language is that of individual characters, the dramatic narratives provide subjective mediation between offstage and onstage space. The world which is out of sight of the spectators is the inverse of the onstage space because the unseen is the place over which subjectivity is dominant. In the case of Cinna, public space is the field over which a dominant private view of the offstage (Livie's prophecy) can ultimately assert itself, consecrating the Emperor's determination to pass from private hesitation and doubt to public resoluteness and control.

26. René Descartes, *Discours de la raison* in *Oeuvres et lettres*, ed. André Bridoux (Paris: Gallimard, "La Pléiade," 1953), 149.

The baroque is, in many ways, an aesthetic and an epistemology of the border; of frames, mirrors, galleries, and gardens. The dramatic *récits* focus attention on the border of theatrical space by bringing the outside distant space into the center of the stage. Yet Cinna's narrative shows that the all-important concept of the border is itself unbounded. How can we tell when Cinna is *here* and when he is *there?* When is he fully present and in the present and when is he elsewhere, merely representing the Cinna who was or who will be? The tension between presence and absence in this dramatic narrative can only be traced by Pascal's circle of which the circumference is everywhere and the center nowhere.[27]

---

27. Blaise Pascal, *Pensées*, Lafuma edition, fragment 199.

II. Descartes and the Site of Subjectivity

KEVIN DUNN

"A Great City Is a Great Solitude": Descartes's Urban Pastoral

> **Touchstone.** Truly, shepherd, in respect of itself, it is a good life; but in respect that it is a shepherd's life, it is naught. In respect that it is solitary, I like it very well; but in respect that it is private, it is a very vile life. Now in respect it is in the fields, it pleaseth me well; but in respect it is not in the court, it is tedious. As it is a spare life (look you) it fits my humor well; but as there is no more plenty in it, it goes much against my stomach. Hast any philosophy in thee, shepherd?
>
> —*As You Like It*

In March of 1629 René Descartes, citing the lack of privacy allowed him by the social life of Paris, removed himself to Amsterdam, where, he tells the reader of the *Discourse on Method*, "amidst this great mass of busy people who are more concerned with their own affairs than curious about those of others, I have been able to lead a life as solitary and withdrawn as if I were in the most remote desert, while lacking none of the comforts found in the most populous cities" (I.126).[1] Despite this neat formulation, he seems quickly to have grown tired enough of the "crowded throng" to move to a smaller town across the Zuider Zee; as one of Descartes's biographers has pointed out, "in spite of his remarks on Amsterdam, he evidently preferred a country life, or else to live in the outskirts of town."[2] And not only was his urban retirement more suburban, even rural, than urban; his letters from this

---

1. Unless otherwise noted, all translations are from *The Philosophical Writings of Descartes*, trans. John Cottingham, Robert Stoothoff and Dugald Murdoch, (Cambridge: Cambridge University Press, 1985) and cited in the text. All translations from Descartes's letters are my own and are cited from the standard edition, *Oeuvres de Descartes*, ed. Charles Adam and Paul Tannery (Paris: J. Vrin 1965), abbreviated here *A & T.* I received many helpful comments in preparing this essay, and I would like to acknowledge in particular those of Jeffrey Knapp and my colleagues Lawrence Manley, Thomas Greene, Jonathan Freedman, and Nancy Wright.

2. Elizabeth S. Haldane, *Descartes, His Life and Times* (New York: E. P. Dutton, 1905), 119.

YFS 80, *Baroque Topographies*, ed. Timothy Hampton, © 1991 by Yale University.

period, liberally peppered with requests for friends to visit him, show that his dedication to a life of solitude was more figurative than real.[3]

Yet if Descartes led a life that was neither solitary nor urban, his actual choice of abode serves only to underscore the importance of his "fictional" choice, with its conceptually tidy paradox. Having more philosophy in him than even Touchstone, Descartes attempts to take the conflicting sentiments of his time toward a number of dichotomies—city and country, civic engagement and retirement, labor and *otium*—and turn contradiction into a paradox that could describe his philosophical project. It is the content of that fictional paradox that I wish to explore, remembering, however, Descartes's *real* address, an address that registers his difficulty with the spatial and ideological construct that he articulates through his narrative of urban retirement. Like Touchstone in his assault on the shepherd's sensibilities, Descartes is performing an ideological operation upon the landscape, assigning social functions to spatial configurations. Unlike Touchstone, however, he is also questioning traditional dichotomies and attempting tentatively to bridge them. The compromise implied by his yoking together of the discourses of retirement and civic engagement, and his uneasiness with his own compromise, stand very close to the center of his concerns in the *Discourse on Method* and in his philosophical work as a whole.

Descartes's urban retreat is situated in an old literary neighborhood. The topos he adapts in praise of urban anonymity is at least as old as Strabo: ἐρημία μεγάλη 'στὶν ἡ Μεγάλη πόλις "A great city is a great desert."[4] In its original context, the proverb comments on urban blight at a time when many Hellenistic cities had become depopulated, and the pun on the Peloponnesian city of Megalopolis betrays the tone of the phrase. Guarino renders the tag accurately: "Megalopolis idest ampla civitas ampla fit desolatio."[5] The phrase was canonized, however, by Erasmus in his *Adagia* in the form "*Magna civitas, magna solitudo,*" "A great city is a great solitude."[6] The ambiguity of the

3. See for instance his letter of 18 June 1629 to Monsieur Ferrier and that of 25 April 1631 to Jean de Balzac (*A & T*, I.13–16 and I.199–201).

4. Strabo, *Geographica*, xvi. Otto Steinmayer, a former colleague in classics, updated the tag for me with a loose translation: "The Big Apple is rotten to the core."

5. Strabo, *De situ orbis* [*Geographica*], trans. Gregorius Tifernas and Guarino Veronese (Venice, 1494), 75r.

6. *Opera omnia*, vol. 2 (Hildesheim, 1961), 540. Erasmus's commentary on the proverb shows that he understood the original well: "Seleuciam ad Tigrim ait Babylone majorem fuisse, sed pleraque sui parte desertam. . . ." Nevertheless he chose to use the ambiguous word "solitudo," rather than adopt the translation, for instance, of Guarino.

Latin translation of *eremía*, "solitudo," which can mean both "solitude" and "a place of solitude," "a desert," opened up the social and
psychological context in which the Renaissance understood the tag.
Bacon assumes this context when he explicates the topos: "*Magna
civitas, magna solitudo*, because in a great town friends are scattered,
so that there is not that fellowship, for the most part, which is in less
neighbourhoods."[7] The strictly demographic content of the original
has turned into a lament over the lonely anonymity of the contemporary city. Descartes's adaptation of the phrase retains this interpretation of "solitudo" but gives the commonplace a positive valence by
grafting it onto the discourse of retirement, the *beatus ille* topos,
thereby making the city the ideal location for the philosophical
eremite.[8]

Descartes gives his fullest exposition of "the lonely crowd" motif in
a letter of 1631 to Jean de Balzac, a letter that provides much of the
context for the motif as it appears in the *Discourse on Method*. Balzac
had already built a literary reputation on his letters, many of which
debate the time-honored opposition between a contemplative country
retirement and an active public life. In his letter, which predates the
Discourse by six years, Descartes explains to Balzac why he prefers
Amsterdam as a place of retirement to the rural retreat his friend
praises:[9]

> However perfect a house in the country might be, it always lacks count-
> less comforts, that are only found in towns; and even the very solitude

7. "Of Friendship," in *Works*, ed. James Spedding et al. (1857–74; New York: Garrett
Press, 1968), VI.437.

8. The topos thus became an ideal tag for Neo-Stoic moralizers; in *The Great Pre-
rogative of a Private Life: By way of Dialogue* (London 1678), the English translator of La
Mothe le Vayer's *De la vie privée* writes, ". . . our minde findes its *Hermitage* every
where; and in the most numerous *Assemblies* of men in the greatest Towns and Cities in
the world, I very frequently finde my self in a *Desart. Magna Civitas magna mihi
solitudo.* And I am commonly as much alone as could be *Orpheus in Silvis, inter Del-
phinas Arion* provided that my Soul may conserve its liberty. . . " (121–22).

9. Many of the details Descartes responds to are from a letter not to himself, but to
Monsieur de la Motts Aigron, dated 26 September 1622. The literary nature of Descartes's formulation is thus enhanced by the fact that he is probably reacting to a *published* letter, since the first edition of Balzac's popular familiar letters came out in 1624.
The letter in question is I.15. The actual letter from Balzac to Descartes, dated 25 April
1631, does not mention rural retirement, but is full of Stoic reproach for life at court and
acknowledges that "Monsieur des Cartes" is more of "le Sage des Stoïques" than is Balzac
(A & T, I.200). It should also be noted that many of the details of the topos show up in an
earlier letter of Descartes, to Ferrier (18 June 1629): "Nevertheless I dare not invite you to
come here; but I assure you that had I thought about it when I was in Paris, I would have
tried to bring you along. And if you were a brave enough man to make the trip and come

that one hopes for there is never found to be entirely perfect. . . . Whereas in this great city where I am, containing not a single man except me who doesn't pursue a career in trade, everyone is so attentive to his own profit that I could live here my entire life without ever being seen by anyone. I take walks every day amidst the confusion of a great multitude, with as much liberty and repose as you could experience along your footpaths, and I consider the men that I see here no differently than the trees I would encounter in your forests, or the animals that pasture there. Even the noise of their bustle does not interrupt my reveries any more than would that of some brook. If I sometimes reflect on their activities, I receive the same pleasure that you would in seeing your peasants cultivate your fields; because I see that all their labor serves to adorn the place where I reside, and to assure that I lack for nothing here. [*A & T*, I. 203–04]

Descartes develops at length (I have quoted selectively) the topos that has such important implications for the work on method he would soon compose. He shows here that remarkable ability, often commented upon in the poets of the period, to assimilate what would properly be the stuff of georgic, manual labor, into the pastoral ideal.[10]

---

to spend some time with me in the wilderness [*le desert*], you would have ample leisure to exercise yourself—no one would distract you—you would be far removed from the things that can disturb you; in short, you'd be subjected to nothing worse than me, and we would live as brothers . . ." (*A & T*, I.14).

10. I am using "pastoral" and "georgic" in the supraliterary sense developed in recent criticism. The originary moment of this criticism may well be Raymond Williams's *The Country and the City* (New York: Oxford University Press, 1973), but the most extensive treatment is Anthony Low's *The Georgic Revolution* (Princeton: Princeton University Press, 1985). Low argues that the moral and conceptual apparatus of georgic had begun functioning long before Dryden published his translation of Virgil's *Georgics* (prefaced by Addison's laudatory essay) in 1697. Low points to (among other things) the new interest in the study of agriculture itself, to the "new science" with its emphasis on "use" and to Puritanism's insistence on the moral significance of work. See also Alastair Fowler's answer to Low, "The Beginnings of English Georgic," in Barbara Kiefer Lewalski, ed., *Renaissance Genres: Essays on Theory, History, and Interpretation* (Cambridge, MA: Harvard University Press, 1986), 105–25; Annabel Patterson, *Pastoral and Ideology: Virgil to Valéry* (Berkeley: University of California Press, 1987); Michael O'Loughlin, *The Garlands of Repose: The Literary Celebration of Civic and Retired Leisure* (Chicago: University of Chicago Press, 1978); James G. Turner, *The Politics of Landscape: Rural Scenery and Society in English Poetry 1630–1660* (Oxford: Blackwell, 1979); Peter Stallybras, "'Wee feaste in our Defense': Patrician Carnival in Early Modern England and Robert Herrick's 'Hesperides'," *English Literary Renaissance* 16.1 (1986): 234–52; Leah S. Marcus, *The Politics of Mirth: Jonson, Herrick, Milton, Marvell, and the Defense of Old Holiday Pastimes* (Chicago: University of Chicago Press, 1986); and Peter Lindenbaum, *Changing Landscapes: Anti-Pastoral Sentiment in the English Renaissance* (Athens, GA: University of Georgia Press, 1986).

The picture of Balzac, at his ease, watching his peasants cultivate his fields, is a case in point; the labor central to that enjoyment is present, but marginalized as part of the landscape.

Yet Descartes's transposition of this picture onto an urban canvas, even though presented in a playful fashion, cannot dispel the stress lines gathering around the pastoral ideal. His "reveries" among men who are indistinguishable from trees and farm animals not only reflect back ironically upon Balzac's homogenized landscape but also problematize his own attempts to see his work as the fruit of aristocratic leisure. The bustling burghers of Amsterdam will not readily metamorphose into happy swains, even though Descartes goes on to make the somewhat strained argument that they are serving him by importing the commodities he needs for his comfort.[11] The "busyness" of the bourgeoisie played a central role in the changing attitude toward labor,[12] and, in fact, Descartes's urban solitude does not provide repose at all, but rather a means to make uninterrupted intellectual labor possible. He would seem to be moving unwittingly, or at least reluctantly, toward Bacon's georgic conception of scientist as aristocratic laborer in the fields of public welfare.[13]

Descartes's ambivalence toward the choice between retired contemplation and urban activity, however, itself has a tradition;[14] it is as if he is recalling the ironic oppositions of Horace's *Second Epode,* where a vision of the "happy man's" rural retirement is suddenly re-

11. Descartes's social evaluation of the Dutch merchants and their uniform obsession with trade might be usefully compared with Thomas Sprat's observations that while London "is compos'd of Gentlemen, as well as Traders. . . , Amsterdam is a place of Trade, without the mixture of men of freer thoughts." And even the "Traders" themselves, Sprat thought, differed: "The Merchants of England live honourable in forein parts; those of Holland meanly, minding their gain alone. . . ." *The History of the Royal-Society of London* (London, 1667; rpt. St. Louis: Washington University Press, 1958), 87–88.

12. Although Alastair Fowler argues that, "Just as today (although for very different reasons), the work ethic was a matter of dispute," (107) there is no reason to contest the basic outlines of Weber's thesis that the sixteenth- and seventeenth-century Protestant urban bourgeoisie fostered a new interest in the value and significance of labor.

13. On Bacon and georgic see Stanley Fish's well-known essay, "Georgics of the Mind: The Experience of Bacon's *Essays,*" in *Self-Consuming Artifacts: The Experience of Seventeenth-Century Literature* (Berkeley: University of California Press, 1972), 78–155; Low, *The Georgic Revolution;* and especially, James S. Tillman, "Bacon's Georgics of Science," *Papers on Language and Literature* 11.4 (1975): 357–66.

14. For discussions of these concepts in antiquity see Thomas G. Rosenmeyer, *The Green Cabinet: Theocritus and the European Pastoral Lyric* (Berkeley: University of California Press, 1969) and O'Loughlin, *The Garlands of Repose.*

vealed to be that of the usurer Alfius, a momentary daydream in the ongoing world of money-making. By moving his eremite to the city, Descartes does not so much resolve Horace's oppositions as maintain them while laundering out the irony: rather than allowing the vision of the "happy man" to dissolve into the harsh, cynical light of the marketplace, Descartes argues that this glare offers the best protection for a man seeking to avoid the notice of others. In this scheme the "happy man" and Alfius the businessman can never be the same, not even at the level of fantasy, since only the existence of Alfius provides the glare to make the happy man's urban retirement possible. Descartes's implied solution seems to be one of simple contiguity: through his adjacency to the Dutch merchants he can associate his philosophical researches with labor and the pursuit of the public good. And yet the effect of his analogy between Amsterdam and Balzac's country estate is first and foremost to identify his labor with the pastoral pipings of the aristocracy and thus deny its status as labor altogether. The paradox of the urban pastoral, therefore, is generated by Descartes's social ambivalence, an ambivalence that produces in the *Discourse* a kind of internal commuting between the values of urbanized georgic, with its stress on labor for the public good, and the rural values of aristocratic leisure.

Before tracing the itinerary of this commute, I should clarify the source of the ambivalence. Auerbach, in his study of the seventeenth-century French "public," describes Descartes as a *grande robe* who also seemed to possess a noble title.[15] By this time the *grande bourgeoisie* had all but ceased to perform its function as the bureaucratic class, and its mercantile role lay even further in the past. "Like those of many other periods and countries," says Auerbach, "these bourgeois were characterized by a desire to escape from their class and to stabilize their wealth. . . . Spreading side by side with prosperity, humanism and its ideal of *otium cum dignitate* also encouraged the flight of the bourgeois from their class" (171–72). Richard Sennett, following up on the implications of Auerbach's research, notes that if the *grande bourgeoisie* of "la ville" was successfully shaking off its connection to its mercantile origins and merging for all practical purposes with "la cour," it was at the same time creating a new sense of the word "pub-

15. Erich Auerbach, "La Cour et la Ville," in *Scenes from the Drama of European Literature* (1959; Minneapolis: University of Minnesota Press, 1984), 170.

lic." No longer did the word connote only the "public weal"; it also came to stand in opposition to the "private" as the "special region of sociability."[16] No longer could the aristocrat, with his ethic of voluntary public service, consider public action as consubstantial with his own actions. For the French aristocrat of the mid–seventeenth century, be he a member of the *noblesse de robe* or the *noblesse d'épée*, public action connoted a kind of display, defined by his appearance first in the fashionable salons and then later in the century in the theater. It is this "public" that Descartes was fleeing when he left Paris. Having tried and failed to maintain secret lodgings in that city, he felt obliged to seek a place in which he could quietly pursue his work (Haldane, 104–05). At the same time, as the letter to Balzac shows, Descartes was attracted, however condescendingly, to the bourgeois activity of Amsterdam, which offered the kind of anonymous public space to which we have become accustomed.

Amsterdam thus becomes a means for Descartes to gather up and bind together two representations of the same social unease: nostalgia for the intimate social structure of the aristocratic coterie on the one hand, and, on the other, the desire to absent himself from the dynamic urban scene that was replacing this intimate structure. The flight to Amsterdam, then, is both toward and away from his bourgeois origins. He desires to reduce the class that produced him to a picturesque backdrop against which he can perform his laborless toils. By moving his eremite back home, but home to a city that remains foreign, Descartes creates a suburban compromise within the city limits, in which the subject contributes his labor to the common good but remains socially alienated by retaining his private plot of ground. But the business of the burgher contaminates the busyness of the philosopher, and unlike the aristocrat donning the shepherd's weeds for a courtly entertainment, Descartes the *grande robe* can in fact disappear all too easily into the georgic landscape of Amsterdam. It is not surprising, then,

16. Richard Sennett, *The Fall of Public Man: On the Social Psychology of Capitalism* (New York: Knopf, 1977), 16. Auerbach examines this public in terms of theater audiences, and Sennett extends this concept to public play-acting of all sorts. On the class-specific nature of public and private in the seventeenth and eighteenth centuries, see Nicole Castan, "The Public and the Private," in *A History of Private Life*, vol. 3, *Passions of the Renaissance*, ed. Roger Chartier, trans. Arthur Goldhammer (Cambridge, MA: Harvard University Press, 1989), 403–04 and *passim*. Castan argues that the "great" lived an entirely public life, while the life of the commoner was, from a contemporary point of view, "exclusively private."

that Descartes devotes much of the *Discourse on Method* to avoiding such an assimilation, to retaining both a distinct, private voice and the georgic vocation of public utility.[17]

Descartes's social and philosophical ambivalence are woven into the basic stuff of the *Discourse on Method*'s metaphoric fabric. In his famous meditation in the "stove-heated room," he implies that just as a centrally planned city is to be preferred to one that has grown up organically, so his system is superior to traditional philosophy because it is free from the inconsistencies of accretion. The analogy, in effect, argues for the public utility of a private method:

> Again, ancient cities which have gradually grown from mere villages into large towns are usually ill-proportioned, compared with those or-derly towns which planners lay out as they fancy on level ground. Look-ing at the buildings of the former individually, you will often find as much art in them, if not more, than in those of the latter; but in view of their arrangement—a tall one here, a small one there—and the way they make the streets crooked and irregular, you would say it is chance, rather than the will of men using reason, that placed them so. [I.116]

Lewis Mumford seizes on this passage as an illustration of his case against Baroque city planning. The passage describes, according to Mumford, the triumph of mechanical principles over organic ones, of the "baroque despot's" will over the individuation of the Middle Ages that had been rationalized but not destroyed by Renaissance city plan-ning. The hallmark of this new, monolithic city planning was the avenue, with its impersonal vistas and wide traffic lanes that daunt pedestrians but facilitate the movement of the large national armies that had arisen in Europe.[18]

Mumford's observations have direct relevance for Descartes, yet Descartes was by no means the eager spokesman for baroque unifor-mity that Mumford portrays. As we shall see, Descartes not only un-

17. Annabel Patterson traces a similar process in England, particularly in the works of Bacon, whom she sees as attempting to reconcile the individual intellectualism of pastoral with the public "practicalities" of georgic. "A pastoralized georgic, or vice versa, as a program for the intellectual development of the seventeenth century could have served his contemporaries very well." Instead of such a synthesis, Patterson argues, a kind of public spirit entered the pastoral itself through a dialogic engagement with the courtly culture that pastoral represented. See *Pastoral and Ideology*, Chapter Three, "Going Public. Pastoral versus Georgic: The Politics of Virgilian Quotation," 38 and *passim*.

18. Lewis Mumford, *The City in History: Its Origins, Its Transformations, and Its Prospects* (New York: Harcourt Brace & World, 1961), 393–94.

derstood well the threat that authoritarian uniformity represented to him and his work, he also felt keenly how difficult, if even possible, it is to authorize any uniform plan, whether architectural, political, or methodological. Moreover, as Mumford himself admits (without mentioning Descartes), Amsterdam, Descartes's adopted home, does not fit the baroque mould; Mumford dubs it "capitalism's one outstanding urban achievement, rivalled only by elegant Bath" (439). Leonardo Benevolo points to the fact that the political structure of Holland's city states emerged from the Middle Ages relatively intact and notes both the individualized architecture of Amsterdam's houses and its closed visual spaces, limited by the curvilinear nature of the canals and the rows of elms planted along them according to the 1607 plan for the city's expansion. In fact, and it is a fact relevant to Descartes's urban metaphors, Amsterdam was seventeenth-century Europe's most rationally and efficiently designed city, but its design included a closely confined yet nonetheless expressive individualism, as conveyed in the facades of the houses, the only external detail not specifically controlled by city ordinance.[19]

Amsterdam must have seemed a figurative bonanza to Descartes, a place where he could at once represent himself as the aristocratic stranger, standing aloof, and, at the same time, as a participant in a social structure whose ostentatious republicanism and public commerce could not have been more different from the universities and salons of Paris. The Amsterdam compromise between authoritarian plan and individual expression thus epitomizes nicely his own prevarication. Once he has put forward his analogy, asserting that in building a philosophical system, as in building a city, razing is the necessary precondition for raising, he immediately retreats into his apolitical pastoral stance and dissociates himself from any implications the analogy might have beyond describing his internal pursuit of method. "This example convinced me that it would be unreasonable for an individual to plan to reform a state by changing it from the foundations up and overturning it in order to set it up again . . ." (I.117). Moreover, by shifting even his idealized role immediately from great architect to great city planner, he manages to have his cake and eat it too. While avoiding an exemplarity that implies absolutism, he suggests that the example of his method might stand over the product of other indi-

19. Leonardo Benevolo, *The History of the City*, trans. Geoffrey Culverwell (London: Scholar Press, 1980), 706–15.

viduals in a loose, supervisory manner, just as the central planning of
Amsterdam permits individuated architectural expression within defined limits. In the remainder of this essay I will examine how the
"suburban compromise" that Descartes finds in Amsterdam becomes
the basis for what might be called his social epistemology, his exploration of the possibilities for institutionalizing scientific endeavors.

This exploration, which he pursues primarily in Part 6 of the *Discourse*, combines concerns that appear in autobiographical, rhetorical,
methodological—even topographical—forms throughout the *Discourse* and his works as a whole. The social ambivalence that he spa-
tializes in his retirement to Amsterdam takes on a rhetorical form in
the two quite distinct voices with which he could address differing
audiences. The preface to the *Meditations*, where he looks back on the
Discourse, describes his unwillingness to explore the "topics of God
and the human mind . . . in a book written in French and designed to
be read by all and sundry, in case weaker intellects might believe that
they ought to set out on the same path" (II.6–7). These elitist assump-
tions stand, of course, in direct contrast to the famous opening sentence of the *Discourse:* "Good sense is the best distributed thing in the
world" (I.111). Yet if Descartes manages to separate his audiences
neatly between different tracts, the rhetorical motive behind his appeal
to the "natural reason" (I.151) of the audience for the *Discourse* reveals
in itself his autobiographical and even methodological ambivalence.
For if his employment of the "natural reason" of his vulgar readers
works to establish his authority *vis-à-vis* his predecessors, it also suggests that those readers consider the autobiographical element as an
exemplary instance of "reason"; that is, private experience must become public method if any sense is to be made out of the very existence
of the *Discourse*. And, in fact, much of the *Discourse* is given over to
simultaneously denying and establishing the exemplarity of the narrator's story.

The vexed question of Descartes as exemplary figure has been
much commented upon;[20] here I will merely reiterate the extent to

20. Among the many works discussing narrator as exemplum in Descartes's *Dis-
course* are David Simpson, "Putting One's House in Order: The Career of the Self in
Descartes' Method," *New Literary History* 9 (1977): 83–101; John D. Lyons, "Subjec-
tivity and Imitation in the *Discours de la Méthode*," *Neophilologus* 66 (1982): 508–24;
Ralph Flores, "Delusions of Self: Descartes's Authorial Burden," *Kentucky Romance
Quarterly* 25 (1978): 283–95; Dalia Judovitz, "Autobiographical Discourse and Critical
Praxis in Descartes," *Philosophy and Literature* 5 (1981): 91–107; and Jean-Luc Nancy,
"Mundus est Fabula," *Modern Language Notes* 93.4 (1978): 635–53.

which this question is one of adjudicating between public and private voices, voices that Descartes juxtaposes, but does not harmonize, in his paradox of the urban retreat. His self-presentation is from one viewpoint a means of involving his audience in an instructive "ethical" reading, the last gasp of a humanist dialectic that does not offer its model as mere example, but as a complex process with which the reader must grapple. The irresolvability of the public and the private might then be seen as an attempt to avoid the simple didacticism of the "Precepteur."[21] The *Discourse* could also be seen, however, as the foremost example of what Timothy Reiss calls "the surreptitious replacement of . . . [the] 'I' by a *'we'* whose claim is to collectivity."[22] That is, Descartes may be taking here one of the first steps towards creating that hegemonic entity of "common sense" that both grants and masks the writer's authority. The problematic exemplarity of the narrator's persona, then, may be seen as at once a rearguard action in defense of aristocratic flexibility, and a sortie of the vanguard, advancing a quantifiable, univocal method under the banner of middle-class common sense and public utility. The very fact that either viewpoint makes sense of the narrator's stance, however, brings us back to the fundamental irresolvability of the public and private elements in Descartes's agenda.

Turning then to the final part of the *Discourse on Method,* one finds Descartes engaged in an attempt to work out a compromise between public and private, composing in effect an oblique meditation on the possibilities for institutionalizing his method. Hovering over this meditation is the fate of Galileo and the implications of his condemnation for the publication of scientific speculations. In Part 5, Descartes had given a *précis* of *Le Monde,* a work he had suppressed before publication upon hearing the news of Galileo's trial. Although *Le Monde,* a scientific *summa* of sorts, was couched as a fable, describing an alternate world created by God "in the imaginary spaces" (I.132), Descartes felt he could not risk publication.[23] Why, one might ask, did Descartes

21. This view is espoused by Victoria Kahn in "Humanism and the Resistance to Theory," in *Literary Theory/Renaissance Texts,* Patricia Parker and David Quint, ed. (Baltimore: Johns Hopkins Press, 1986), 373–96.

22. Timothy J. Reiss, *The Discourse of Modernism* (Ithaca: Cornell University Press, 1982), 223.

23. The *Discourse on Method* is haunted throughout by Descartes's decision to suppress *Le Monde.* In a letter to Mersenne (April 1634), he speaks of his self-suppression in terms of significance to my argument: ". . . that desire that I have to live in repose and to continue the life I have started by taking as my motto: 'He has lived well, who has

feel unprotected by the fiction of *Le Monde* yet go on to risk publication of the *Discourse* and the accompanying treatises on optics, meteorology and geometry? The answer, I believe, is to a large extent a
hermeneutic one; that is, Descartes had no doubt about the legibility
of *Le Monde*'s fable, but could nonetheless put his faith in the indeter-
minacy of the generic fiction of a "discourse." In a letter to Mersenne of
1637 he explains his choice of title:

> But I haven't been able to understand very well your objections con-
> cerning my title; because I didn't call it *Treatise on Method*, but *Dis-
> course on Method*—which is the same as *Preface or Notice concerning
> Method*—in order to show that I had no design to teach a method, but
> only to speak about it. Because, as one can see from what I said in it, the
> *Discourse* consists more of a praxis than a theory, and I call the treatises
> following some "Essays on that Method," because I propose that the
> things that they contain couldn't have been discovered without it. . . .
> [*A & T*, I. 349]

Not only does the *Discourse* bear a prefatory relation to the texts that
follow, but both sets of texts are presented as conative, exploratory
documents, essays spoken in a private voice rather than imprinted
with the public designs of the written treatise. It is this fiction that
Descartes hides behind, but it is also this fiction that exposes the
difficulties he will have in Part 6 in grounding a public science on an
almost Montaignesque personal discourse.

Part 6, in other words, must return to the now familiar question of
exemplarity: why should he publish a purportedly private discourse
unless he sees himself as a model for the pursuit of scientific research?
Acknowledging once again that "we might find as many reformers as
heads" (I.142), Descartes nonetheless appeals to "the law which obliges
us to do all in our power to secure the general welfare of mankind"
(I.142). In a momentary flush of good-will toward his fellow man, he
seems to forget the problematic nature of self-publication and to suggest the possibility for cooperative research. He reasoned, as he explains to the reader, that the huge scope of the endeavor could be
overcome if he were to publish his findings to date in order to incite
others to contribute their observations and talents. "Thus, by building
upon the work of our predecessors and combining [*joignant*] the lives

---

lived well-hidden . . .' " (I. 285–86). For the connection between Galileo's and Descartes's
ideas that led to the suppression of *Le Monde*, see Pietro Redondi's *Galileo: Heretic*,
trans. Raymond Rosenthal (Princeton: 1987), especially 280ff.

and labours of many, we might make much greater progress working together than anyone could make on his own" (I.143). Yet if this vision seems to partake of a kind of Baconian institutionalization of science, it stalls at key moments. Descartes never admits a truly collaborative project, only a collective one, passed from hand to hand after each experimenter has made his contribution. The translator's metaphor of "combining" is a Baconian label fundamentally foreign to Descartes, whose language of "joining" suggests a system in which one's work does not circulate as a commodity, but rather descends to a new researcher as one's legacy, not unlike an aristocrat's estate. This genealogical model for experimental research, with its comfortingly abstract and hierarchically constituted ligatures binding an experimenter to his indebted progeny, is as far as Descartes finds himself able to proceed into a publicly articulated system of knowledge.

Posthumous publication would seem the mode of transmission most fully fitted to this lonely collective of discrete and solitary acts of scientific inquiry. But if Descartes prefers not to open his researches to the public eye, he also realizes that his labors are of such a magnitude as to require aid. Even the best intentioned whom he had enlisted were hampered by the privacy of the method; "highly intelligent persons" (I.146) to whom he outlined his opinions recount them back to him in such a way that they are hardly recognizable as his own. The only glimmer of hope lies in his limited faith in the "artisan," a faith that implies a mechanization of progress wherein the skilled technician can hammer out the details of a prearranged master plan, a plan not unlike the hierarchic, centralized uniformity of Mumford's Baroque city: "[A]s regards observations which may help in this work, one man could not possibly make them all. But also he could not usefully employ other hands than his own, except those artisans . . . who would be led by the hope of gain (a most effective motive) to do precisely what he ordered them to do" (I.148). Descartes's artisans recall his bustling burghers: anonymous but necessary participants in an otherwise solitary undertaking. Even when he grants his "coworkers" something more than artisanal status, there is no doubt who holds the master plans. Describing why posthumous publication will not suffice to further his work and why he had written Le Monde, he explains: "This would oblige all who desire the general well-being of mankind . . . both to communicate to me the observations they have already made and to assist me in seeking those which remain to be made" (I.144). Publication is therefore a necessary evil designed to "oblige" others to share their research and to reduce them to the status of assistants.

In the end, even this heavily compromised form of collaboration seems too unsystematic, too messily disparate for Descartes. "So if there were someone in the world," he coyly suggests, "whom we know for sure to be capable of making discoveries of the greatest possible importance and public utility . . . I do not see how they [other men] could do anything for him except to contribute towards the expenses of the observations that he would need and, further, prevent unwelcome visitors from wasting his free time" (I.148). Thus, after an elaborate maneuver around the question of collective research and the institutionalization of science, Descartes brings the *Discourse* to an end by suggesting that his fellow workers might best serve as fund-raisers and security guards. While private speculations contribute to the public weal, the public, with its "common sense," can do no better than to appreciate which private discourse deserves its (primarily financial) support. The ironic result of the failure of Descartes's narrator to serve as an intermediary between private accomplishment and public dissemination of that accomplishment is that Descartes himself passes beyond establishing himself as a merely paradigmatic figure in the search for knowledge to exhibiting a truly proprietary interest in the discourse of the new science: "In short, if there was ever a task which could not be accomplished so well by someone other than the person who began it, it is the one on which I am working" (I.148). The *Discourse on Method* thus becomes the prototypical grant proposal.[24]

The spatialized version of these irresolvable public and private discourses, Descartes's Amsterdam compromise, reveals the limited sense in which he can allow himself either to accept the new discourse of common sense or to synthesize it with older notions of an authority that stands outside of public utility. The licensing of individualized facades within a rigid master plan embodies, within the city limits, the kind of compromise we would now call suburban, the subdivision of the public realm into small private plots. Descartes's final rhetorical stance involves just such a retreat to a kind of public privacy: "I have never tried to conceal my actions as if they were crimes. . . . For if I had done this I thought I would do myself an injustice, and moreover that

24. As David Simpson puts it, "[T]he final resting point of the debate is a surreptitious appeal for the patronage necessary to allow Descartes to carry on with his own work in his own way, undisturbed by having to take account of the attentions of others to different objects." "Putting One's House in Order," 88.

would have given me a certain sort of disquiet, which again would have been opposed to the perfect peace of mind I am seeking" (I.127). He describes here a delicately poised *otium,* one that depends on "going public" just to the extent required to defuse curiosity and idle gossip about the product of his "perfect peace of mind." Once again, since Descartes is quick to add that he seeks leisure for the sake of the public good that it will produce, this leisure must be understood in the context of a scientific georgic. Yet public service that requires public exposure is nonetheless clearly at odds with an older tradition of aristocratic privacy that he is unwilling to abandon. His solution is to offer only a partial version of his researches, a partial version of his self.

Descartes leaves the reader with this paradoxical amalgam of public and private. He has taken up residence in the city, but he retains his solitude. He cannot speak clearly and univocally the public discourse of universal scientific method that he himself was instrumental in shaping: there is an "I" that remains distinct from the "we" of common sense. But he has already pointed the way to a new rhetoric in which the author is figured as a public judge, a spokesman for a shared discourse, rather than a private advocate arguing for the relevance and legitimacy of his words vis-à-vis an authoritative tradition to which he can make reference but not ever fully represent. Bacon, as spokesman for the new forces of "method," asserts, "I cannot be fairly asked to abide by the decision of a tribunal which is itself on its trial" (Spedding, IV.21). Descartes, arguing against the value of academic disputation, uses the same figure: ". . . [T]hose who have long been good advocates do not necessarily go on to make better judges" (I.146). Through his narrative of urbanization, Descartes gives Bacon's new venue a local habitation in the georgics of public technology, although he seems unwilling to settle there himself. The *Discourse on Method* is the register of this social and ideological commuting.

TIMOTHY J. REISS

Descartes, the Palatinate, and the Thirty Years War: Political Theory and Political Practice

> In the course of their conversations they happened to discuss the principles of statecraft—as they are called—and methods of government, correcting this abuse and condemning that, reforming one custom and abolishing another, each one of the three setting up as a fresh legislator, a modern Lycurgus or a brand-new Solon. To such a degree did they fashion the commonwealth that it was as if they had taken it to the forge [fragua] and brought away a different one.
>
> —Miguel de Cervantes, *Don Quijote de la Mancha*, II. i

Descartes has become a familiar myth of Western thought as the lonely semihermit in Holland, despite the evidence of his considerable correspondence with many important intellectual and political figures in the Low Countries, France, England, and Sweden. Consistent with this image of an isolated philosopher, later exegeses have concentrated on those matters held capable of having sprung fully developed from the thinker's powerful subjective brow: on the Method and issues of epistemology, on scientific theory and practice, on philosophy of mind, on an "ego-psychology" of the passions and ethical inquiry.

The vast library of Cartesian studies contains little on political theory: a scattering of essays, an elderly and slightly foolish work by Maxime Leroy on *Descartes social* (Paris: Vrin, 1931), viewing the philosopher as a forerunner of Saint-Simon and Comte, even as some sort of proto-Marx, and two volumes directly addressing political philosophy. Antonio Negri's *Descartes politico o della ragionevole ideologia* (Milan: Feltrinelli, 1970) takes Descartes's philosophy to provide the foundations of a bourgeois political ideology, although not itself specifically political. For his part Pierre Guenancia argues in his *Descartes et l'ordre politique: critique cartésienne des fondements de la politique* (Paris: PUF, 1983) that the philosopher had established the

YFS 80, *Baroque Topographies*, ed. Timothy Hampton, © 1991 by Yale University.

individual as the basis of social organization, and that such a premise made the state a simple matter of coercion (as the political imposition of authority, whether mild or harsh, upon that individual), and contradicted any truly political organization of society.

I will take an entirely different tack. Starting with a number of pointers in the *Discourse on the Method*, I will show the avowed importance of Descartes's relations with the Royal House Palatine, and of his firsthand knowledge of European political and military conditions: particularly the events of the Thirty Years War and the polemics constantly accompanying them, emanating especially from the exiled Palatine court and that of Sweden. I will place the philosopher in the more general political and cultural crisis characterizing an increasingly "self-conscious" Europe in the second half of the sixteenth and the first half of the seventeenth centuries. I will also take some note of his awareness of prior political theory. These points will enable me to argue not only that Descartes has an important and specifiable political philosophy, but further that his philosophy as a whole (all those aspects mentioned at the outset) was the product and rationalization of a particular political conjuncture.

This last claim obviously involves a long-term project and, if sufficiently proven, will have profound implications as to the meaning of subsequent Western philosophy, for which Descartes and Cartesianism have provided the main focus of reference or rebuttal. What follows is essentially introductory to that overall project. It is divided into three parts. The first seeks to make the connections between Descartes and the political context in which he lived, to observe his relations with certain important political figures intimately involved in that context, and to emphasize the way in which certain aspects of his early thinking "corresponded" with it. The second studies the theoretical (and a priori) grounds Descartes developed to understand the nature of a new political establishment, and it examines the idea of society conceived from the viewpoint of a thinking, self-possessed and self-contained subject. The third deals with how Descartes considered the relations between numbers of such individuals, linking them to an ordering subject (the good "Cartesian prince") whose job was to build an ideal society founded upon the interplay of enlightened self-interest.

A final theme running through this essay involves Descartes's efforts (especially in the late 1640s) to tie this basically theoretical scheme to the concrete political realities of his time—particularly as they pertained to the Royal House of the Palatinate. This was, after all, deeply and inextricably embroiled in the most complex and weighty political problems of the time: its prince, Frederick, had made the moves in 1619 that provoked the outbreak of a war whose resolution thirty years later would determine European order for the next three centuries. His loss of the Palatinate was the engine that kept war going. And for Descartes that very loss made the Palatinate into a base of "zero power" entirely analogous to the mind in a state of radical doubt—from which a new order could be developed by a methodological ordering of the common foundations of state and society, as Method ordered common sense.

Descartes's first published writing, the *Discourse on the Method*, used such political reflection to frame its ostensibly merely epistemological argument and indeed to facilitate many of its more particular aspects. In 1619, we are told, Descartes had a dream, "involving the Seventh Ode of Ausonius, which begins *Quod vitae sectabor iter* [What road in life shall I follow?]." In the "Olympics" he noted the exact date as 10 November, and added: "full of enthusiasm, convinced [I] had discovered the foundations of a marvellous science."[1] In the *Discourse on the Method*, we learn that this illumination occurred in the celebrated *poêle* ("a stove-heated room") somewhere "in Germany, where [he] had been called by the wars that are not yet ended there," and while he was "returning to the army from the coronation of the Emperor." David Lachterman has aptly termed this "a retreat from the *polis* to the *poêle*."[2]

What Descartes chose to emphasize, however, was that the retreat took place just at the beginning of the Thirty Years War. Ferdinand's accession and his Catholic fervor was what provoked the Bohemians to revolt and elect a Protestant monarch to their throne. The Duke of Bavaria's army, to which Descartes was "returning," was the force that defeated Frederick and the Bohemians outside Prague in 1620 and then went on to occupy and despoil the Palatinate itself. The war was still

---

1. René Descartes, "Observations" and "Olympian matters" in *The Philosophical Works of Descartes*, trans. John Cottingham, Robert Stoothoff, Dugald Murdoch, 2 vols. (Cambridge: Cambridge University Press, 1985), 1: 4. References to the French are mostly to the *Oeuvres philosophiques*, ed. Fernand Alquié, 3 vols. (Paris: Garnier, 1963–73). Henceforth these will be referred to by the initials *PW* and *OP*, followed by volume and page number. I thank Patricia J. Hilden for her work on the awkward style and confusion of an earlier version of this essay.

2. *PW*, 1: 116; *OP*, 1: 578–79. David R. Lachterman, "Descartes and the Philosophy of History," *Independent Journal of Philosophy* 4 (1983): 31–46.

being fought while Descartes was writing the *Discourse* in 1627–37, which were almost exactly its middle years. The conflict was not over until October 1648, with the signing of the Treaty of Westphalia (although Spain and France continued hostilities until 1659 and the Treaty of the Pyrenees). Descartes's choice of framework for the Method indicated a field of principal concern: one that has been too long ignored.

Historians often argue that the Treaty of Westphalia marked the beginning of modern Europe. It was not an isolated event. In England, in November 1648, Parliament decided to bring Charles I to trial. In France, at the end of August, the parliamentary Fronde had begun with insurrection in Paris, justifying Anne of Austria's and Mazarin's fear that their country might follow England's path.[3] For Descartes, who wrote about all these matters, the moment was also personally uncertain. He was in Paris from May 1648 when the chain of events began which concluded in the outbreak of the first Fronde, and he wrote of them in a letter to Elisabeth Princess Palatine. Although he had seemingly wanted to quit Holland for a more peaceful Paris, he was thus disappointed. At the same time, while the Lower Palatinate had been restored to Elisabeth's older brother by one of the clauses of Westphalia and Descartes had been invited to go there, he felt it was too entirely ravaged by the wars, and would be truly "agreeable" only "after two or three years of peace." Thus it was that Queen Christina of Sweden's March 1649 invitation to Stockholm came just at the right time.[4]

Descartes's epistolary remarks on the political events of the last years of the Thirty Years War suggest that if he did "retreat" from the political arena in 1619, he returned to the fray some twenty-five years later. But the retreat was anyway more symbolic than real. It is more or less certain that he fought at Prague in 1620, and he did not in fact withdraw to Holland until 1627. Even then, he was by no means detached from public events. He corresponded frequently with some of those most closely involved. His civil retreat may be considered en-

---

3. See on this subject, Philip A. Knachel, *England and the Fronde: The Impact of the English Civil War and Revolution on France* (Ithaca: Cornell University Press, 1967), especially 18–49.

4. Letter to Elisabeth, 22 February 1649 (*OP*, 3: 891). In a letter to Chanut of 31 March 1649, Descartes expressed surprised hesitation about accepting Christina's invitation (*OP*, 3: 899). Some of the correspondence has been translated in René Descartes, *Philosophical Letters*, trans. and ed. Anthony Kenny (Oxford: Oxford University Press, 1970). Most letters mentioned in what follows are not in that collection, and I have preferred to keep my own translations for all.

tirely analogous to the project "to undertake studies within myself too," the thinking that finally ended (in the 1630s) in the "discovery" of Method (*PW*, 1: 116; *OP*, 1: 578). That process, too, had been accompanied by constant material inquiry: in medical and anatomical matters, in optics, in meteorology, physics, and more.

Once the *Method* was completed (1637), Descartes was sure of having provided a tool capable of obtaining all possible knowledge—even though, as he wrote in the Preface to the French edition of the *Principles of Philosophy*, most people's uncertainty (among other difficulties) would mean that "many centuries may pass before all the truths that can be deduced from these principles are actually so deduced" (*PW*, 1: 189). By the end of the 1640s Descartes had an equally clear idea of the consequences of Method applied to political dilemmas. In other words, he thought his Method could order authority in a state society, as well as power relations between sovereign and subjects, and among subjects themselves. It is by no means clear that he did not already think this as he wrote the *Discourse*.

This work had doubtless been put in its final form between the end of 1635 and the first half of 1637, in time to be published on 8 June by Jean Maire at Leyden. These dates are murky, however. According to his friend, Jean-Louis Guez de Balzac, he had already undertaken "a project on the story [*histoire*] of his Mind," as early as 1627–28.[5] Was this the first part of the *Discourse*? If the writing of this text indeed occupied the ten years from 1627 to 1637 as the evidence suggests, we are then speaking, as I indicated, precisely of the middle years between the time of the dream, when he first concerned himself seriously with epistemological and metaphysical problems, and the year of his flight to Sweden away from European tumult. These were also the exact years of the Thirty Years War, and he never stopped commenting on events and sending advice to the Princess Elisabeth about her family's political situation. This timing of the *Discourse* may be anecdotal. I do not think it is trivial.

Before its real significance can be properly understood, and then guide an analysis of Descartes's writings perhaps more revealing of their political weight, we need to recall the details of the military and political events which Descartes assumed to be familiar to his readers. Because I will insist that the *Discourse* is as crucial to our understand-

5. Letter from Balzac to Descartes of March 1628, mentioned by Gilbert Gadoffre in his important introduction to the *Discours de la méthode*, 2nd edition (Manchester: Manchester University Press, 1961), xxi.

ing of Descartes's political ideas as the more usually cited letter of September 1646 to Elisabeth about Machiavelli's *Prince*, it is important to remember these contextual facts.

Frederick V, Elector Palatine, had been Ferdinand's rival for the Empire. After the latter's election and coronation (witnessed by Descartes), his active anti-Protestant behavior swiftly alienated the Bohemians, who finally offered their crown to the young and inexperienced Frederick. Over much opposition, this prince unwisely accepted. He entered Prague in late summer 1619 with his Queen, Elisabeth, daughter of James I of England, from whom Frederick expected in vain military aid (a failure for which James was popularly castigated at home by such as John Reynolds and Thomas Scott). Known later as the Winter King, because that was the length of his reign, Frederick was defeated at the Battle of the White Mountain in spring 1620. His lands were expropriated. He and his family were exiled, soon receiving asylum at The Hague.

Frederick's winter was the same whose "onset detained" Descartes "alone in a stove-heated room" in Germany (*PW*, 1: 116). The future philosopher of Method had gone to Holland to do his military apprenticeship, like so many others of his age and class, under the celebrated Maurice of Nassau. After the Emperor Matthias's death on 20 March 1619 and the coronation of Ferdinand, for which Descartes had left Breda, he was now hopefully on his way to sign up with Duke Maximilian in Germany, even though, he wrote to his friend Isaac Beeckman, he "suspected there would be a lot of men under arms, but no fighting" (Letter of 23 April 1619, *OP* 1: 41; Gadoffre, xvii). Letters to Beeckman at this time are an astonishing mixture of mathematical discoveries, tales of his travels, expressions of ambition concerning his new science, and comments on the political and military troubles (*OP*, 1: 35–44). The mixture continued, and Frederick's defeat corresponded to another date given by Descartes himself: "in the year 1620, I began to understand the fundamental principles of a wonderful discovery" (*PW*, 1: 3; *OP*, 1: 49). The discovery foretold by the 1619 dream, of course.

From all of this we may safely assume, since the philosopher himself chose to emphasize the events, that during the writing of the *Discourse*, the instability of the sociopolitical situation, in 1637 no less than in 1619–20 at the very beginning of his original thinking, could be seen only as counter to the stability desired of Method. The counterpoint would be the more evident in that by the time of the

Discourse's publication, several of the chief personages involved in these events were almost certainly already at least known to its author, and would soon be even more so.

I have said that Frederick's Queen was James I's daughter. The (ex-)Elector died in 1632, but two of his sons, Rupert and Maurice, were to fight for their uncle, Charles I, in the English civil wars (Rupert, indeed, was to head the British Navy for his cousin, Charles II, in the wars against the Dutch after the Restoration—something ungrateful to his Dutch hosts, one might think). Frederick's and Elisabeth's daughter, Sophia, was to become mother of the Elector of Hanover, future George I of England. During the 1640s (and long before being a mother), it was Sophia who became the intermediary in the correspondence between Descartes and her sister Elisabeth, when the latter thought the exchange was becoming too risky—probably because they were now writing of political matters, on Machiavelli, reason of state, the behavior of princes.

I will show that such questions were already raised in the *Discourse*, and that the remarks on the Florentine contained ambiguities not foreign to the *morale par provision* advanced ten years before. It was Elisabeth of course to whom Descartes dedicated the *Principles of Philosophy* in 1644, and at whose request he elaborated (in letters) and then published the *Passions of the Soul*. It was also to her that he wrote in January 1646 praising the "prudence" of another brother, Edward, Prince Palatine. He had married Anne of Gonzaga, the King of Poland's sister, and converted to Catholicism. Elisabeth had been outraged, but Descartes argued that such behavior was a way of laying firm foundations for their House once again, in the absence of real force. No doubt, he wrote, such conversion was a sign that God used all means to bring humans back to Him, but it was especially an indication that her brother was capable of the "worldly prudence" (*la prudence du siècle*) required to restore "fortune" (*OP*, 3: 633).

Such an argument might be drawn directly from Machiavelli: the idea of religion in service to the state, the thought that the truly powerful prince was the one who knew how to attract fortune by prudence, and how to "tame" it by *virtù*. Pierre Mesnard has spoken of Descartes's "so-called Machiavellianism," and has been followed by most other commentators on this aspect of Cartesian thought.[6] They may be

6. Pierre Mesnard, *Essai sur la morale de Descartes* (Paris: Boivin, 1936), 190. Descartes could have drawn his concept of prudence less from Machiavelli than from Pierre Charron who defined prudence as: "the knowledge and choice of things to be desired or

correct to reject Machiavelli as a direct source of Descartes's thinking, for such ideas were not unique to Descartes. The polemics of the French civil wars had made them commonplaces. To Le Bret and Richelieu, to Balzac and Naudé they were clichés. The analysis of Mazarin's diplomatic correspondence in the 1640s has been used to show how he, his ambassadors, and his spies were all convinced that the English parliamentarians were using religion only as a pretext for seizing power. Mazarin himself thought Charles fundamentally mistaken not to accept the puritans' religion, and to destroy them after consolidating his power (Knachel, *England and the Fronde*, 26–32). Such action would have been a matter of rational prudence, of political virtue. That such "Machiavellian" ideas were stock, is one thing; that Descartes *always* shared and used them in political arguments, is quite another.

It was again in writing of her family that Descartes gave Elisabeth further evidence of accepting this sort of thinking. On 12 February 1649, he wrote to console her on her uncle's execution, which marked, he said, "the grievous conclusion of England's tragedies." At least, he remarked, this death was "more glorious, more fortunate and sweeter" than that suffered by "common men." Was it to be taken as a sign of the greatness of the Princess's Royal House? Were admiration for the King's gracious self-control and sympathy for his death to be turned to prudent advantage? Perhaps not, but there was surely some ambivalence in Descartes's going more or less immediately from consoling Elisabeth to discussing the Palatinate's power. Charles's death took place on 9 February, but since the signing of the Peace of Westphalia in October of the previous year, Descartes remarked, *"en peine,"* he had yet to hear whether Elisabeth's older brother, Karl-Ludwig, had accepted it. Although it had not restored all their father's territories, the Treaty had given the prince the Lower Palatinate and created a new Electorate (the original remaining with what was now the Bavarian Palatinate). Descartes's distress was elicited by the thought that nothing could come of nothing, and Karl-Ludwig had to begin building somewhere.

As before, his concern was to use all possible means toward power,

---

avoided, the just estimate and selection of things, the eye that sees, directs, and orders all. It consists of three things of importance: consulting and deliberating well, judging and resolving well, directing and effecting well" (*De la sagesse*, in *Toutes les oeuvres* [Paris, 1635; rpt. in 2 vols. Geneva: Slatkine, 1970], 3: 1).

and to be aware that all that really counted was to possess force. Failing that, whatever subtlety was at hand should be used.

> When what is in question is the restitution of a state occupied or disputed by others who have the upper hand in force, it seems to me that those who only have justice and the rights of people on their side should never insist on satisfying all their claims. They have far greater cause for gratitude to those who get some of them redressed, however small a part it be, than hatred of those who retain the rest.

Additionally, he continued, the "prudence" that encouraged one to remain friends with all might create a further advantage toward "maintaining one's position." The great powers might have restored his lands to avoid any one of them becoming too powerful. Firstly, they obviously would rather not have a second Palatinate at all than have yet another rival for power. Secondly, he implied, the balance in question might eventually lead to the very mutual destruction it was designed to prevent, and then to the Palatinate's resurgence as a real force—a matter of biding time. Descartes did not make this explicit, but it would agree fully with the kind of advice he had given about her brother Edward (*OP.* 3: 888–91).

This union of reason and force, of prudence and utility, of experience and interest, marked all Descartes's thinking about politics. Restoration, or inception of power occurred according to an entirely linear, progressive scheme. To secure your interests, first you had to refer to concrete historical event and actual experience (knowing that humans always place *their* own interests first). To this end, you had to confirm right away what was certain, the necessary basis for all political maneuvers, and the equivalent of the epistemologically clear. You had to be ready to do good to others, he wrote to Elisabeth in January 1646, not for ethical reasons, but because of the likelihood of being rewarded with "numerous good services" in return (*OP,* 3: 646). That was how you could gradually (re)acquire a certain power and authority from a condition of impotence.

This position of impotence, I suggested, was equivalent to the isolation of 1619, that Descartes would never stop seeking however he might move from it over the years. Lack of power was a moment of suspension and expectancy entirely analogous to that of radical doubt. In its first Part, the *Discourse on the Method* gave the story (the "fiction," *fable*) of a mind. That story or history had to be set aside so as to allow the rediscovery of the pure good sense characterizing all humans *in potentia*, and the methodical reason able to guide it and let it function as it should. Similarly, Descartes sought initially to set aside the history of his age: not only in the *poêle* of winter 1619, but in Holland from 1628, whence he wrote in 1631 to Guez de Balzac lauding the United Provinces' calm situation, comparing it to the turbulence everywhere else (*OP*, 1: 292–93). He repeated this commentary at the end of the *Discourse's* third Part:

> Exactly eight years ago this desire [to become worthy of the reputation that was given me] made me resolve to move away from any place where I might have acquaintances and retire to this country [Holland], where the long duration of the war has led to the establishment of such order that the armies maintained here seem to serve only to make the enjoyment of the fruits of peace all the more secure. Living here, amidst this great mass of busy people who are more concerned with their own affairs than curious about those of others, I have been able to lead a life as solitary and withdrawn as if I were in the most remote desert, while lacking none of the comforts found in the most populous cities. [*PW*, 1: 126; *OP*, 1: 600]

This was a constant refrain, one repeated for example to Chanut in February 1649 when he regretted having been in Paris at the outbreak of the first Fronde (*OP*, 3: 894), and often to Elisabeth. He sought to make these world events, this historic tumult, all his concrete experiences, as it were, wholly incidental. At least initially they were to be entirely contingent. We will see later what became of them. But concerning the early stages of his thought at least, Henri Gouhier's insistence that reason and experience were quite separate is right enough. Indeed, such a separation followed quite naturally from the logic of the system.[7] Descartes emphasized the fact in a May 1646 letter to Elisabeth:

> I have no doubt that [the maxim on "civil life"] Your Highness proposes is the best of all: that it is better in such matters to follow experience than reason, for one rarely has to deal with reasonable people, as all should be, so that one could judge what they will do from mere consideration of what they should do. And often the best advice is not the most fortunate. That is why one is obliged to guess, and put oneself in the power of fortune. [*OP*, 3: 653–54]

Guesswork, fortune, inconstant experience, human unreason. . . . No doubt, and seemingly much à la Montaigne, as Brunschvicg ob-

---

7. Henri Gouhier, *Essai sur Descartes*, 2nd. edition (Paris: Vrin, 1949), 271–80.

served (although we shall soon see just what Descartes did with the reminiscence of Montaigne). But we have already seen the philosopher suggesting reasonable (political) means for getting fortune onto one's side. Besides, the inevitability of the opposition between experience and reason in civil affairs was explicitly tied here to the fact that humans do not habitually use their rational good sense. It followed that if the use of right reason could be learned by Method, then social experience should be capable of being brought to order by the same Method: just as in the *Passions of the Soul,* those "passions" would be controlled by reason. Descartes was clear that *rational* experience was always better than raw experience (an opposition used only a few years earlier both by Bacon and Galileo: for whom "raw experience" was unusable—perhaps strictly *meaningless*).

We can then draw an "equation" showing how good sense is to Method as civil society in history is to the rational and methodical power of the state. In the sixth Part of the *Discourse,* Descartes himself indicated this, comparing the progressive and linear acquisition of methodological scientific knowledge to that of financial and military power:

> Those who gradually discover the truth in the sciences are like people who become rich and find they have less trouble making large profits than they had in making much smaller ones when they were poorer. Or they may be compared with military commanders, whose forces tend to grow in proportion to their victories, but who need more skill to maintain their position after losing a battle than they do to take towns and provinces after winning one. For attempting to overcome all the difficulties and errors that prevent our arriving at knowledge of the truth is indeed a matter of fighting battles; we lose a battle whenever we accept some false opinion concerning an important question of general import, and we need much more skill afterwards to regain our former position than we do to make good progress when we already have principles which are well founded. [*PW,* 1: 145; *OP,* 1: 639]

We will later see how important to the issue of relations between individual and society were habit and the knowledge of truth discussed in that passage. For the moment I would like to highlight three ideas: the creating of a foundation; the linear process of growth;[8] the relation between the search for truth and power civil and military, between Method as an order of reason and Method as an order of society.

8. On this linear process of growth see Alexandre Matheron, "Psychologie et politique: Descartes—la noblesse du chatouillement," *Dialectiques* 6 (1974): 90.

All this implied that one must remove oneself from political and social history *for precisely the same reason* that one must remove oneself from the prior history of one's mind. For right practice to be possible, you must first find right rule. Utopianism? no doubt. But Descartes had after all written to Mersenne in November 1629 that Method itself presupposed "great changes in the order of things. The whole World would have to be a terrestrial paradise—something one might propose only in the realm of fiction" (*OP*, 1: 232). Yet eight years later, in 1637, he placed this utopian Method before the public. Later, in 1647, as we saw in the Preface to the French translation of the *Principles*, he could assert this Method would eventually permit everyone to accede to a knowledge of all truths. So why not the state and society as well?

Until this enlightened time, it was true, humans would have to live and order their social life according to experience, not reason, since they did not function like "reasonable people." If rational "prudence" ruled events, a true sovereign would have no difficulty, but "all humans would have to be perfectly sensible, so that knowing what they must do, one [would] be sure of what they will do." Even that would be insufficient, for all humans had their "free will," and only God could know its motion. Still that would not be enough: for to judge what someone would do, one needed to share the same intellectual capacity. What all this meant, as Descartes implied in the November 1645 letter to Elisabeth from which I have been quoting, was that methodical reason was in fact essential if anarchy was to be avoided (*OP*, 3: 628). Therefore, unlike James V. Schall and others, I am convinced that Descartes did indeed imply "that agreement in civil affairs [would] result from his philosophical method"[9]

On one side were actual society and common sense, experience and history; on the other were the rational state and Method, reason and the invention of a new instauration. The will of the thinking subject was to create fresh knowledge to replace the former knowledge of age-old authority. The will of the individual subject would create for itself new relations with the social and the political. These were one and the same subject. The old "public being," as Montaigne had called it, would be relegated to the *morale par provision*, to concrete history that was to be removed and changed. The old "private being," inconstant passage caught in perennial motion, and above all outside the political

9. James V. Schall, "Cartesianism and Political Theory," *The Review of Politics* 24 (1962): 263–64.

arena, had now been established and asserted as willful subject, in the bright stability of the *cogito*.[10] Reason, "virtue," habit, and the good conduct to follow, would let the new subject be concretized in its new history: that history where force and reason, virtue and power drew each to the other. The second and third Parts of the *Discourse* provided the needed bridge.

The work was presented, we know, as a history of the thinking self. First it narrated the rejection of an authoritarian past, the abrogation of a certain history. But if I have spoken at some length of Descartes's relations with the Palatine court and more briefly of the general European crisis, that is because, second, Descartes himself gave his search for a method, supposedly "nothing" but philosophical, an immediately political meaning. Apart from the frame already mentioned, Descartes emphasized an architectural metaphor long applied to theory of state and at least since Bacon to the idea of a new discursive and conceptual instauration. He now undertook, he wrote, a new construction (even as he claimed to set bounds to it):

> Admittedly, we never see people pulling down all the houses of a city for the sole purpose of rebuilding them in a different style to make the streets more attractive; but we do see many individuals having their houses pulled down in order to rebuild them, some even being forced to do so when the houses are in danger of falling down and their foundations are insecure. This example convinced me that it would be unreasonable for an individual to plan to reform a state by changing it from the foundations up and overturning it in order to set it up again; or again for him to plan to reform the body of the sciences or the established order of teaching them in the schools. [*PW*, 1: 117; *OP*, 1: 581]

He insisted that he only wished to correct his own thinking, to conduct his life on principles more solid than the "old foundations," that he did not want to reform "even minor matters affecting public institutions," even though these did reveal, if needs be said, some "imperfections" (*PW*, 1: 118; *OP*, 1: 582). He assured his reader that any stable situation was preferable to change. This he said despite having just asserted that the best ordered states were certainly those that from the outset had "observed the basic laws laid down by some wise law-

10. On the stability of the *cogito*, see Timothy J. Reiss, "Montaigne and the Subject of Polity," in *Literary Theory/Renaissance Texts*, ed. Patricia Parker and David Quint (Baltimore and London: The Johns Hopkins University Press, 1986), 115–49. A shorter version is available as "Montaigne et le sujet du politique," in *Montaigne*, ed. Steven F. Rendall, Jr. (Paris: J.-M. Place; Tübingen: Gunter Narr, 1984), 127–52.

giver" (*PW*, 1: 117, *OP*, 1: 580). Indeed, a close reading of the long passage just quoted leads to the same conclusion as before: Descartes situated state reform, scientific reform, and reform of education all at the same level. Given that, we should consider the following fact: the *Discourse* already contained and was immediately followed by the first steps in scientific reform (*Dioptrics, Meteorology, Geometry*). It was further followed by the *Meditations*, as far as foundations went, and then by the psychology of the *Passions of the Soul* (to say nothing of the *World* and the *Treatise on Man*). Educational reform was continued in the *Principles of Philosophy*, deliberately written as a student manual to replace other school texts.

May we not then see in Descartes's relations with the Palatinate (and eventually with the Swedish Queen), and in his correspondence with Elisabeth, no less concrete an effort, if not to reform the state, at least to act in a way such that little by little his ideas would filter into the political arena? An arena, as he noted from the *Discourse* on, far more intractable and ungracious than those of science and education— more dangerous as well. That Descartes so saw it was indicated by the precautions taken to keep part of the correspondence with Elisabeth secret, with him even proposing that they write in cipher.[11] Such concern is easily explained if he really was thinking of some new establishment, and is indeed *only* explained by the fear that *others* would think he was working toward a new concept of power and new individualized social relationships. This would simply be an application to himself of the prudence applauded in Prince Edward, and desired more generally in humankind.

At this point I would like to make what may seem to be an aside. Its significance will soon be evident. Léon Bruschvicg has reminded us that some important points in Descartes were already to be found in Montaigne. One was the idea of widely distributed good sense. Another was the importance of military apprenticeship in the development of youth.[12] That for Montaigne such apprenticeship was irrevocably bound up in the civil wars of his time goes without saying. Good sense and armies bring us inevitably to the memory of Descartes's *poêle*. We saw how the philosopher related his illumination in

11. Elisabeth to Descartes, 10 October 1646, in *Oeuvres*, ed. Charles Adam and Paul Tannery, new presentation, 11 vols. (Paris: Vrin, 1964–76), 4: 524. This edition henceforth referred to as *AT*.

12. Léon Brunschvicg, *Descartes et Pascal, lecteurs de Montaigne* (New York and Paris: Brentano's, 1944), 115–16, 126–27.

the room in Germany at the outbreak of a war that began as that of Protestant Bohemia against Catholic Empire, upstart Palatine versus entrenched Hapsburg. By 1637 Descartes was certainly not recounting his German adventure and his *poêle* unaware that the wars in whose onset he had participated were remaking the face of Europe, as an earlier Protestant/Catholic conflict had remade that of France. Perhaps, indeed, his celebrated *poêle* was as much a literary as a real memory; for the image was not unfamiliar as a metaphor of revolt and renewal.

At the start of the earlier French wars, Pierre de Ronsard had written in praise of Lorraine, opposed to Germany, in strikingly similar terms. In his "repetition" Descartes chose to put himself in the position of those whom the poet saw in 1560 as the originators of rebellion:

> O bien-heureux Lorrains, que la secte Calvine,
> Et l'erreur de la terre à la vostre voisine
> Ne deprava jamais! d'où seroit animé
> Un habitant du Rhin en un poësle enfermé,
> A bien interpreter les Saintes Escritures,
> Entre les gobelets, les vins et les injures?

> O happy Lorrainers, whom the Calvinist sect and the mistake of the
> land bordering on yours never perverted! How could a Rhine dweller
> closed up in a stove-heated room come to interpret the Holy
> Scriptures well, between cups, wine and abuse?[13]

This elegy was written in 1560, dedicated to the poet Louis des Masures, who had himself converted to Protestantism just two years earlier. In view of the images of city and concept building with which Descartes followed his own repetition of the *poêle*, it is surely not irrelevant that the next two lines of Ronsard's poem made a not very oblique reference to the same matter, commenting on a statue owned by Des Masures: "Y croye qui voudra, Ami, je te promets / Par ton bel Amphion de n'y croire jamais" [Let whoever will believe it, my friend, I promise you on your beautiful Amphion never to believe it]. Amphion was of course the poet-builder of Thebes. The irony surely was not lost on Descartes that Ronsard was addressing his disbelief in the legitimacy of (Protestant) revolt to a friend who had converted, who was thus already a rebel, and to whom, further, belonged the statue of the city-building poet. When the poet continued that "L'autre jour en dor-

13. Pierre de Ronsard, "Discours a Loys des Masures," *Oeuvres complètes*, ed. Gustave Cohen, 2 vols. (Paris: Gallimard, 1950), 2: 571 (ll. 49–54).

mant" [The other day, while sleeping], he saw the skeletal presence of
Du Bellay, are we not reminded of Descartes's own later dream—also in
his *poêle?* In Ronsard's dream, Du Bellay counselled his friend not to
accept change. Since Descartes would be adopting the situation of the
Germans in their *poêle*, it was scarcely surprising that he also accepted
change and the new.

The importance of the literary model, whether from Montaigne or
from Ronsard, is not that it undermined in any way the reality of
Descartes's experience. On the contrary, it placed it in a quite specific
context: in this case, one of political and religious rebellion. Much
earlier, in Antoine de la Sale's *Petit Jehan de Saintré*, the metaphor of
the German *poêle* had been used to debase the chivalric ideal. When
the evil Abbot derided Saintré before his Lady (the two interlocutors
being guilty of betrayal), reversing the chivalric ideal in a text sym-
pathetic to it, he chose the very metaphor of the stove: "encores, ma
dame, vous dy plus. Quant ces chevaliers ou escuiers vont faire leurs
armes et ont prins congié du roy, se il fait froit ilz s'en vont a ces pales
[poêles] d'Allemaine, se rigollent avec ces fillectes tout l'iver" [Further,
my lady, I will tell you more. When these knights or squires go off to do
their knightly deeds and have bid farewell to the king, if it is cold they
go off to these German stove-heated rooms, and play around with girls
all winter].[14] Once again, what you had here was an overturning of
norms: in this case of the chivalric ideal; in Ronsard of religion. In
Tasso's *Jerusalem Delivered* (1: 41–42), Guelpho and his Germanic
soldiers were wont to spend their nights drinking in such rooms, while
in Ariosto's much earlier first Satire (which Descartes almost certainly
knew), the poet gave "il caldo de le stuffe" [the heat of the stoves] as a
reason for not going to Hungary, and therefore breaking with his pa-
tron, Ippolito d'Este.[15]

I do not suggest of course that Descartes was referring specifically
to any of these predecessors, however well he may have known them;
the point is simply that the *poêle* metaphor was a familiar one for a
break with the past and an implication of revolt and renewal. In the

14. Antoine de La Sale, *Jehan de Saintré*, ed. Jean Misrahi and Charles A. Knudson
(Geneva: Droz, 1965), 277.

15. *The Satires of Ludovico Ariosto: A Renaissance Autobiography*, trans. Peter
Desa Wiggins (Athens, OH: Ohio University Press, 1976), 8. It is worth noting that in his
Colloquy, *Diversoria* ("Inns"), Erasmus pilloried the German inns, the drinking and
overheated stove rooms ("*alemmanica hypocausta*"): Desiderius Erasmus, *The Collo-
quies*, trans. Craig R. Thompson (Chicago and London: University of Chicago Press,
1965), 147–52. For him, they represented the opposite of culture and spirit.

eighteenth century therefore, d'Alembert was perhaps not at all mistaken when he wrote that Descartes could "be thought of as a leader of
conspirators who, before anyone else, had the courage to rise against a
despotic and arbitrary power and who, in preparing a resounding revolution, laid the foundations of a more just and happier government,
which he himself was not able to see established."[16] To take up Descartes's own image of the state or science as a building to be constructed on new foundations, and to add to it the philosopher's own
sense of secret political revolt was quite perspicacious. For, of course,
in Descartes himself these background references lay hidden: a further
evidence of prudence. Additional confirmation that Descartes's *Larvatus prodeo* was to be taken seriously. Yet the spirit underlying the
prudence was there for all to see (the prudence would have been unnecessary, were it not).

Indeed, Descartes's selection of a literary reference in order to
switch its apparent value (to "hidden" but vital effect) was clear in
what was arguably his most important literary borrowing. Brunschvicg
was surely correct in finding the origin of the *Discourse*'s opening
sentence in Montaigne's essay, *De la praesumption* (2: xvii). Yet in
implying a lack of originality (not only good sense as what all ascribe to
themselves, but also the following ironic remark), Brunschvicg ne-
glected altogether Montaigne's context—which was most significant.
For we should consider what Descartes had done with an earlier sentence from the same essay: "It is a cowardly and servile temper that
disguises and hides itself under a mask, not daring to appear as it is.
That is how men prepare themselves for perfidy." Descartes had not
hesitated to adopt just this masking of the self as his motto.

Now, Montaigne's whole purpose in the essay on presumption was
to show how we all fool ourselves as to the truth and our own worth.
While it was indeed the case that he wrote: "It is commonly said that
the fairest division nature has made of her benefits is that of sense: for
no-one is unhappy with the portion she has dealt them,"[17] his goal in
the ironic qualifying phrase was to query the thought. He was empha-
sizing further the inconsistency and unreliability of all human reason.
Not so Descartes, who added that doubtless people were not mis-

16. Jean Le Rond d'Alembert, *Preliminary Discourse to the Encyclopedia of Diderot*
trans. Richard N. Schwab, with the collaboration of Walter E. Rex, introduction and
notes by Richard N. Schwab (Indianapolis and New York: Bobbs-Merrill, 1963), 80.

17. Brunschvicg, *Descartes et Pascal*, 115–16. Michel de Montaigne, *Oeuvres complètes*, ed. Albert Thibaudet and Maurice Rat (Paris: Gallimard, 1962), 630, 641.

taken—they simply did not know how to use that good sense properly. *That* was the question. That Descartes more or less announced a switch in values was thus important. He was claiming that matters did not need to depend on human inconstancy and unreason, on fortune and guesswork. He was implying that the thinking subject could act rationally in history. Such would be the result of the (hidden) revolution. Descartes's use of literary reference was then subtle and significant: the textual precedents clarified a revolutionary meaning, one that can better help us understand the full implications set out in the *Discourse*, as well as his agreement with other thinkers of political *instauration*.

Between the expression of prudence about the state, urged in the "reform" passage in the second Part of the *Discourse* which I earlier quoted, and the tale of the *poêle* and his German journey there appears a series of significant similes. First, "works composed of several parts and produced by various different craftsmen" usually had not "so much perfection" as "the works of one man." Second, "buildings undertaken and completed by a single architect are usually more attractive and better planned than those which several have tried to patch up by adapting old walls built for different purposes" (*PW*, 1: 116; *OP*, 1: 579). Descartes then applied these dicta without delay to the construction of entire cities, to "the constitution of the true religion, whose articles have been made by God alone," and to the excellence of the laws establishing Sparta's constitution, which were "devised by a single man and hence all tended to the same end" (*PW*, 1: 116–17; *OP*, 1: 580).

Doubtless these were commonplaces of political theory—a fact in itself of importance in understanding Descartes's purpose. With this in mind, it may be useful to quote a passage from Machiavelli's *Discourses*, even though Descartes wrote to Elisabeth that he only read them after summer 1646 (*OP*, 3: 681):

> Happy indeed should we call that state which produces a man so prudent that men can live securely under the laws which he prescribes without having to emend them. Sparta, for instance, observed its laws for more than eight hundred years without corrupting them and without any dangerous disturbance. Unhappy, on the other hand, in some degree is that city to be deemed which, not having chanced to meet with a prudent organizer, has to reorganize itself. And, of such, that is the more unhappy which is the more remote from order [from the outset]; and that is the more remote from order whose institutions have

missed altogether the straight road which leads to its perfect and true destiny. For it is almost impossible that states of this type should by any eventuality be set on the right road again; whereas those which, if their order is not perfect, have made a good beginning and are capable of improvement, may become perfect should something happen which provides the opportunity.[18]

Where did Descartes situate himself in this accounting? Well, we will see easily later, because in his well-known letter about *The Prince* addressed to Elisabeth in September 1646, he adopted many aspects of such a concept of state and sovereign authority, while adjusting it to his own notions of prudence and right, of virtue and interest, of reason and utility.

But first I must discuss another discursive component of the Descartes passage just quoted, one of prime importance when we speak of an *instauration* in the context of the European seventeenth century. It can be seen in the order, "true religion"/methodical constitution of the state: the order proceeding from God to Sparta. In this movement appeared once more that purely human *Fiat* with which Hobbes ushered in the "Pacts and Covenants" founding Leviathan. The premises of the *Fiat* were already in Bacon, whose Great Instauration and "Novus Atlas" (sic) were praised by the anonymous author of the preface to *The Passions of the Soul* (perhaps Descartes himself, perhaps the abbé Picot), as the only attempts before Descartes at a systematic construction of something truly new.[19] In this very treatise Descartes would emphasize just which aspect of mind permitted such an analogy between a divine and a human *Fiat:*

> I see only one thing in us which could give us good reason for esteeming ourselves, namely, the exercise of free will [*libre arbitre*] and the control we have over our volitions [*volontés*]. For we can reasonably be praised or blamed only for actions that depend on this free will. It renders us in a certain way like God by making us masters of ourselves, provided we do not lose the rights it gives us through timidity. [*PW*, 1: 384; *OP*, 3: 152]

It was this same free will that Descartes had associated with the requirements of worldly prudence in the quoted letter of November

18. Niccolò Machiavelli, *The Discourses*, ed. Bernard Crick, trans. Leslie J. Walker, s.j., revised by Brian Richardson (1970; rpt. Harmondsworth: Penguin, 1978), 105 (1: ii).

19. *AT*, 11: 320. For the wider implications of the *Fiat*, see Timothy J. Reiss, *The Discourse of Modernism* (Ithaca and London: Cornell University Press, 1982), 203–05, 216, 222.

1645. The word here translated as "timidity" is *lâcheté:* precisely the word used by Montaigne to qualify the contrary viewpoint when he spoke of concealment in his essay on presumption.

In his "Author's Epistle to the Reader" (printed by Sir William Molesworth at the Beginning of *The Works*), Hobbes wrote that like the spirit of God moving over the deep in the second verse of *Genesis*, the true philosopher must let his "reason move upon the deep of his [own] cogitations and experience." The "method must resemble that of the creation." A direct analogy existed between "the order of the creation" and the necessary "order of contemplation." It was almost as if the very processes of reason had been hypostatized into their object of study: here the object was the state and civil society.[20] The very organization of mind meant that God, the philosopher, and the legislator acted in the same way: true rational order would thus apply to every domain of action. For free will was not just any old element of mind. By definition, it was directed to action, and whatever *rights* we might have lay in taking full and prudent responsibility for such action.

Descartes had already made the assimilation of the human to God by means of this supreme free will, in a letter to Queen Christina of 20 November 1647. He had indeed made the point even more strongly:

> besides that free will is in itself the noblest thing in us, insofar as it makes us somehow like God and seems to exempt us from being subject to him, so that its good use is thus our greatest benefit, it is also the one most properly ours and most important to us. It follows that it alone can beget our greatest satisfactions. [*OP*, 3: 747–48]

The "volitions" of which he spoke in the article from the *Passions* were linked, precisely, to the diverse passions. *Libre arbitre* was the higher will, the freedom that enabled us to organize all actions of life. It was readily assimilated to the "will" that "used reason" to create and institute an ordered system. As Spinoza would later say: "Voluntas et intellectus unum et idem sunt" ["Will and intellect are one and the same thing"].[21]

It is worth remarking here that this concept of free self-directing human will was of an order wholly different from what could have been thought before. I have mentioned its absence from Montaigne. I

---

20. Thomas Hobbes, *The English Works*, ed. Sir William Molesworth, 11 vols. (London: John Behn, 1839–45), 1.

21. Benedict de Spinoza, *Ethics* in *Ethics and De Intellectus Emendatione*, trans. A. Boyle, introduction by G. Santayana (London: Dent; New York: Dutton, 1910), 76, 2: 49.

may also take a representative sample from that supposed apostle of reason the poet François Malherbe. He ended his "Consolation à Monsieur du Périer": "To will what God wills is the only wisdom / That gives us rest."[22] Written in 1598, this expressed a quite typical, even banal, sentiment of subordination of the human to the divine. Yet just because the consolation was a set piece, which often reflected at this time, rather, a stoical reliance on human reason, the idea of its absorption into the divine will was the more significant in its difference from what we find in Descartes and others. Indeed, it was entirely the opposite (compare for example Descartes's consolation to Elisabeth on her uncle's execution; and think of what he had done with texts by Ronsard and Montaigne). The claim to a powerfully free human will was something new in Descartes's time.

Without mention of Machiavelli, Bacon or Hobbes, however, the mere exposition of the elements observed in the *Discourse* may make us doubt the genuineness of those limits Descartes pretended to place on the use of Method. The more so, when we see him insisting on the architectural metaphor at the beginning of the third Part of the text. He used it to compare his provisional morality to a comfortable temporary dwelling, useful while building his new home, allowing him to follow meanwhile habitual laws, but whose only conceivable superiority was just that of being habit. For there was no reason to suppose that there were not people "as sensible among the Persians or Chinese as among ourselves," although they might obey quite different opinions and laws (*PW*, 1: 122; *OP*, 1: 593). Such a thought implied another cliché of the time: namely that beneath the laws, habits, and opinions of the various known nations, it should be possible to discover the elements of universal law. In 1642, that was precisely what Hobbes declared as his goal as he began the *De Cive*.[23] Descartes insisted that humans became

22. François Malherbe, *Oeuvres*, ed. Antoine Adam (Paris: Gallimard, 1971), 43.
23. His aim, he wrote, was not "to point which are the laws of any country, but to declare what the laws of all countries are" (*Philosophical Rudiments Concerning Government and Society* in *Works*, 2: xxiii). Descartes would have read the slightly more prescriptive Latin: "ne quicquam dissererem de cujuscunque civitatis legibus speciatim, id est, ne quae sint, sed quid sint leges, dicerem" (*Opera philosophica*, ed. Sir William Molesworth, 5 vols. [London: John Bohn, 1839–45], 2: 152). Hobbes had read the *Discourse* as early as 1637, when Kenelm Digby had lent him a copy (Samuel I. Mintz, *The Hunting of Leviathan: Seventeenth-Century Reactions to the Materialism and Moral Philosophy of Thomas Hobbes* [Cambridge: Cambridge University Press, 1970], 10). From his arrival in Paris in 1640 Hobbes kept close contact with French philosophical circles. He soon fell out with Descartes but stayed in touch with Mersenne (who had him

different because they had been "raised from infancy among the French or German" or "among the Chinese or cannibals" (*PW*, 1: 119; *OP*, 1: 583–84). But what made the difference was not common good sense; simply the diversity of custom and upbringing.

The *Discourse* was not the only place where he insisted on the need to accept common experience while awaiting the discovery of the one true Method. Later on, Method in hand, he would still warn the readers of his *Principles*, his philosophical textbook, that patience was a necessity: "As far as ordinary life is concerned, the chance for action would frequently pass us by if we waited until we could free ourselves from our doubts, and so we are often compelled to accept what is merely probable" (*PW*, 1: 193; *OP*, 3: 92). The provisional morality was thus intended to permit the supreme will of the thinking individual to function on the basis of *doxa* only while waiting for it to be able to do so on that of Method.

While insisting from the first sentence of the *Discourse* on the universality of good sense and the need of methodical reason, Descartes further stressed (in the second Part) that a city, society, or state guided only by fortune would be no more effective than good sense failing to follow the only right path: that of Method. The experience and habit guiding the provisional morality were thus to be eliminated—as soon as possible. Further, he declared, "the will of [a few] men using reason" risked leading to just as fantastic and disordered an organization as what resulted from mere fortune or chance (*PW*, 1: 117; *OP*, 1: 580). What was needed, in politics as in the case of mind and knowledge, was the will of one man using reason, guided by this almost divine will, guaranteeing the rights of the thinking subject in action. This was strikingly close to Machiavelli's claim that "One should take it as a general rule that rarely, if ever, does it happen that a state, whether it be a republic or a kingdom, is either well-ordered at the outset or radically transformed *vis-à-vis* its old institutions unless this be done by one person. It is likewise essential that there should be

---

write the third Objections to the *Meditations*), with Pierre Gassendi and his future translator, Samuel Sorbière (Adrien Baillet, *La vie de Monsieur Des-cartes*, 2 vols. [1691; facsimile rpt. New York and Hildesheim: George Olms, 1972], 2: 167–74). It was surely not chance that Hobbes's *Elements of Law* and the English translation of Descartes's *Traité des passions* were published by the same editors, John Martin (future printer to the Royal Society) and John Ridley, just three weeks apart, 4 May and 24 May 1650 (Thomas Hobbes, *Les Éléments de droit naturel et politique*, trans. and ed. Louis Roux [Lyon: Hermès, 1977], 31).

but one person upon whose mind and method depends any similar process of organization" (Machiavelli, *Discourses*, 132 [1: xi]).

Both the question of power, as the relation between individual and society, between subject and state, and the problem of the opposition between historical experience and methodical reason applied to society (that is, between opinion, habit, and custom on the one hand, and interest, prudence, and creation of the new on the other), were inscribed in Descartes's thought at least from the *Discourse* on. The provisional morality therefore needs to be read politically. As the old history of being was to be set aside to permit the building of a new order of thought, so the provision of a civil morality, adopting common habit and opinion, was to be set aside with the creation of a new reason of state. His determination to advance "slowly," "like a man who walks alone in the dark," did not alter his goal of "seeking the true method of attaining knowledge of everything within [his] mental capacities" (*PW*, 1: 119; *OP*. 1: 584). This certainly included science, education, and those things pertaining to the social. Descartes again emphasized the connection when he at last enunciated the four rules of Method, comparing their reduced number to laws whose rarity meant "that a state is much better governed" (*PW*, 1: 120; *OP*, 1: 586). Exactly so, he wrote, reaching the end of the third Part of the *Discourse*, he had managed to pull down the "old house" and build "more certain opinions" (*PW*, 1: 125; *OP*, 1: 599).

He then indicated another side of the social implications of his thinking: the matter now of putting his text itself into social action. Having reached this stage in his discoveries, he wrote, he felt obliged to communicate them to the public—to avoid sinning against society's rules:

> as soon as I had acquired some general notions in physics and had noticed, as I began to test them in various particular problems, where they could lead and how much they differ from the principles used up to now, I believed that I could not keep them secret without sinning gravely against the law which obliges us to do all in our power to secure the general welfare of mankind. [*PW*, 1: 142; *OP*, 1: 634]

Here we are already in the midst of future discussions by Descartes of the relation between the individual and society, examined theoretically elsewhere, but whose concrete implications he now put forward as they concerned himself. Given life's brevity and the inevitable poverty of an individual's ability to experiment, one had to turn to the collectivity to avoid the effects of "these two obstacles," and create a scientific community: hence the obligation "to communicate faithfully to the public what little [he] had discovered, and to urge the best minds to try and make further progress" (PW, 1: 143; OP, 1: 635). Nonetheless, some more or less perilous situations arose in which this reaction was not desirable, and then it was best to restrain oneself and keep things secret: the subject of knowledge, the individual, had to decide (shades of Bacon's Atlantan scientists and Galileo's secretive mathematicians). Descartes gave an example:

> Every man is indeed bound to do what he can to procure the good of others, and a man who is of no use to anyone else is strictly worthless. Nevertheless it is also true that our concern ought to extend beyond the present, and that it is good to neglect matters which may profit the living when we aim to do other things which will benefit posterity even more. [PW, 1: 145; OP, 1: 638]

Beyond this ground of personal obligation, Descartes was indeed concerned with the creation of a new civic order, a new concept of princely power and the individualist state (or at least with providing firm grounds for a view already expressed by Bodin, elaborated and confirmed by such contemporaries as Le Bret, Richelieu, and his friend Guez de Balzac, although Descartes added an interesting and unusual utopian twist). Clearly the new prince had to be identified with the subject of the *cogito*, as the willful self acting through Method. Here Descartes spoke of *himself* as possessing a new knowledge and alone able to understand its implications—and so alone able to decide what others should be told (whatever obligations he might have to their improvement). He set himself, that is to say, in the place of the prince described in his September 1646 letter to Elisabeth. Nor need we be surprised to see approval of princely secrecy: "the chief motives for the actions of princes are often such special circumstances, that unless one is oneself a prince or has long participated in their secrets one could not imagine them" (OP, 3: 670). Bacon and Hobbes expressed just such a view (Reiss, *Discourse*, 190–93, 203–04).

Only the thinking subject then could make such decisions. For it alone knew the truth in question. Here of course we return to that free will guiding all of an individual's actions. It was at work in the first and second maxims of the provisional morality, where Descartes declared himself determined not to be shaken from this ethic. Such stubbornness was likewise the mark of the good prince who, wrote Descartes in the same letter, had to be "inflexible with respect to such things as he has been seen to have decided even if they are harmful to him" (*OP*, 3: 669). Such will, he said in article 153 of the *Passions*, was entirely bound by our "firm and constant resolution to use it well"; a resolution, he added, showing how we followed the path of virtue and the knowledge of truth.[24]

The relation between the truly rational individual, the possessive subject of methodical knowledge, and historical society always implied a relation of power and interests. The state, Descartes intimated, had to be ordered in such a way as to recognize these diverse aspects of the social arena, first, the necessity binding the individual to all, at the same time as the whole could not undermine the radical individuality of each. Descartes made this point in the same letter of September 1646, insisting that "everyone's happiness depends on oneself," explaining that this was why you "must keep yourself so firmly beyond the sway of fortune" (*OP*, 3: 670). A year before, in another letter to Elisabeth, Descartes had linked this last question to the need for socialization:

> Once we have thus recognized God's benevolence, our soul's immortality and the immensity of the universe, a truth yet remains whose knowledge I think most useful. This is that although each of us is a person separate from others, whose interests are consequently somehow distinct from everyone else's, yet you must be aware you cannot survive alone, that you are indeed one of the parts of the universe, and more especially one of the parts of this earth, one of the parts of this state, this society, this family, bound to it by your abode, your oath, your birth. And you must always prefer the interests of the whole, of which you are a part, to those of your individual person: yet with restraint and caution. For you would be wrong to expose yourself to great harm, wanting to obtain but a small benefit for your kin or country. And if a man is alone worth more than all the rest of his town, he would not be right to want to ruin himself to save it. [*OP*, 3: 606–07]

Again the decision was left to the individual. The self came first. To use one's will against one's own interest (at least when the issue was

24. *PW*, 1: 384; *OP*, 3: 1067. Again, Descartes could have found this twofold need in Charron, who spoke of it as he began his chapters on political matters: "the first thing needed before any action, is knowledge of state: for the first rule of prudence is knowledge." He added, "after this knowledge of state, which is a sort of preparatory matter, the first thing required is virtue" (*Sagesse*, 3: 2). The order in which Descartes set them was even the same.

disproportionate) ran counter both to reason and free will: "il n'aurait pas *raison* de *se vouloir* perdre." Descartes himself, we recall, before being positioned to give such counsel, removed himself from his state, his society, his family, changing his abode to be completely *isolated* (a choice constantly reiterated). Of course, Descartes's separation aimed at building a new order, a kind of falling back the better to spring forward: a question of individual authority and self-interest.

Moreover, for the individual, the most sensible reason for participating in society was not at all primarily a matter either of ethics or ontology. It was, he said to Elisabeth (6 October 1645), self-interest itself: "For if we think of ourselves alone, we can enjoy only our own particular stock [*biens*]. Whereas if we think of ourselves as part of some other body, we share its common stock, yet without thereby being deprived of any of our own" (*OP*, 3: 613). Such a remark embodied the same idea of constant accumulation that we saw in the *Discourse*, as to knowledge and power, both military and financial. Participation was a way to increase one's power, to augment possessions and pleasure. The thinking individual partook of the public to serve its own interests (the advice given to Elisabeth about her two brothers aimed at nothing else). Actually Descartes went much further, approaching the argument deployed a century later by Bernard Mandeville in *The Fable of the Bees*. He imagined a social process that endured because it reinforced the interest of each, because it increased benefits enjoyed by each individual. He ended the letter just quoted with the following advice:

> I confess it hard to tell how far reason commands us to be interested in public affairs. But anyway the issue needs no great nicety: it suffices to satisfy one's conscience, and to that end we may largely go along with our fancy. For God has so ordered things, and joined men in such close community, that even if each tied everything to himself and had no care for others, he would not fail to work for them usually on everything in his power, provided he did so with prudence. Especially if he lived in an age when manners were uncorrupted. Besides, just as doing good to others is better and more glorious than obtaining it for oneself, so it is the greatest souls who are most inclined to it, and make least fuss of the wealth they possess. [*OP*, 3: 619]

This was close indeed to private vice as public virtue and *laissez-faire*, except that Descartes had in mind an *obligation* as much social as individual.

In fact he had already given a practical example of how to serve one's own interest, while seeming not to and to remain publicly available. Pretending, he said, to lead a life of pleasant leisure, he achieved his only aim of "pursuing [his] project" and thus of making "progress in the knowledge of truth" (*PW*, 1: 126; *OP*, 1: 600). *Larvatus prodeo:* "I go forward masked" (*PW*, 1: 2; *OP*, 1: 45). Here again, we find a concept applicable to the good prince: as he wrote in his September 1646 letter to Elisabeth, such a prince had to be able to retain the "honours" and "respect the people believe due to him," letting "appear publicly only his solemnest actions, or those that all can approve, keeping his pleasures for his private life" (*OP*, 3: 668). The problem stayed that of balancing personal interest and social obligation. The long passage just quoted showed a sort of break. The first two sentences seemed to argue how to keep oneself to oneself and serve one's own interests in the face of present society: where one had to go forward masked, if one was to obtain knowledge of truth and have breathing space. The last sentence appeared to envisage a society of good custom and great souls, where all interests converge. (God was here the reassuring mediator, as in the argument of the *Meditations*.)

This utopian state would be possible only when the truth was finally known, and even then only when it had become a *habit*. As Descartes again wrote (to Elisabeth, on 15 September 1645): "only two things are required, it seems to me, for one to be prepared always to make good judgment. One is knowledge of truth, the other the habit of recalling and accepting that knowledge whenever occasion requires" (*OP*, 3: 605). It was a point he chose to emphasize: "I have said above that apart from the knowledge of truth, habit is also needed to be prepared always to judge well." This had to be, for otherwise the concrete event, the actual experience might divert us from it: "which is why," he added, "the School is right to speak of virtues as habits" (*OP*, 3: 609). The whole argument was summarized in the *Passions of the Soul* where he insisted that conduct had to be ruled by those "weapons" proper to will: "its 'proper' weapons are firm and determinate judgments bearing upon the knowledge of good and evil." Judgments allowing will to go into action had to be based on "knowledge of the truth" (*PW*, 1: 347; *OP*, 3: 992, 994). That passions produced action only through the mediation of desire was, he said, morally essential, for such desire was properly regulated by knowledge (*PW*, 1: 379; *OP*, 3: 1059). Such knowledge, we know, came from Method.

However, before such knowledge became general, before the creation of this utopia of great souls and habitual good judgment (a deeply individualist idea), a way had to be traced through society as it was, sheltering individuality. To that end, and perhaps for the last time before suggesting the possibility of something else, Descartes pursued the idea of a relation between individual and society showing all the signs of that *laissez-faire* which developed clearly only a century later. Yet another letter to Elisabeth (January 1646) elaborated this:

> What makes me think those who do nothing but to their own advantage must like other people be working for others and trying to please all, as much as is in their power and so long as they are prudent, is that it usually happens that those thought socially serviceable [*officieux:* a word with clear Ciceronian overtones] and quick to please, receive many good services [*offices*] from others, even those they have never helped. They would not get these if they were thought of a different temper, and the trouble they go to to please is not so great as the benefits [*commodités*] received from the amity of those who know them. . . . As for me, the rule I have chiefly obeyed in the conduct of life has simply been to follow the high road and believe the best part of guile is not to want to use guile at all. The common laws of society, all tending toward our doing good to one another or at least doing no harm, are I think so well established that who follows them honestly, without deceit or fraud, leads a far happier and safer life than those who seek their advantage by other paths. It is true they sometimes succeed by other men's ignorance and fortune's favor. More often they fail, and thinking to make their place, are ruined. [*OP*, 3: 636–37]

Again he was dealing here with knowledge of truth, habit of virtue coming from judgments based on that knowledge (derived from Method), self-interest, and individual morality. They lived in a society that worked badly—as the general crisis demonstrated: religious wars, Thirty Years War, revolts against Spain in the Low Countries, in Portugal, in Sicily, Naples and Catalonia, internal emergencies in Poland, Russia, Sweden and Switzerland, civil war and revolution in England, universal questioning of old forms and ways of knowledge, major crises in educational methods and processes, grave economic and commercial dislocation, first stutterings of a rising technology, and so on.

How were they to live in all this? In fact, he had been arguing, there was at first no choice. Provisionally one had to live as if nothing were happening, agreeing to adopt accepted customs and opinions. At the same time, one could not but work toward something more stable and more "pleasing." What could that something be?

Beyond the social, Descartes saw only one fixed and trustworthy element: the thinking self, endowed with good sense capable of being ordered by true Method. That would permit a knowledge of truth, and truth would enable good judgment and habitually virtuous action based on such judgment. That "set" in turn made possible a good use of the will, of that free will in which we equal God. The action available to such will, through "officious" prudence and interest, collective and personal advantage and utility, had to create the society of great souls benefiting all. In another field, Method would allow access to complete and true knowledge; in the political realm, it could build the good society.

But how could one get from individual action, benefiting private interest in an imperfect society, by means of mask and morality provisional, to this new society where all acted to everyone's benefit?

This was the good prince's role. Fully to understand this we need to know first that new habit based on knowledge of truth could be established extremely fast. In the *Passions*, Descartes asserted the utility of knowing we could change even those habits which seemed most permanently engrained, and no less rapidly: "Indeed this habit can be acquired by a single action and does not need long practice" (*PW*, 1: 348; *OP*, 3: 995). In the political arena such an idea had weighty implications: the wise prince could quickly be effective for change. If only there were a leader who possessed all the qualities of one who had acquired the means of true knowledge, of good judgment, the use of methodical reason, and was thus able to direct the will to the common interest, then such change and a new establishment would be entirely possible. This Cartesian prince able to benefit from the lessons of Method was the one he opposed (wrongly) to the Machiavellian prince. And we must understand the name of "Prince" as it was frequently understood at the time, as the name given to sovereign authority whatever its actual form. It is with all this in mind that we should read the celebrated letter to Elisabeth of September 1646, where he answered her query about *The Prince*.

Her own letter of 10 October, which fiercely criticized Descartes's remarks, makes it clear that the princess did not at all miss the implications of Machiavelli's text. She declared that the proposed actions did indeed "lead to the establishment" of a state, but to a state where "at least in popular opinion the prince is a usurper" (*AT*, 4: 520). It was the case that her own House would not have been illegal should it return to the Palatinate (as it later did), but the phrase, "au moins en l'opinion du peuple," surely referred to its situation (out of its throne for a generation), and certainly lets us know the discussion was serious and concrete. As early as June 1643, Elisabeth had lamented to Descartes that she lacked time for meditation in part because of "the interests of [her] House, which [she] could not neglect" (AT, 3: 684). Descartes's advice about her brothers and his comments on her uncle targeted actual political conditions. (Although he did not react, Elisabeth's mention of her brother Philip's "treaty with the Republic of Venice," in an April 1646 letter about quite other matters had doubtless not been innocent: AT, 4: 404.)

In his reply to her October letter, Descartes agreed on the issue of legality, suggesting that if the situation had not been such as Machiavelli actually faced in Italy, his argument would doubtless have been different: a point giving eloquent testimony to her interlocutor's awareness of concrete political situation. When you had, he wrote, "no reason to fear," the establishment of authority could be "more generous" (OP, 3: 681). Throughout his correspondence, as in the Discourse and the Passions, Descartes implied that he faced a radically different situation from the one to which Machiavelli had reacted. The power of his new prince, thinking subject, a willful power founded on the truth enabled by Method, allowed him to tend his own interest as he responded to everyone's, to act with virtuous prudence, and to elaborate a *"generous"* instauration.

This was the sense in which Descartes returned, at the start of the Prince letter, to the architectural metaphor of the Discourse. Now it was no longer the image of a mental trajectory. First, the issue at hand was indeed to build a new state. Second, and as important, the Method enabling the building now existed. We can view his arguments about the prince, the state, and sovereign power no longer as the merely possible knowledge implied in the Discourse, but as a real example of a civic science: equal to the Dioptrics, the Meteorology, or the Passions.

Supposing, first, the possibility of acquiring "a state by just means" and of a "generous" instauration, Descartes then continued: "just as when you build a house whose foundations are so bad as to be unable to support high and thick walls, you are forced to make them weak and low, so those who have begun their establishment by crimes are usually obliged to continue committing crimes, and could not stay in power if they tried to be virtuous" (OP, 3: 666). The state therefore *had* to be established and maintained on the foundations of Method, knowledge of truth, and that habit of virtue which meant you supported other's interests *because* you were attentive to your own.

In a state based on crimes, everyone could become prince, and the first to succeed, wrote Descartes agreeing with Machiavelli, would replace the usurper—a potentially endlessly repetitive process (*OP,* 3: 666). For although he elsewhere denied it (speaking for example of Hobbes's *De Cive* in a letter of 1643), Descartes was far from believing humans to be other than bad (*OP,* 3: 61; Baillet, *Vie,* 2: 173–74). For that reason the good prince would prudently distrust people: "For whatever loyalty you plan to use, you must not expect the same in return. You must assume others will deceive you whenever it is to their advantage. And the stronger may indeed succeed when they wish, but not the weaker" (*OP,* 3: 668). He practiced this advice, we saw, when he tried to counsel the Prince Palatine, Karl-Ludwig, after the Treaty of Westphalia just three and a half years later.

Descartes could certainly have gleaned this assumption of human evil from the skeptic, Pierre Charron, whose work he knew well, and who spoke of the absolute need of prudence especially in political matters: "the principal reason for this necessity is the wicked nature of man, the most savage and hard to tame of all animals" (Charron, *Sagesse,* 3: 1). It was also a cliché of the wartime polemical writings (which Descartes knew) and of argument from Machiavelli to Bodin. Although disapproving of the *Prince*'s Chapter 16, where Machiavelli asserted the good man would always be ruined, Descartes immediately replied that such would indeed be so if "by good man, he means a superstitious one," if, that was to say, the Florentine was opposing the prudent prince (aware of general corruption and acting accordingly) to the prince who had a naïve idea of religion. Now that, as François Regnault has observed, was just exactly what Machiavelli *was* talking about.[25]

So Descartes now introduced another kind of good person: "he who does everything that right reason dictates" (*OP,* 3: 669). And there we are: the rational prince was the one who, knowing among other things "the wicked nature of man" (for he knows how to make moral judgments), could tame him and guide him toward new habit, in the same way exactly as the philosopher of Method would teach everyone to use right reason. In the *Principles of Philosophy,* Descartes was explicit on the matter: "the power which men have over each other was given

25. François Régnault, "La Pensée du prince," *Cahiers pour l'analyse 6: la politique des philosophes* (Paris: Seuil, 1967), 30–31.

them so that they might employ it in discouraging others from evil" (*PW*, 1: 205; *OP*, 3: 114. Echo of Charron, *Sagesse*, 3: 2). The claim implied that power always accompanied true knowledge and good judgment and that such characteristics created a definitive division among humans: those who were wicked, irrational, and ignorant of the methodical use of good sense, and the others: philosophers and princes. In 1647 he thus wrote to Chanut: "It is true that I ordinarily refuse to write down my thoughts about morality. I do so for two reasons. One is that nothing provides the ill-disposed with an easier pretext for calumny. The other is my belief that it is only for sovereigns, or those delegated by them, to be concerned to regulate others' behavior" (*OP*, 3: 749).

We already saw in the *Passions of the Soul* that the prince (sovereign mind) was the site of power able to change others' habits. That was the very source of difference between prince and subjects.[26] The prince was not bound by the same rules as others. The new prince was above the simply self-interested strife of (other) subjects. It depended on him, exactly, to establish something new. The prince who relied on right Method *could not* go wrong:

> in the instruction of a good prince, though new to his state, I think quite different maxims [from Machiavelli's] must be proposed, and we must *suppose* that the means used to establish himself were just—as indeed I believe they almost always are when the prince using them believes they are. For justice among sovereigns has other limits than among private people, and I think in these affairs God gives right to those to whom he gives might. [*OP*, 3: 666]

There is a legitimate might: that of the new methodical prince. We are not dealing here with the simplistic equation that might gives right, even less that they are the same thing. Rather was it that the justice of an absolute monarchy in the domain falling under its sovereign power was by definition legitimate—as among others Bodin, Charron, and Hobbes had already argued.[27] For Descartes it really was

26. See Simone Goyard-Fabre, "Descartes et Machiavel," *Revue de Métaphysique et Morale* 78 (1973): 325.

27. Charron certainly contributed as much as Hobbes to this line of thought. He wrote: "We know that the sovereign's justice, virtue, and probity function rather differently from those of private people. Their character is larger and more free, because of the weighty and dangerous burden he bears and directs. For this reason it is appropriate for him to walk with a step that in others would seem wild and unruly, but which on his part is necessary, honest and lawful. On occasion he must dissemble and equivocate, mix prudence with justice, and, as we say, sew to the lion's skin, when it does not do, the fox's

a question of the prince's *will*, governed by Method, knowledge of truth, and the good judgments that inevitably result. Since this sovereign knew good and evil (as it was said in the *Passions*), it obviously knew what justice and legitimacy were. Habit, he wrote to Elisabeth, agreeing with "conscience" and "inclination," would necessarily make such a prince act to protect others' interests with his own (*OP*, 3: 619).

That is the sense, too, in which we need to understand what Descartes wrote about friendship: that you should never abuse it with falsehood (*OP*, 3: 667). Amity marked the obligation one owed as an individual to others. The word "obligation," as we saw, signalled a sort of enlightened play of everyone's interests allowing the proper working of the new society. To fail such friendship was to cause the failure of all effort to build this new society. For the individual's interest, protected by this amity, was to be equated with the very thinking subject whose will permitted the institution of Method. To fail friendship was thus to fail knowledge of truth, prudence, good judgment, and the thinking subject itself. It was to go against the *cogito,* and the essence of being human.

The meaning of friendship is clear when one looks at its limits. You should not have too much friendship, nor "alliances" that were too "restrictive"; nor could you let amity interfere with the needs of power: to the very degree that others' interests might then "incline to confuse the state" (*OP*, 3: 668). The prince always had to attend to the advantage he might draw from doing good to others, from keeping his promises, for instance, never therefore making any he could not keep (a matter of which Descartes elsewhere gave concrete examples).[28] A balance had always to be kept between one's own and others' interests, between the needs of this sort of amity and the protection of one's own just claims, the security of the thinking subject. The prince's power proceeded from the action of the rational will, based on the methodical

---

skin" (*Sagesse,* 3: 2). Descartes did not disapprove of the Machiavellian advice to "couple the fox with the lion, and join trickery to force" (*OP*, 3: 667). Returning to the right of sovereigns, he could also have read in Hobbes: "ideoque quod legislator praeceperit, id pro *bono;* quod vetuerit, id pro *malo* hadendum esse." And immediately after: "reges igitur legitimi quae imperant, justa faciunt imperando; quae vetant, vetando injusta" (*Opera philosophica,* 2: 285; *De Cive,* 3: xii. 1).

28. *OP*, 3: 667, 668. In his letter about Karl-Ludwig, Descartes spoke of such promises (*OP*, 3: 891), as he did in a letter to Chanut (also 1649) reacting to the fact that certain promises made to him had not been respected on his visit to Paris during the first Fronde (*OP*, 3: 894).

knowledge of truth and consequent good judgment. Thus could it handle the diversity of social action and organize individual interests into a stable society.

Finally, therefore, Descartes could bring back history and concrete experience, kept at arm's length during his early lonely retreat. Again he played on the difference between the good prince and his people, subjects, to whom he had to show, "with exactness, justice *in their style* (that is according to the laws with which they are familiar)" (*OP*, 3: 668). He did not now return to a provisional morality, effective because it adopted common opinion, custom and accepted habit. On the contrary he emphasized that idea of transformation noted in the *Passions*: change that the true prince had to direct gently and almost secretly. After all, it was no easier to "persuade" people of what was "just" than to offend them with what "they imagine unjust" (*OP*, 3: 670). All depended on the prince's prudence and *savoir faire*: "you must not attempt to draw people abruptly to reason, when they are not accustomed to understand it; but you must try little by little, whether by public writings, through the words [*voix*] of preachers, or any other means, to make them comprehend it" (*OP*, 3: 670).

Reason and reason of state had become identical. History had returned. But it was a *new* history, created by the prince as the thinking and willful subject of Method, the site of a power able to usher in a society composed of such (improvable) subjects. That would create another dilemma: for this subject, willful, self-interested, possessive of certain rights, now able to be socialized but tending to self-concern, would inevitably come into conflict with all other such subjects. What would happen when everyone was a Descartes; when all were beings of the *cogito*? What would happen when everyone was an enlightened prince? (One might consider an itinerary leading from Voltaire's view of Frederick the Great, Diderot's of Catherine, Carlyle's of Frederick or Napoleon, to H. G. Wells's ironic notion of the common statesman in *The New Machiavelli*.)

Thus before Hobbes, Locke, and the eighteenth-century thinkers, Descartes raised the contractual issue. One of the important differences between Hobbes and Descartes was that the former was convinced the prince occupied a unique position (once the contract was in place) and that absolute sovereignty removed him permanently from his subjects—or at least as long as the original conditions continued. Descartes (without really facing the issue, since rational equality lay in the future) thought the good prince could eventually bring about "reason" and "prudence" everywhere. Locke would then reply to everything utopian in Descartes's view and everything seemingly constrictive of individual freedoms in Hobbes's, by supposing the sovereign (as much as everyone else) to be bound by the fact that the contract was not a merely originating instance but a living condition for maintaining civil society. In that way, Locke could deny the equal value of individual civic judgment, much like Hobbes, but by replacing it with a kind of "contractual judgment" whose duration would be that of civil society itself. Like Descartes, he could insist on the (eventually) rational equality of all members of such society. That would bring us directly to Rousseau and his efforts to articulate individual and general will.

Both these oppositions (between individual and collectivity, between one's own and others' interests, power and freedom, equality and will, even state and society), and attempts to reconcile them (that Descartes seemed to assume overcome—as he helped set them in place), would be the very terms of the future political thinking of Western "liberalism." Like Descartes (not to mention Richelieu), Leibniz asserted that *any* action resulted from the combination of knowledge and will. The elements were so imbricated however, that you could equally well say that will and power were founded on knowledge. In that respect Leibniz's idea of power and its potential could have been drawn directly from Descartes:

> Justice is nothing else than that which conforms to wisdom and goodness joined together: the end of goodness is the greatest good, but to recognize it wisdom is needed, which is nothing else than knowledge of the good. . . . Thus wisdom is in the understanding and goodness in the will. And justice, as a consequence, is in both. Power is a different matter, but if it is used it makes right become fact, and makes what ought to be also really exist, in so far as the nature of things permits.[29]

Leibniz may have fallen on the Cartesian side, but it was rather the Lockean effort to reconcile contradictions that tended to furnish the foundations for future discussion.

Much later for instance, during the Revolution in France, precisely the opposition between Descartes and Hobbes seemed to furnish the

---

29. Gottfried Wilhelm von Leibniz, "Meditation on the Common Concept of Justice" in *The Political Writings of Leibniz*, trans. and ed. Patrick Riley (Cambridge: Cambridge University Press, 1972), 50. On the foundational nature of the concept of justice see my *The Meaning of Literature*, forthcoming Cornell University Press: chaps. 3 and 6.

terms of dispute between Burke and the English Dissenters, his first adversaries. In his *Reflections on the Revolution in France,* Burke insisted that the maintenance of government authority was virtually the sole means of preserving true liberty: social justice was then guaranteed (he assured us) by the invocation of sovereign power to counteract the chaotic turbulence of his notorious "swinish multitude." Against such as Wollstonecraft and Paine, this viewpoint was essentially Hobbesian, and a Calonne would grasp with exactness its central idea that any reform could and had to be carried out from above.

But the major provoker of Burke's diatribe, Richard Price, took just the opposite tack, insisting on common sense and the precisely equal and individualist division of rights. In his *Discourse on the Love of Our Country,* preached in favor of the French Revolution on the anniversary of the English, Price spoke of three gifts. The first was knowledge: "enlighten [the people] and you will elevate them." Enlightenment in turn prepared "the minds of men for the recovery of their rights, and hastened the overthrow of priestcraft and tyranny." Knowledge thus produced virtue and enabled liberty. For the Dissenters, "liberty" had a precise meaning. "It especially denoted the free exercise of reason and freedom in matters of conscience, together with the freedom to pursue any career according to talent" (and therefore interest).[30]

A century and a half after Descartes's death, it would be hard to imagine a more exact echo of what he set forth. We would of course expect the individual subject no longer to have need of the prince, be he good or bad. The individual now has automatic access to reason, equality, and right. Descartes's subject of reason and will has become the subject of society (the provisional world being unnecessary). English Dissenters have America and France as concrete (if idealized) examples of establishing "a completely new government on the principles of *equal liberty* and the *rights of men,* without nobles, . . . without bishops, and without a king."[31]

Such arguments draw their strength from the fact that all have confidence in a reason no less Hobbesian than Cartesian. The former's idea of equivalence between ethical and mechanical forces, justifying his "Galilean" method, no less than Descartes's universal *mathesis,*

---

30. James T. Bolton, *The Language of Politics in the Age of Wilkes and Burke* (London: Routledge and Kegan Paul, 1963), 91. On Price's arguments see, too, *Meaning,* chap. 9.

31. Joseph Priestley, *Letters to the Right Honourable Edmund Burke* (1791), 40: quoted in Bolton, *Language,* 92.

was behind much of the opposition to Burke: "Geometry . . . bears nearly the same relation to mechanics that abstract reasoning does to politics. The *moral forces* which are employed in politics are the passions and interests of men, of which it is the province of metaphysics to teach the nature and calculate the strength, as mathematics do those of the mathematical powers." So did James Mackintosh in 1791. And Bolton's criticism that human institutions are not reducible to the causal laws of mechanics is irrelevant: (James Mackintosh, *Vindiciae Gallicae* [1791], 118; quoted op. cit. 153–54) for the point is that *this* concept of reason now provided the terms in which *all* discourse was carried forward. Half a century later, Mill would dispute Comte in just such terms (in which his antagonist also wrote).

Burke, Paine, Price, Wollstonecraft and the rest, Saint-Just, Robespierre, Mirabeau, de Gouges, Roland and their companions, Fichte, Schiller, de Staël, Constant, and others, still all spoke the same language and used the same terms, for good reason. The thinking of a Hooker or a Montaigne, even more that of an Erasmus or a Budé, was fundamentally foreign to the kind of thinking instituted by Descartes, Bacon, or Hobbes. But the new terms *they* constructed, the adjustments added by a Leibniz, or, more, by a Locke, remained inevitable terms of reference: right conceived in terms of interest and property; society imagined in those of the voluntaristic and reasonable subject; the individual as the basic "building block," and thought equal to all others, having (for just that reason) an equal right to possess and use "his" prudent but aggressive talents in entire "freedom." The main difficulties would then clearly be those of deciding who got how much and what was shared: what was the relation between the individual and that sovereign power whose existence alone maintained the order necessary to any society? What power did the individual possess, and what was its nature, in regard to that sovereign power whose nature was unique? Did those powers in fact differ in any basic way? Where should one situate sovereign power? What rights did the individual have in relation to it? And so on: what was shared? And then, too: what was the relation between the individual and others? What were the individual's rights as opposed to those of all others? What free will could the individual retain, however reasonable and prudent, when battling others? Walpole against Bolingbroke, Mandeville versus Gay? Or at the end of the century, Heine against de Staël, or Paine versus Burke. What, precisely, were the relations of force obtaining between discrete, monadic individuals in an ordered society which was not to sink into anarchic chaos? How much was common?

Descartes, Hobbes, Leibniz, and Locke might well discuss the exact terms and quantities of liberty and power, of freedom and right, might well dispute the functioning of the subject's will, reason and knowledge, virtue and prudence. But they discussed variables within a discourse whose constants remained the same. They remain our own; and that is why we can understand them so readily. Yet it was Descartes, who, by relating the new prince (subject) of Method to the old society of custom, provided the means to found a new political subject, a new subject within the field of the political, and finally a subject that had to create from its now fixed and assured place *its* own political adventure. Political *obligation* had been transformed into political *right*. Descartes here threw down a gauntlet that subsequent "liberal" political theory picked up.

ERICA HARTH

Cartesian Women

Major epistemic shifts are often accompanied by changes of discursive sites. The early seventeenth century witnessed such a change with the rise of Cartesian thought and modern rationality. In the sixteenth century, Henri III was host to the *Académie du Palais*, one of several courtly, salonlike gatherings of men and women in which the delights of poetry and music blended with the interests of humanist scholars in the search for an encyclopedic knowledge uniting the arts and the sciences.[1] Conceptual and linguistic imprecision that blurred the lines between the salon and the academy persisted into the seventeenth century, but by Louis XIII's reign, informal, all-male academies specializing in scientific and erudite pursuits were distinguished from the female-led salon. The academy cultivated those aspects of Descartes's philosophy that were to have the greatest impact on the development of modern rational discourse: his dualism, mechanism, and objectivity. The salon was home to a poetic discourse of metaphor and analogy, akin to the episteme of resemblance which Michel Foucault has seen as characteristic of the Renaissance.

Reputedly, the seventeenth-century salon was also a major conduit for Cartesian discourse. But the famous Cartesian salon women of the time, such as Mme de la Sablière, Mme Deshoulières, and Mmes de Bonnevaux, d'Outresale, d'Hommecour, de Guedreville, have proven elusive.[2] Most of the *Cartésiennes* left few or no writings, and little of what remains concerns Descartes. Even Mme de Bonnevaux, who sup-

1. See Frances A. Yates, *The French Academies of the Sixteenth Century* (London: The Warburg Institute, University of London, 1947).
2. Most of these women are mentioned in contemporary lists of learned women. See Marguerite Buffet, *Traité sur les Eloges des Illustres Sçavantes, Anciennes et Modernes*,

YFS 80, *Baroque Topographies*, ed. Timothy Hampton, © 1991 by Yale University.

posedly held lectures on Descartes in her home and figures in the correspondence of Christian Huyghens, seems to have left no written trace of her activities (on Mme de Bonnevaux, see Buffet, 264–66). More is known about Descartes's two royal patrons, Queen Christina of Sweden and Princess Elizabeth of Bohemia, but even they left no counterpart to the scholarly work of male Cartesians. The lack of evidence cannot be argued away by the fact that the salon's major contribution to cultural life was conversation, for much writing by learned male habitués has survived.

Initially, Cartesian philosophy and the prominence of the salon combined to offer women a unique historical opportunity to partici- pate in the construction of rational discourse. The clear, jargon-free French of the lay learning that Descartes proposed was especially ap- pealing to women. In fact, the philosopher acknowledged that he pur- posely omitted from his *Discourse on Method* some complexities in his proof of God, because they didn't seem to him appropriate for a book "of which I wanted even women to understand something."[3] However, the exclusivity of the academies soon left women on the margins of the new intellectual culture. Whereas in the sixteenth cen- tury the intellectual functions of salon and academy overlapped, in the seventeenth century there was only a small nonreciprocal overlap in personnel (some academicians frequented some of the salons) and a small but significant overlap in discourse (Cartesian philosophy was discussed in the salon). The discussion of the salon did not exactly parallel that of the academy, which was eventually to predominate, but rather constituted a sort of discursive "wild zone," shaped by a critical stance taken from the outside.[4]

Much has been written about the hostile reaction to Descartes in

in *Nouvelles Observations sur la langue françoise* (Paris: Jean Cusson, 1668) and [Jean de] La Forge, *Le Cercle des femmes sçavantes* (Paris: Jean Baptiste Loyson, 1663). For women as catalysts in the diffusion of Cartesian philosophy see: Antoine Adam, *Histoire de la littérature française au XVIIe siècle* (Paris: Del Duca, 1962), 3: 18–19; Francisque Bouillier, *Histoire de la philosophie cartésienne* (Paris: Durand; Lyon: Brun, 1854)1: 420–26; Gustave Reynier, *La Femme au XVIIe siècle* (Paris: Tallandier, 1929), 174–77. Mme de la Sablière is particularly well known as the addressee of Jean de La Fontaine's "Discours à Mme de La Sablière" (in Book IX of the *Fables*), in which the poet debates Descartes's theory of animals as automata.

3. Letter to Father Vatier, in René Descartes, *Oeuvres*, ed. Adam and Tannery (Paris: Léopold Cerf, 1897), 1: 560. Henceforth referred to as *AT*.

4. For the concept of the "wild zone," that (perhaps imaginary) space for women's culture which falls outside the dominant male culture, see Elaine Showalter, "Feminist Criticism in the Wilderness," in *Writing and Sexual Difference*, ed. Elizabeth Abel (Chicago: University of Chicago Press, 1982), 9–35.

the universities and schools. Very little is known about the critique that emanated from the salons and which is embedded in the writings that I will discuss. This critique adumbrates what I will call a feminist alternative to the developing rational discourse. The founding of the Académie des Sciences in 1666 marked a point of no return in discursive construction. In formally institutionalizing the exclusion of women from the new rationality, this event foreclosed development of the feminine alternative. The retrieval of the critique points to a reconceptualization of the Cartesian woman and her relation to modern rationality.

REFLECTIONS ON DESCARTES

Three learned women who have been known as Cartesians since their own day receive nothing more than a footnote in a recent study of women in seventeenth-century France.[5] But in their own time, Anne de la Vigne, Marie Dupré, and Catherine Descartes achieved a small measure of renown for their erudition, and in particular for their command of Cartesian philosophy. The three friends had much in common. Each acquired her learning with the help of male family members. (Such was the traditional means to a solid education for women. [See Gibson, 24].) Anne de la Vigne (1634–1684) was the daughter of a physician to Louis XIII and dean of Paris's Faculté de Médecine. Michel de la Vigne is said to have commented on his two children: "When my daughter was conceived, I thought I was conceiving my son, and when my son was conceived, I thought I was conceiving my daughter."[6] It was said of Catherine Descartes (1637–1706), a niece of the philosopher, that her uncle's mind fell to the distaff side. Her father, René's older brother Pierre, was a *conseiller* in the *Parlement* of Brittany. Marie Dupré (dates unknown, roughly a contemporary of her two friends) is the most mysterious of the three women. She seems to have left no writings at all on Descartes. In the meager amount of poetry and correspondence that she did leave we can only infer her attitudes toward Cartesian philosophy.[7] Dupré had two illustrious uncles in the

5. Wendy Gibson, *Women in Seventeenth-Century France* (Houndmills: Macmillan, 1989), 273, n. 147.

6. Titon du Tillet, *Le Parnasse français* (Paris: Jean-Baptiste Coignard fils, 1732), 1: 369.

7. Dupré's writings are of particular interest for what is perhaps a Cartesian variety of the "refusal of love" which figures in much of seventeenth-century salon writing. The "tendre amitié" that she favors is akin to Descartes's theory of the passions in his

scholar and *littérateur*, Roland Desmarets, and Jean Desmarets de Saint-Sorlin, one of the first members of the Académie Française. Roland took charge of her education, teaching her Latin, Greek, rhetoric, poetry, and modern philosophy.[8] Dupré was known as "la Cartésienne;" Catherine Descartes was dubbed "l'illustre Cartésie" by Madeleine de Scudéry, and Anne de la Vigne was so linked to Cartesianism that it was she to whom Catherine Descartes addressed her poem, "L'Ombre de Descartes." None of the women married.

The women were seen in the most fashionable salons. Both Catherine Descartes and Anne de la Vigne frequented Mme de Rambouillet's *chambre bleue*. Catherine Descartes was friendly with Mme de Sévigné and her daughter, Mme de Grignan. All three were in Mlle de Scudéry's orbit. Marie Dupré appears in Somaize's seventeenth-century compendium, the *Dictionnaire des précieuses*, and Anne de la Vigne alluded to herself as a *précieuse*.[9] As "femmes savantes," the three friends stood out in the milieu of the *précieuses*, only a minority of whom could be qualified as "docte" or "savante." We may well wonder what might have prompted *mondaines* such as these to run the risk of ridicule in the apparent earnestness with which they pursued their interest in Descartes.

Cartesian dualism held undeniable attractions for women. It may read as an endorsement of either the separability or the inseparability of mind and body. Seventeenth-century literature by and about women was generally consistent with the first reading and included variations on the theme, "the mind has no sex." With the diffusion of Cartesianism, this phrase became something of a feminist rallying cry. The concept of a soul freed from bodily and therefore sexual impediments lent philosophical weight to the commonplace. Poullain de la Barre used it as the linchpin of his Cartesian arguments in support of women.[10] My contention is that the writings under consideration here

---

Passions de l'âme. A full discussion of her writings will be included in my forthcoming book, *Cartesian Women*.

8. See Louis Moréri, *Le Grand Dictionnaire historique*, new ed. (Paris, 1759), 4:295.

9. See the last stanza of her "Réponse à une lettre galante qui lui fut ecrite des Champs Elizées, aprés une grande maladie dont elle pensa mourir," in Le R. P. Bouhours, *Recueil de vers choisis* (Paris: George [sic] & Louis Josse, 1693), 15. Hereafter referred to as Recueil Bouhours.

10. See Poullain de la Barre, *De l'égalité des deux sexes* (Paris: Jean Du Puis, 1673). On the implications for women of Descartes's departure from Aristotelian sex-linked theories of the soul, see Londa Schiebinger, *The Mind Has No Sex? Women in the Origins of Modern Science* (Cambridge, Ma.: Harvard University Press, 1989), 170–75. Cf.,

reflect the first reading. Not only do the texts themselves support this premise; the values and outlook of the *précieuses* would naturally have inclined them to such a reading, which would in turn have reinforced their views. Both neo-Platonism and neostoicism combined to aid the *précieuses* in their question for relationships that would free them from the obligations and prejudices attached to their female bodies. A dualism that emphasized the separability of soul and body lent dignity to the intellectual enterprise of the salon and validated women as thinking subjects.

Nevertheless, it was precisely Descartes's dualism, read in the first sense, that the *salonnières* also contested. On the one hand, Cartesian dualism seemed to support them as thinking subjects; on the other, it seemed to drain the thinking subject of all feeling and emotion connected to the body and to reduce the body to a mere machine. The women's simultaneous attraction and resistance to dualism epitomizes the critical distance from which they reflected on Descartes's philosophy and makes problematic their designation as Cartesian. The fact that history has lost track of the critical side in its assimilation of the women to the "Cartesian" group is an instance of that absence which is the obverse of hegemony.

In all fairness, however, there is no straightforward route to the women's thinking. Insufficient documentation does not permit conclusions about the specific Cartesian concepts they may have accepted or rejected. They left no counterpart to the treatises of such Cartesians as Jacques Rohault, Claude Clerselier, and Pierre-Sylvain Régis. Instead, they couched their ideas in the *précieux* language which has come to be considered as foreign to modern rationality. The poetry and personal correspondence which they did leave is characterized by the

---

Timothy J. Reiss, "Corneille and Cornelia: Reason, Violence, and the Cultural Status of the Feminine," *Renaissance Drama* 18 (1987): 10; and Reynier, 116–17. I am very grateful to Amélie O. Rorty for her comments on an early draft of this paper. Although she and I still undoubtedly disagree, our discussions have been an invaluable help to me in my considerations of women's relation to Cartesian dualism. I am also grateful to her for having made available to me a draft of her forthcoming paper, "Descartes on Thinking with the Body." This paper articulates what I will call the inseparability position on Cartesian dualism. See also her "Cartesian Passions and the Union of Mind and Body," in *Essays on Descartes' Meditations*, ed. Amélie Oksenberg Rorty (Berkeley: University of California Press, 1986), 513–34. At the other end of the spectrum is Susan Bordo's *Flight to Objectivity*. A highly useful discussion of the separability/inseparability question is to be found in Marjorie Grene, *Descartes* (Brighton: Harvester Press, 1985), 23–52.

metaphor, veiled allusion, hyperbole, and circumlocution that was the standard fare of the salon.

This linguistic medium makes it difficult to determine the value that Cartesianism may have held for *le monde.* How seriously, for example, are we to take the fact that Mme de Sévigné's daughter referred to Descartes as her (spiritual) "father?" Mme de Sévigné's good friend Jean Corbinelli enthused in the usual aristocratic style to Sévigné's cousin, Bussy-Rabutin:

> During your stay in Paris, I advise you to learn Descartes's philosophy. Mlles Bussy [Bussy-Rabutin's daughters] will learn it faster than any game. For my part, I find it delicious, not only because it disabuses us of a million commonly held errors but also because it teaches us how to think properly. Without it, we would die of boredom in this province.[11]

A poetic exchange between Catherine Descartes and Anne de la Vigne raises the possibility that *précieux* language could also serve as a protective shield for women's learning. (On the need for the educated woman to hide her learning, see Gibson, 19; 30.) Catherine Descartes's "Shade of Descartes" ("L'Ombre de Descartes") (1673) was meant as a compliment both to her uncle and to her friend. In it she invited La Vigne to spread the Cartesian word in order to help combat the misunderstanding and prejudice surrounding the new philosophy. La Vigne replied with a polite refusal. The poems, conceived more in admiration than in criticism of Descartes, illustrate the ways in which the *salonnières'* playful language could conceal a certain commitment to the logic and clarity of Cartesian truth.

Love is the organizing metaphor of Catherine Descartes's poem. She adopts the persona of her uncle, who urges La Vigne to avow her love for him openly. The poem ends with Descartes's humorously plaintive self-defense: "Is there anyone as worthy as myself? And, entre nous, do you see / Any lover more illustrious than I and worthier of you?" (Catherine Descartes, "L'Ombre de Descartes," *Recueil Bouhours,* 27–30, especially 30). Within this *précieux* framework the poet imagines a new philosophical union of the masculine and the feminine. The language of love that she adopts poses an implicit challenge to a dualism that would have emotion be an object of investigation for the dispassionate mind.

11. Letter of 23 August 1673, in Mme. de Sévigné, *Correspondance,* ed. Duchêne (Paris: Gallimard, 1972–78), 1: 589–90.

The poem's Descartes describes himself as a militant Modern fighting for Truth against the "ignorance" of the scholastics. Of scholastic philosophy he says, "This proud one, with her Aristotle / Is still the fad of today's scholars; / Everything said against her is a novelty, / And without further examination should be dropped; / As if the errors of those great men merited respect in our time; / And ceasing to be errors by their antiquity, / Finally proscribed truth" (28). But, through the intervention of La Vigne, "novelty," which in the Quarrel between the Ancients and the Moderns had a distinctly pejorative ring, will give way to truth; "Great truths, which seemed new, / Will henceforth appear clear, solid, beautiful" (28). In uniting philosophical truth and feminine beauty, Catherine Descartes plays on the conventional allegorical portrait of truth as a woman: "When truth comes from such lovely lips, / It convinces the stubbornest mind" (29).

The poet's vision of Descartes as clearing away the prejudices of earlier times recaptures the philosopher's own view of himself as a lone herald of enlightenment.[12] Catherine Descartes places herself in solidarity with her uncle as his mouthpiece and with her friend as his champion, thereby proposing an alliance of men and women in the service of Truth. The errors and prejudices of outworn philosophy to which the poet refers conceivably include those that theorized the mental inferiority of women from an inferior body. So although the poet initially casts her friend as Descartes's disciple, La Vigne emerges ultimately as his equal: "To false dogma destroyed and errors stifled / You will raise me [Descartes] a hundred illustrious trophies; / By your illustrious offices my writings, in turn, / Will become the love of all true scholars. / I see our two names joined together, / Bringing to posterity my glory with yours; / And I can already hear it said in many climes, / 'Descartes and La Vigne have instructed the world' " (29).

The use of the word "love" ("amour") in these lines prepares us for the final conceit, Descartes as La Vigne's suitor. The precious language also carries a deeper layer of meaning in which truth is beauty and knowledge is love. Cartesian truth is "clear" and "solid," but it is also "beautiful" and must be nurtured with love. For it is only with loving attention to its diffusion, the poet suggests, that error can be conquered. One senses in these lines a passion akin to the "dynamic objectivity" that Evelyn Fox Keller has glimpsed as a possible feature of

12. This view is especially apparent in the *Discourse on Method* and in Descartes's correspondence with Princess Elizabeth of Bohemia. See my "Classical Discourse: Gender and Objectivity," *Continuum* 1 (1989): 155–56.

feminized science. In this type of objectivity, subjective experience is not effaced before the object of knowledge, but is used in "a form of attention to the natural world that is like one's ideal attention to the human world: it is a form of love."[13] Catherine Descartes corrects a dualism that in freeing the mind from the fetters of the body also detaches it from the emotions. She challenges what Susan Bordo has identified in Descartes's *Meditations* as the "purification of the mind" and the "transcendence of the body."[14]

The dualism underlying this poem has a twofold, conflicting value. On the one hand, through the demystification performed by Descartes's methodical doubt and his campaign against prejudice and error, it bears the liberating message to women that "the mind has no sex."[15] On the other hand, the mind severed from body and purified of emotion results in what I have elsewhere called a "spectatorial subject," one which in its detachment and impartiality is antithetical to the thinking and feeling subject addressed in "L'Ombre de Descartes" (for the spectatorial subject, see my "Classical Discourse, 165; cf., Bordo, 88).

The message of philosopher's shade to Anne de la Vigne is that the battle for truth should be waged with the heart as well as with the mind. As a final paean to La Vigne, the poet ranks her above Elizabeth of Bohemia, "wise Elizabeth, the glory of the Empire," in the roster of illustrious women surrounding Descartes. La Vigne's mission is to bring about universal intellectual harmony: "I expect from you a special miracle. / That at last truth will find no more obstacle, / And despite error and prejudice, / The entire universe will hold but one opinion" (29). But Catherine Descartes fears that her hopes will be frustrated by her friend's reluctance to display her erudition. Interestingly, the poet views this hesitation as a failure of commitment and love. She urges La Vigne to abandon her silence and secrecy and to give free rein to eloquence; she should "not scruple to garner love" for Descartes's philosophy.

The refusal that Anne de la Vigne delivered to her friend in her "Reply to the Shade of Descartes" ("Réponse à L'Ombre de Descartes")

13. See Evelyn Fox Keller, *Reflections on Gender and Science* (New Haven and London: Yale University Press, 1985), 117.

14. Susan R. Bordo, *The Flight to Objectivity: Essays on Cartesianism and Culture* (Albany: SUNY Press, 1987), 75–95.

15. It is this aspect of Cartesian doubt that Ruth Perry stresses in her "Radical Doubt and the Liberation of Women," *Eighteenth-Century Studies* 18, no. 4 (Summer 1985): 472–93.

suggests the force of the social stigma attached to women's learning. La Vigne was well-known and generally praised for her "feminine modesty," as were her two friends. When Esprit Fléchier, the future bishop of Nîmes, asked La Vigne to distribute his Latin poetry to some of their mutual friends, she initially demurred, with a hint that she didn't want to show off her knowledge (albeit imperfect) of Latin.[16] It was only after some coaxing by Fléchier that she consented to run the risk of being labelled a "dona Bachellera" (lady graduate).

La Vigne's refusal to the shade's invitation is consistent with her reputation: "I have neither the appearance nor the manners of an old Doctor; / And don't feel that I'm fit to give lessons" ("Réponse de Mademoiselle de la Vigne à l'Ombre du M. Descartes," *Recueil Bouhours*, 30–32, especially 31). It requires more understanding than she possesses, she says, to establish "great truths." "I leave it to our scholars to display them, / And I learn them only not to speak of them" (31). Nevertheless, beneath her docile exterior, a consciousness of what Juliet Mitchell has called "social coercion" creeps in.[17] La Vigne's answer to the question put to her by the shade in Catherine Descartes's poem, "Why do you make a crime of showing [your estime for me]?," is typical of the learned lady's enlightened bow to social pressure in the early modern period. For La Vigne, as for so many others, the risk wasn't worth the effort: "I know that the loveliest, most forceful eloquence / Is often not worth a modest silence; / That for us custom has made it almost a duty / To speak rarely and to know nothing; / And that if perchance a lady follows other maxims / She should hide them as one hides crimes. / Whether it be a well-founded custom / Or only the law of the mightiest: / Without doubt she'll find it surer and wiser / To submit to this tiresome practice" (31). As La Vigne reweaves the threads of Catherine Descartes's argument, her impatience at the restrictions on women's education shows through the surface of her compliance. Certain women, she says, exceptional for either their mind or their rank, can dispense with social restrictions on learning. Did "wise Elizabeth," for example, submit to such "bizarre laws?" Would she have been worthy of Descartes in doing so (31–32)?

16. See Abbé A[ntonin] Fabre, *La Jeunesse de Fléchier* (Paris: Didier, 1882) 2: 108–09; and [Jules-Antoine] Taschereau, "Correspondance galante de Fléchier," *Revue Rétrospective* 1 (1833): 242–54, especially 252–54. Fléchier commented elsewhere on her modesty. See Fabre, 2: 71.

17. Juliet Mitchell, *Women: The Longest Revolution* (New York: Pantheon, 1984), 27–28.

Finally, La Vigne resigns to others the glory of celebrating the works of her friend's uncle—to Elizabeth of Bohemia, but especially to Descartes's male friends, as the stress in the French alexandrines (to which my emphasis corresponds) indicates: "Pour porter votre nom au temple de Memoire, / J'en laisse à vos amis le plaisir & la gloire: / J'en connois quelques-uns dignes de cet emploi, / Qui s'en font un honneur, qui s'en font une loi; / Par eux bientot la Cour, le Barreau, la Sorbonne / Croiront votre doctrine & la seule & la bonne; / Par eux tous vos Ecrits, tous ces savans Traitez / Seront lus hautement sans etre contestez: / Par eux mille succez dont le bonheur extreme / Passera votre espoir, passera vos voeux meme, / Rendront egalement celebres parmi nous, / Votre profond savoir, & leur amour pour vous" (Recueil Bouhours, 32). [I leave *to your friends* ["amis"] the pleasure and glory [of immortalizing your name] / . . . *By them* soon the Court, the Bar, the Sorbonne / Will believe your doctrine alone is good; / *By them* all your writings, your scholarly treatises / Will be read openly, without contestation: / *By them* a thousand successes / . . . Will have made famous both / Your deep knowledge and their love for you.]

In one move, La Vigne leaves to men (or to very exceptional women) two problematic spheres of activity for women: love and learning. She adds a twist to Catherine Descartes's conceit of love in repudiating that poet's vision of women uniting love and knowledge: "For me not even the love of a dead man is permitted; / Pure as it is, I could be blamed; / There is always some shame in loving" (32). The *précieuses* were of course notorious for their "refusal of love." Although to observers in some circles, identified by Carolyn Lougee as antifeminist, the *précieuses* appeared to be loose women, the ideal of Platonic and spiritual love that was articulated in fashionable salons was probably taken quite seriously in the Scudéry circle. It was certainly compatible with the Cartesian "transcendence of the body."[18] On one reading of Anne de la Vigne's poem, then, she would be more Cartesian than the Cartesians, the purest of the pure. Her refusal of love and learning and her attachment of shame to both mark an extreme reaction (but one which may have been typical) to the dilemma of the learned lady in her social milieu.

Some twenty years after Catherine Descartes composed her "Shade of Descartes," her "Account of M. Descartes's Death" [Relation de la

18. On the antifeminist view of love in the salons of the *précieuses,* see Carolyn C. Lougée, *Le Paradis des Femmes: Women, Salons, and Social Stratification in Seventeenth-Century France* (Princeton: Princeton University Press, 1976), 70–84.

mort de M. Descartes] appeared. In two decades, the writer had developed a critical stance toward Cartesianism that was only intimated in the earlier work. The "Relation" introduces motifs of contestation that begin to define the features of a feminine alternative.

Unlike other *relations* of Descartes's death, such as those by Claude Clerselier, Philibert de la Mare, and Adrien Baillet, the niece's departs from a supposedly factual narrative as she meditates on the meaning of the philosopher's system (for the other relations, see *AT,* 3: 481–94). Why did she wait forty years to write her account? Her story is that she was motivated by a Huguenot minister on his way out of France after the Revocation of the Edict of Nantes, who had been in Stockholm at the time of Descartes's death. Perhaps in this critical moment of the Counter-Reformation Catherine Descartes wanted to rehabilitate the image of her uncle for posterity by her depiction of his pious death. Whatever the reason, the time intervening between her "Ombre de Descartes" and the "Relation" gave her more distance on her uncle.[19] The "Relation" no longer portrays Descartes as the bearer of a universal Truth, but rather as a mere mortal who himself must yield to a higher truth. Of course the writer respected the conventions of the *relation de mort,* which was meant to commemorate an illustrious person: it is after all in one's dying moments that truths of a higher order are glimpsed. Nevertheless, the convention also provided her with a convenient framework for questioning her uncle's achievements.

This *relation* gives us a retrospective view of the philosopher's life as destiny. Queen Christina of Sweden has a vision in which she decides to send for Descartes to help her resolve her difficulties with the problem of attraction. Her summons is a fateful call: "To instruct a Queen he hastens; / Thinking he goes forth to glory he rushes to his death" (Catherine Descartes, "Relation de la mort du M. Descartes, Le Philosophe," *Recueil Bouhours,* 129–39, especially 131). All that remains of Descartes's dualism in death is the soul's transcendence of the body. The philosophical conflicts in which he has been embroiled are dissolved by divine truth: "Whoever sees truth, sees also / The multitudes divided by conflicting errors" (138).

In a gender role reversal that ironizes the convention of the *relation,* Catherine Descartes seriously challenges the masculine framework of

19. Leonora Cohen Rosenfield views the "Relation" as Gassendist. See her *From Beast-Machine to Man-Machine: Animal Soul in French Letters from Descartes to La Mettrie,* new ed. (New York: Octagon, 1968), 113: 158–59.

her uncle's philosophical discourse. The writer offers both a poetic and a prosaic version of the philosopher's death. The prosaic version agrees with other accounts in attributing his demise to a pulmonary inflammation that followed his exposure to the harsh Swedish winter. The poetic account, however, subverts the prose in having him punished by Nature for invading her privacy. His lessons to Christina are an instance of his insistent prying into Nature's secrets: "It is said that then astonished Nature / Was indignant at finding herself discovered. / Rash mortal, audacious soul, / Learn that one doesn't view the Gods with impunity. /" Nature revealed to Descartes is compared to Diana discovered at her bath by Actaeon: "[Like Diana] seeing herself open to René's view, / Nature was angered and swore his destruction" (131–32). In becoming an agent, this avenging Nature loses her conventional pose of receptivity to the male creative principle, it is as if the poet deliberately confounds her uncle's desire for philosophers to become "masters and possessors of Nature."[20]

Descartes must relearn his own neostoical lessons in a different key. It is no longer the active soul or mind that prevails over the passions, but an active Nature that presides over human destiny. Thus the writer has Descartes's good friend Pierre Chanut, France's ambassador to Sweden at the time of Descartes's death, tell the philosopher to forget his physical pain and to entrust his body to Mother Nature: "It's a tribute that we owe her: / Let us pay it freely, and follow without a murmur / The command of Nature. / She is good, she is wise, and her rich presents / Like those of a good mother / Showered on all, are long savored / And her great woes soon pass" (133).

Feminine principles rule Descartes's life as his niece revises it. It is the allegorical Lady Philosophy who appears to Queen Christina in her vision, urging the monarch to seek "illustrious René." This Philosophy, a "modest woman," is, however, an ominous figure, with a "gaunt face" (131).[21] She eventually gives way to Nature, suggesting that Descartes needed to reorder his priorities. In a final dialogue between Chanut and Descartes, the ambassador pictures his friend leaving life "like a great conqueror" whose name will resound through the universe. To Chanut's expression of grief over the approaching loss of his

20. *AT*, 6: 62. Cf. Carolyn Merchant, *The Death of Nature: Women, Ecology and the Scientific Relvolution* (San Francisco: Harper & Row, 1980), 188.

21. For a recent discussion of the iconography of feminine allegorical figures, in this case ones relating to early modern science, see Londa Schiebinger, "Feminine Icons: The Face of Early Modern Science," *Critical Inquiry* 14, no. 4 (Summer 1988): 661–91.

friend, Descartes replies that they will be reunited in heaven, where the chastened philosopher will leave the investigation of Nature forever behind. He will "never more cast his eyes on Nature" (137–38).

We don't know the reasons behind Catherine Descartes's reevaluation of her uncle's accomplishments in her later work. We do know that she rejected the theory of sensation that he outlined in the *Principles of Philosophy* (1644).[22] Perhaps with age her own approaching death modified her views. But there may be more continuity between the "Ombre" and the "Relation" than my discussion suggests. In both works a previously subordinate feminine takes a leading role—first as a teacher (Anne de la Vigne), then as a guiding principle of life (Nature). The later work seems a revision of Descartes's *Passions of the Soul*, in which the poet adopts its neostoical moral philosophy and ignores its mechanistic dualism. This strategy allows her to divinize nature. For if in the Cartesian system soulless *res extensa* defines nature precisely as that which is *not* spiritual, Catherine Descartes rehabilitates a vitalistic Nature by reinfusing her with soul and with moral value (on Descartes's soulless definition of nature, see Bordo, 102).

Her *relation* of Descartes's death is therefore also an account of a figurative death. It kills Descartes's discourse by feminizing it. Lady Philosophy bows to Mother Nature, as we are reminded of a nature that nurtured instead of obeying mechanistic laws imposed on her. The Descartes whom we see breathing his last in utmost piety may be a monument to a great man, but it may also be a warning against the pride of intellect and rationality.

CHAMELEONS OF A DIFFERENT COLOR

Distrust of Cartesian mechanism was prevalent in the Scudéry circle. In this connection it is of great interest that Catherine Descartes, Anne de la Vigne, and Marie Dupré were among "Sapho's" friends. Catherine Descartes certainly shared Scudéry's hostility to animal mechanism, as her verses on a much-fêted warbler in her hostess's garden make clear: "Here is my compliment / To the loveliest warbler, / When it returns to you. / Ah! I then exclaimed in surprise: / With all due respect to my uncle, it has judgment."[23]

22. See Mme de Sévigné's letter of 30 June 1677 to Mme de Grignan in Mme de Sévigné, *Correspondance*, 2: 479; and 2: 1325–26, no. 4; also her letter of 15 May 1689 to Mme de Grignan, 3: 600.
23. As quoted in Titon du Tillet, *Le Parnasse français*, 1: 505. Cf., Rosenfield, 159–60. Rosenfield does not attempt to explain the Scudéry circle's rejection of animal mech-

A feminist alternative to Descartes's rationalism—specifically, his mechanism and his objectivity—underlies Scudéry's "Story of Two Chameleons" ("Histoire de deux caméléons"). On 1 June 1672 the consul of Alexandria sent her a gift of two chameleons. They reached her at the end of September, and for the short time that they survived they were the subjects of much experimentation, discussion and creative effort in her circle. The account of this episode, which appears in her *Nouvelles Conversations de morale* (1688), includes a collection of poems on the two animals by various members of the group, among them Anne de la Vigne (who delivered the funeral oration on the death of one of the chameleons). To my knowledge there is no concrete evidence that Catherine Descartes and Marie Dupré were present for the activities, but I know of no reason why they could not have been there. Frédéric Lachèvre attributes one of the poems in Scudéry's collection to Catherine Descartes, but he appears to have been mistaken.[24] In any event, the three friends' views were consistent with those prevalent in Scudéry's salon. The narrative of the chameleons typifies the blending of metaphor and the new science that characterizes the construction of the feminist alternative.

Scudéry's *conversation* is presented as an actual alternative to Claude Perrault's *Anatomical Description of a Chameleon* (1669) (*Description anatomique d'un caméléon*), published under the auspices of the newly founded Académie royale des Sciences. The little treatise was part of an ongoing effort by the academicians to compile a taxonomy of animals, which would result in the two magnificent folio volumes of the *Mémoires pour servir à l'histoire naturelle des animaux* (1671–76).[25] Scudéry's conversation opens with an allusion by the narrator, Bérénice, to the *Anatomical Description* (never mentioned by name): "a very lovely, ample Treatise, which is in everyone's

anism other than by the sentimentality of ladies about animals (159). She adds that "the fair sex was prone to reject animal mechanism" (201) . . . .

24. Frédéric Lachèvre, *Bibliographie des recueils collectifs de poésies publiés de 1597 à 1700* (Paris: H. Leclerc, 1901–05), 3: 293–94. Lachèvre cites the first line of a poem by Catherine Descartes that appeared elsewhere and that appears nowhere in Scudéry's collection. All but two of the poems in the 1688 edition of Scudéry's *Nouvelles Conversations* are signed. One of these two was supposedly written by a man who wished to remain anonymous. It is of course possible that Catherine Descartes was the author. The other poem is said to have been by "the same hand as that of the person who did the funeral." Was this another poem by Anne de la Vigne, in addition to the signed one? See [Madeleine de Scudéry], *Nouvelles conversations de morale* (1688), 2: 607–19.

25. On the *Mémoires pour servir à l'histoire naturelle des animaux*, see my *Ideology and Culture in Seventeenth-Century France* (Ithaca: Cornell University Press, 1983), 261–78.

possession." Bérénice proposes a different description of the chameleon: "I won't step in to speak as a Physician or a Philosopher; I don't have the ability. I will simply relate what I very carefully and precisely observed."[26]

The convergences and divergences between the official academic description and Scudéry's unofficial *conversation* are apparent even in this brief statement of purpose. Although the feminine narrator claims no special expertise or training in the natural sciences, she does purport to conform to the academicians' standard of objective observation. Similarly, academic discourse had not yet become completely disengaged from the older discourse of metaphor and analogy to which the Scudéry circle remained attached. Scudéry and the author of the *Anatomical Description* were friends. Perrault and his fellow academician Jean Pecquet dissected Scudéry's chameleons when they died. However, power and privilege separated the Académie from the salon. This gulf was even wider than that which separated women from the Académie Française. Neither academy admitted women. Yet Scudéry had won a prize from the older academy, whereas she received no official recognition from the Académie des Sciences. This academy's links to Colbert's program of mercantilist expansion helped to define a new arena of economic power from which French women were definitively banned (on the relation of the Académie des Sciences to Colbert's mercantilism, see my *Ideology and Culture*, 222–309). Claude Perrault wasn't a Cartesian, but he spoke what was to become the dominant discourse of a rationality that Descartes was instrumental in establishing. Scudéry and her three women friends did not shrink from an understanding of the new rationality, but, excluded as they were from official participation, their enthusiasm was qualified.

Perrault's effort was to observe and to describe. To this end he attempts in his *Description anatomique* to divest the observer of any prejudices or sentiments that could interfere with an exact transcription of the "truth." In his introductory remarks he discards as false much of what had been written on the chameleons and gives us to understand that in substituting the truth of observation for conjecture and myth he writes against the Ancients. Scudéry also claims to report from direct observation, but whereas she writes empathically of her animals' feelings (for instance of the male chameleon's grief at his

26. [Madeleine de Scudéry], *Nouvelles Conversations de morale*, 2nd. ed. (The Hague: Jacob van Ellinkhuysen, 1692), 296. All further references will be to this edition.

female companion's death) (Scudéry, *Nouvelles Conversations*, 305–06), Perrault treats the chameleon dispassionately as an object of investigation. Although he too rejects Descartes's beast-machine theory, he is interested only in the explanatory value of animal feelings. He hypothesizes, for example, that cautiousness and not fear, as had been thought, is responsible for the chameleon's measured gait.[27]

Perrault, like Descartes, wanted a signified truth to shine transparently through the signifier, and so he aimed to avoid metaphor and other forms of rhetorical ornamentation. It is as a comparative anatomist that he likens the chameleon's head, structure by structure, to that of a fish (Perrault, 12). Scudéry's corresponding comparison, by contrast is metaphorical. Her chameleon's head, also like that of a species of fish, resembles an "antique helmet" (Scudéry, 297–98). Perrault did not of course entirely desert metaphor for "plain-speaking." It is from Perrault that Scudéry borrows her image of the chameleon's tongue as an elephant's horn (ibid., 301; cf., Perrault, 32). Yet although the two writers describe the living chameleon's eye similarly, there is nothing in Perrault's description of the dissected animal's eye to match the magic that Scudéry finds in it: "The whole body of the eye appeared like a pearl, perfect in its roundness, whiteness and sheen; the lively little black pupil surrounded by a tiny circle of the most beautiful gold in the world and this golden circle bordered by another tiny circle of pink. . . ."[28] Perrault largely confines his description to the eye's anatomy (Perrault, 28–29).

In general, the observations that resulted from the informal experimentation with the two chameleons in Sapho's salon agree with those of the academicians. Both groups, for example, reached no conclusion as to the reasons for the animal's change of color, but refuted the notion that the chameleon takes on the color of surrounding objects. There were two major areas of disagreement. Perrault reported no evidence of any organ of hearing or sound in the chameleon. Scudéry agreed that the animal was voiceless, but insisted that her male chameleon responded to his given name of "Méléon." We sense that just as Perrault was writing against the Ancients, Scudéry was writing against him: ". . . I can guarantee that those who have said that chameleons don't hear are mistaken. . . " (Scudéry, 306–07; cf., Perrault, 30).

27. [Claude Perrault], *Description anatomique d'un caméléon, d'un castor, d'un dromadaire, d'un ours, et d'une gazelle* (Paris: Frédéric Léonard, 1669), 20–21.

28. Scudéry, 315. For the descriptions of the living chameleon's eye, see Scudéry, 299–300; Perrault, 15.

The second and major point of disagreement was that of the chameleon's nourishment. Perrault reported that the animal ate flies and dismissed as a fable of the Ancients the idea that it lived on air. The academicians observed that the function of the animal's distinctive tongue was to trap insects. When they dissected their chameleon they found flies and worms in its intestines and inside its excrement. Scudéry, on the other hand, goes to great pains to prove that the chameleon lives only on air. She asserts that her female chameleon refused all offers of worms and insects and that when its tongue darted out it took in no insects. In an apparent refutation of Perrault, she describes the chameleon's excrement superficially and reports that her observations "don't disprove that air is the chameleon's natural food. However it may be, I conclude nothing. I relate only what I've observed." (Of course she doesn't mention that only when the academicians dissolved the pebblelike excrement in vinegar were the flies inside it visible.)[29]

Why did Scudéry decide directly to contradict evidence that seems to us irrefutable, and in the "objective" language of the academicians? Scudéry was intensely interested in the scientific experimentation that she followed from outside academic walls. Yet for her, animals fully retained their metaphorical and moral value. Her treatment of the chameleons illustrates both her attachment to the language of metaphor, an attachment which entailed rejection of Cartesian mechanism, and her curiosity about a scientific practice from which she was excluded. At the end of the conversation "On Praise" ("Des Loüanges), which precedes the "Story of Two Chameleons," chameleons are used as an image of pride, which "feeds only on air" (Scudéry, 293). Although the chameleon does not have the same metaphorical meaning in the following conversation, Scudéry needed to "prove" that it lived on air in order to make her point. Because she observed that the living animal became puffed up (Scudéry, 309–10), her image seemed justified.

In the *conversation* on the chameleons, the animal that lives on air becomes an image of the spirituality that Cartesian mechanism denied it. At the outset of the *conversation*, Scudéry announces her anti-Cartesian position: ". . . It's easy to observe that [the chameleon] sees with intelligence and with judgment, whether it walks, climbs a tree, or chooses a resting place. . . " (Scudéry, 300). Louis Le Laboureur's sonnet, like the other poetry included in the conversation is a homage to "Sapho" that turns on a spiritualization of the chameleon. In the

29. Perrault, 33–35; Scudéry, 301; 312–11 (misnumbered in this edition).

second quatrain the poet brushes aside accusations of the chameleon's notorious inconstancy, and offers a counterimage that ends in a conceit of praise for Sapho: "Our body [of the chameleon] is almost nothing but spirit, / A bit of sun nourishes it, / It animates us, it inspires us; / And we come to live with you, / Because the air that you breathe here, / Is the purest of all" (ibid., 365). The metaphorical correspondence between the human Sapho and the animal bears a moral truth: the spirit that infuses life, human and animal alike, carries a spark of divinity. Like Catherine Descartes in the *relation* of her uncle's death, the poets in this collection divinize nature. The relation between the human and the animal is not that of thinking subject to soulless object, as in Cartesian mechanism, but an empathic one between creatures of nature.

In her poem, "Les Caméléons à M.D.S.," Anne de la Vigne repeats the correspondence between the human and the animal in using the chameleon as an image of Mlle de Scudéry's creative genius. She likens the "lively pictures" and the "variety of noble sentiments" in Scudéry's novels to the chameleon's changing colors. Scudéry's "divine genius" appears in different guises in the various subjects she chooses: "Philosopher, *galant*, warrior, statesman, / Into anything it [her genius] wants it can be transformed, / And uniformly elevated, brilliant, tender, heroic, / It always instructs, it always charms" (ibid., 368).

Scudéry did, as she claimed, report what she saw. But she and her friends saw differently from the academicians. If the "Story of the Chameleons" adopts the discourse of objective observation and experimentation, it also draws on the language of metaphor to figure an empathic correspondence between the animal and the human realms. Scudéry couldn't "see" the flies in the dissected chameleon's body because for her the higher truth was moral. In her view, natural philosophy was subordinated to moral philosophy. Perrault, on the other hand, rejected moral lessons that were inconsistent with the facts. "For in order to teach that flatterers lack candor and that vain, ambitious spirits feed on nothing, it doesn't have to be true that the chameleon turns all colors but white and that it lives only on air." If you want to moralize, he says, at least get your facts straight (Perrault, 30). The discourse of objectivity subordinates moral to natural philosophy.

The juxtaposition of Scudéry's *conversation* on the chameleons with Perrault's *Description anatomique* reveals that learned women in seventeenth-century France could participate in the construction of rational discourse, but from afar. As scientific objectivity became increasingly identified with the economic interests of the state, women were excluded from its practice. From the other side of the academic door they had a distinctive contribution to make: the conciliation of an older metaphorical and analogical language with the new rationality. We cannot now, to be sure, take Scudéry's description of her chameleons to be serious "science." But her refusal to bracket moral considerations along with her own subjectivity in her investigation of nature points to the possibility of a science that incorporates the ethical demands of the thinking subject.

If the feminist alternative was a contestation of Cartesian objectivity, how did the Scudéry's three friends come to be known as Cartesian? The women did not completely reject Descartes's philosophy. As the academicians did not leave metaphor and analogy totally behind them, so the salon embraced Cartesian thought selectively. The "precious" transcendence of the body and the refusal of love, which characterize the writings we have examined, can be seen as consistent with Descartes's dualism and his theory of the passions. However, the feminist alternative dismantles the epistemological barrier between thinking subject and object. Why, after all, would Cartesian objectivity have appealed to learned women in early modern times? Their struggle was precisely to overcome their status as physical objects and to gain recognition as thinking subjects.

To call the women discussed here "Cartesian" is to tell only half the story. The label elides their distance from a discourse which prompted them to formulate alternative propositions on moral issues and the value of the thinking subject. In applying the term advisedly, we glimpse women's part in initiating the debates on Cartesian objectivity which have persisted into our own day.

III. Cultural Landscapes

LOUIS MARIN

Classical, Baroque: Versailles, or the Architecture of the Prince

There is no doubt something paradoxical about making Versailles out to be one of the high places of baroque architecture. The huge façade by Louis LeVau and Jules Hardouin Mansart, which spreads out onto the gardens, has passed, and continues to pass,—perhaps rightly so—for the classical model of the royal palace: each element of the construction, although perfectly defined in itself, is subordinated to a center where, at the level of the principal floor—the royal floor—an independent portico of six columns interrupts with its powerful relief the repetitive rhythm of the façade in favor of a stable and firmly determined foyer.

Whatever Versailles's legitimate right in laying claim to "classicism," it is nonetheless true that, in Anglo-Saxon countries in particular, classicism in art and notably in architecture is often considered a French peripeteia of a great baroque period which is born of international mannerism in the sixteenth century and ends in the precious and spiraled graces of rococo, while awaiting the so-called "neo-classic" resurrection around 1750.

It is not a matter here of resolving (either by a combination of formal and stylistic features, or by an even finer diachrony of historical developments particularized according to cultural and geographic areas) the problems, indeed the aporias in method and theory, in periodization and chronology, raised when a work of art, a construction plan or form of reception is designated as baroque or classical. I will therefore set aside this endless query to evoke only in its broadest

A French version of this text appeared in the *Journal of the Faculty of Letters. The University of Tokyo. Aesthetics*, vol. 14, 1989.

YFS 80, *Baroque Topographies,* ed. Timothy Hampton, © 1991 by Yale University.

167

scope the architecture of the Prince, the palace of the absolute Monarch, the place of his greatest power, Versailles, soon after Bernini's journey to Paris (1665). I want to try to distinguish how in Versailles, through what may conditionally be called a tension between the baroque and the classical, the representation of State power in the modern age is expressed and—in every sense of the word—constructed.

The architecture of the Prince: straight off it is fitting to emphasize the double value—objective and subjective—of the phrase which gives its title to this study. The Prince, Louis XIV as it were, was—as we know—a great builder. "Baroque" passion, excess? In a sense, his function as King found its fulfillment, its monarchal dignity, its privileged manifestation, in the edification of the palace; the King is an arch-architect, the architectural Subject of Versailles through which the Kingdom receives its most perfect consecration. But the architecture of the Prince means just as much the construction, the edification of the King as Monarch in and by his palace. In this sense, the castle and gardens of Versailles, "architect" the Prince to make him not only the absolute of political power, but the center of the cosmos in its entirety. To this double extent, Versailles is the result of a production, of a construction at once real, imaginary, and symbolic. Real, in that the palace exists: one can still visit it today. Imaginary, in that it reveals "baroque" desire, the fantastic, the phantasmatic desire to show (oneself) as absolute power. Symbolic—since in some manner it is the sovereign Norm, the "classic" Law of universal subjection to signs constituting a transcendent cultural and political universe devoid of civil and natural exteriority.

Three notions seem to me to be essential to an understanding of the architecture of the Prince as absolute Monarch (at Versailles): first, the notion of place in its relation to space and time, to space (that is, to landscape and site), and to time, (that is, to history and the historical event). Second, the notion of power in its historically and philosophically complex relation to representation. And finally, there is what constitutes perhaps the sense and the essence of the place of power and of the architecture of the Prince. This is the notion of the monument as the location where power puts on its representation and becomes absolute in a "universal place," as the site where the representation of the Prince and of his history is presented in a permanent and definitive presence.

I- PLACE-SPACE-EVENT

What is a place? How is a place different from space?[1] It is perhaps not unnecessary to recall the extreme polysemy of the notion of place in the seventeenth century. Under the entry on *lieu* [place] Furetière's dictionary (which is, in many respects a genuine treatise on cultural anthropology) gives a fine example of this polysemy. Furetière begins by presenting, not without some irony, the Aristotelian definition of *lieu:* "Surface première et immobile d'un corps qui en environne un autre ou, pour parler plus clairement, l'espace dans lequel un corps est placé" [*place:* Primary and immobile surface of a body which surrounds another or, to speak more clearly, the space in which a body is placed]; and in the example he gives it is suitable to insist on the use of the possessive "chaque corps occupe son lieu" [each body occupies its place]; "il ne peut y avoir deux choses dans le même lieu" [there cannot be two things in the same place], etc. This is the motif he then develops: "Endroit destiné à placer quelque chose soit par nature, soit par art. Dieu a rangé tous les êtres en un lieu convenable. Chaque chose est dans son lieu naturel, quand elle est dans son élément. On appelle également "lieu" un endroit fixe et déterminé qu'on veut marquer et distinguer des autres" [Spot intended for setting something either by nature, or by art. God put all beings in a suitable place. Each thing is in its natural place, when it is in its element. "Place" also designates a fixed and determined spot which one wishes to mark and distinguish from all others]. This last notion is not without interest for our purpose, as can be seen by these few examples; "cet homme a voyagé en divers lieux, c'est à dire en diverses contrées; c'est le seigneur du lieu." [this man has traveled in various places, that is in various regions; he is the lord of the place]. Or again with the definition of *county seat* (*chef-lieu*): "Le manoir principal d'une seigneurie où on est obligé de porter la foi et l'hommage" [The principal manor house of a seigneury to which one is obliged to bring fidelity and respect]. Furetière then comes to the more specifically architectural meaning. One calls "place" a "maison particulière à la ville ou à la campagne; l'état des lieux; la clef des lieux; il y a bien du lieu dans cette maison" [private house in the city or in the country; the condition of the place; the keys

---

1. I am keeping the distinction I began in *Utopiques: Jeux d'espace* (Paris: Minuit, 1973), and which Michel de Certeau later admirably developed and synthesized in *L'Invention du quotidien* (Paris: 10/18, 1980), vol. 1.

to the house; this house is a big place]. This architectural notion of place is immediately linked, in the seventeenth century, to the sociocultural understanding of the term: a place is distinguished by the privileges attributed to the various uses it is intended for; "l'église est un lieu sacré; les hôpitaux sont des lieux pieux; le lieu d'honneur, c'est le premier rang à la guerre, c'est à dire le lieu où il y a du danger à courir et de la gloire à remporter" [the church is a sacred place; hospitals are pious places; the place of honor is the front line in battle, that is the place where there is danger to be faced and glory to be reaped]. This last definition leads Furetière to the notion of "place aux rangs d'honneur qui sont établis dans la république ou dans l'opinion des hommes; le président tient le premier lieu dans sa compagnie" [position in the ranks of honor which are established in the republic or in the opinion of men; the president takes first place in his company]. And finally: "Origine, extraction, maison, famille; cet homme vient d'un bon lieu, il est allié en bon lieu, il a fait un bon mariage" [Origin, extraction, house, family; this man comes from a good place, has connections in good places, he has made a good marriage].

All of these definitions may be generalized by noting that "Est lieu, ou relève de la notion de lieu, *l'ordre* dans tous les sens du terme, l'ordre selon lequel des éléments sont distribués dans un rapport de coexistence" [That which is a place, or falls within the domain of place, is *order* in every sense of the term, the order in which elements are distributed in a relation of coexistence]. There cannot be two things in the same place and, to quote Michel de Certeau, "le lieu obéit à la loi du propre et de la propriété" [place obeys the law of the proper and of property].[2] Things, in the local order, are one next to the other and local order is a synchronic configuration of positions. Thus any and all places necessarily imply an indication of stability and thereby, any place produces a law. A "Classicism" of the place?

On the other hand, there is space when one takes into consideration direction vectors, speed quantities, temporal variables, movements. Space, one could say, is animated by the movements within it, or, more precisely, spaces are effects of these movements. Space is the effect produced by operations of orientation which, by the same token, "temporalize" it. In another way, it can be said that *place* is determined by "beings-there," by presences (the dead body as the foundation of a

2. See Michel de Certeau, *The Practice of Everyday Life*, trans. Steven Rendall (Berkeley: University of California Press, 1984), chap. 9.

place, for example), as opposed to *space* which would be determined by the operations which specify it, that is by the actions of subjects, of historical subjects.

Let us take two examples from the series of tapestries depicting Louis XIV entitled *Histoire du Roy*. In the one representing the historical event called "Renewal of the Swiss Alliance" (1662), Louis XIV is shown inside his palace, immobile, as the sovereign figure of the Law of monarchic place. He is the principal "actant," the subject of monarchic place; he figures its property of location. By contrast in the tapestry which shows "The Entry into Dunkirk," the King, agent and actor of the history, a history in the making, is represented as an "actant" in space. A process of spatialization is figured, a movement of the appropriation of space through orientation in a scenario of conflict. Representation is thus essentially an organization of movements in space, movements whose effects are spaces. The King is situated on an eminence, a site and, with his commanding cane, while looking at the spectator, he points to Dunkirk, the city that he is about to enter, and which can be seen in topographic form in the background of the tapestry. In other words, the act of the historical subject designates space in every sense of the term. He points to it as the direction of his power from a (strategic) site he occupies. Moreover, the gesture of the commanding cane corresponds exactly with the definition of the "rex," of the one who outlines a course. This gesture is simultaneously the gesture in history, of the order given his troops to march toward Lille, and the indication, for the spectators, of the city occupied by him, "Baroque" space?[3]

It seems that these examples show that "space" is linked rather to action and to the process of history, to its movement, while place seems reserved for the term of a movement, for the conclusion of an action, for the accomplishment of process. On the one hand, the battle, the conflict, the conquest; on the other, the contract, the treatise, the alliance. Place, space, and event: the dialectic at play between these three notions is no doubt constitutive of the notion of place. The

3. In the famous example of the *Rencontre des deux rois*, an enclosed place, the palace, or what takes its place, is defined as the place of the Prince; figures are placed according to an order of coexistence. The place of the prince is the palace or that which takes its place (since the meeting takes place in the île des Faisants, at the Franco-Spanish border, in 1660), but in this place the law of the Pyrénées treaty appears, and precisely, an exchange takes place between the Infanta who will become queen of France and peace as secured by this marriage.

notion of event is very complex in its definition. Indeed, an event is conceived of, in the seventeenth century, as the result of an intention, of a project, as the outcome of an action. An event is also "une chose grande, surprenante et singulière, qui arrive dans le monde" [a momentous thing, surprising and singular, which happens in the world]. The importance of an event is then measured by its singularity. An event-accident escapes the homogeneity of causal series. What is event by its singularity, conceived or presented as such, surprises and provokes astonishment in the face of its apparition.[4] And at the same time, the result of this semantic tension between these two meanings of the word "event" implies that an event always involves a certain form of theatricality. This is shown both by dictionaries and by the contexts in which the word is used: "ce drame est fait d'événement," "l'événement change la face des choses dans une tragédie ou dans une comédie" [this drama is made of event, the event changes the face of things in a tragedy or in a comedy]. Therefore, it is undoubtedly not excessive to say that in the seventeenth century there is an event only inasmuch as it is taken up, constructed or invented by a theatricality. The event is "baroque" and it is an apparatus of representation which institutes it as such.

The architecture of the Prince, in the double and most general sense of the expression, constitutes just such a *dispositif* [apparatus] of construction and disclosure of the historical event. It is in this space and in this place that the event is revealed as the miraculous manifestation of the perfection of "royal substance." In secular time, it is this peripeteia, this "epiphany," this *merveille* [marvel] by which an act of the king shows itself as the sudden and dazzling apparition of his Power, of his Wisdom, of his Clemency, or of his Justice. The architecture of the Prince, in its place of power, constitutes the theatrical scene which institutes and constructs the representation of the royal act as the revelation of the "Monarch" in time and space.

II-POWER-REPRESENTATION

Hence the necessity of taking into account relations between power and representation in order to grasp the meaning of the architecture of

4. In the *Entrée à Dunkerque* tapestry, Lebrun gives the peasant represented on the right and who is watching the event, a "tête d'expression" [an expressive face] which he had drawn to represent the combined passion of astonishment and admiration.

the Prince. Political power, state power, produces, constructs and in turn appropriates the apparatus of representation, since this apparatus of representation constructs itself as a power of effects. In other words, representation, within the framework of this thought about absolutism, would be this "façade," this palatial "orthography," as the architectural treatise of the time put it, where the grounding, the somber background of power emerges, is presented, and summed up. And yet inversely, (though in the same movement), representation is no longer a façade, but a machine for producing effects. Representation develops a visual theatricality which strikes the eye and subjugates the gaze. From this point of view, how does the exchange between power and representation function? What is power? Is it being "capable" of force, having a reserve of force, a force which is not expended but is expendable? And what would be a force that would not be expended? It would exist at the moment that representation comes into play, turns force into signs—in other words, at that moment in which the external act where force is manifested is replaced by the signs of force which need only be presented (that is, seen), in order for their signified, force, to be believed. What is at play in this play of signs is not the concealment of force, but a process which induces belief in the reality of what they simulate. Signs, to this extent, are power and power is but the irresistible effect of what may be called their "text," the text of the place constructed by signs.

This is what appears, it seems to me, in Bernini's first two projects for the Louvre, where the façade is a text which represents, as their effects, forces internal to the edifice as a whole—forces which persuade by offering the royal absolute, tending potentially to integrate this exteriority and make the architectural edifice a virtually absolute place.

Pouvoir [power] is also a valorization of the capacity for *puissance* [power] which as an obligatory constraint, generates duties. In this sense, to be able [*pouvoir*] to institute as law the capacity for power [*puissance*] is also the operation of its foundation. Not only does it modalize potential force, but it valorizes the capacity for power as a legitimate and obligatory state. It justifies it.

This was again Bernini's intention with the project for the Louvre which could ultimately be executed at Versailles. The text of architectural signs constituted a modality of forces as potential power [*puissance*]. At the same time, in its façades, it raised the palace to a symbolic totality where the apartment of the King, his *proper* place, would, by its central position, find its legitimate foundation, while authorizing and justifying its universal appropriation.

What does it mean to represent? If not to present again . . . or in the place of, instead of . . . ? For someone, for something which was present but is no longer, for an absent, for another, there is substituted a "same" of this other, *in its place*. Such is the first effect of representation, to do as if the other, the absent, were here now the same, present, not presence, but the effect of a local presence—the divine force of painting which, according to Alberti, not only makes the absent present as we say friendship does, but moreover makes the dead seem almost alive. This effect is its power; it is constituted by the contact between a divine force and the transitive dimension of representation: to represent someone, whether it be force by its signs, the king by his portrait or palace, as does Hardouin-Mansart still today in the façade of Versailles that gives onto the gardens of Le Vau.

But to represent means also to show, to intensify, to redouble a presence. Here representing someone no longer means being his herald, his ambassador, but instead it means to exhibit him, to show him. For this someone, it is a matter of presenting himself and of constituting himself by this presentation, of constructing his legitimate identity. To represent is to present oneself: such would be the second effect of representation, the constitution of a subject, of one's own subject; a subject-effect, that is a power of institution, of authorization, and of legitimation resulting from the reflexive functioning of the apparatus on itself. This double power of representation appears: through delegation, the effect and power of presence in the place of absence and death; through self-presentation, the power-effect of a subject, that is of an institution, an authorization, and of legitimation. On the one hand, to represent is to make the absent or the dead imaginarily present once again. On the other hand, it is to construct an identity which is legitimate and authorized by the ostentatious exhibition of qualifications and justifications.

It is at the crossing and at the exchange of these various significations and processes that the representation of state power is constituted as an absolute monarch. The place of power, the local order of the absolute, as we have seen, is force's tendency toward absolutism, it is the desire for the absolute. Therefore, representation is the imaginary fulfillment of this desire. In the political realm, the essence of all power is to tend toward the absolute, it is part of its reality never to console itself for not reaching it. Representation (of which power is the effect and which, in turn, allows it and authorizes it) will be the infinite work of a mourning—that of the missing Object, of the Absolute. Thus representation would transform the infinity of this real lack into the absolute of an imaginary which stands in its place. Such would be the dialectic of the "baroque" and of "classicism" in the sphere of state power. Such would be the place of the King as the position of the absolute Monarch's space, his monument or more precisely the monumentality of his place.

III-THE MONUMENT, EVENT MEMORIAL AND TOMB OF PRESENCE

It is from this point that an investigation of the architectonics of the place of state power, of its representation, in the local order, as absolute Monarch might proceed. And in order to do this, it is useful to pause for a moment to consider the notion of monumentality while attempting to construct it as the very essence of the place of absolute power, of its representation and of its structure. To broach the subject, we will quote, not without some anachronism, (through this will be all the more significant for our purpose) a text of the "Enlightenment," an article from the *Encyclopédie* written by the chevalier de Jeaucourt on the notion of monument. He calls *monument* "tout ouvrage d'architecture et de sculpture fait pour conserver la mémoire des hommes illustres ou des grands événements, comme un mausolée, une pyramide, un arc de triomphe et autres semblables." [any work of architecture or sculpture intended to preserve the memory of illustrious men or great events, such as a mausoleum, a pyramid, a triumphal arch and others similar]. The monument is thus first of all and fundamentally a place of memory, of the memory of the hero, of the Prince, of the King. It is the place for remembering that event, the greatness of which is essentially measured only by the greatness of the one who was its participant and about whom it reveals, in secular time, one of his infinite perfections. The monument, as a memorial, *consecrates* the event, it makes it sacred by its edification; just as, conversely, the edifice is *consecrated* by the event, insofar as it is first and essentially an act of the Prince, hero or demigod. Thus, for example, the triumphal arches at the Porte Saint Martin and the Porte Saint Denis that edify, at the "edge" of the Kingdom's capital, the representation of an act of the King, that is of the immutable and eternal body of Royalty. It is this body which is here constituted, constructed, in the shape of a triumphal entryway into Paris and which, in this commemoration, accomplishes the immutable gesture of appropriating the City, to itself and to the Monarch.

De Jeaucourt goes on:

> Les premiers monuments que les hommes aient érigés n'étaient d'abord que des pierres entassées, tantôt dans une campagne pour conserver le souvenir de la victoire, tantôt sur une sépulture pour honorer un particulier. Ensuite l'industrie a ajouté insensiblement à ces constructions grossières et l'ouvrier est enfin parvenu à se rendre lui-même plus illustre par la beauté de son ouvrage que le fait ou la personne dont il travaillait à célébrer la mémoire. Quelques nombreux et quelques somptueux que soient les monuments élevés par la main des hommes, ils n'ont pas plus de privilèges que les villes entières qui se *convertissent* en ruines et en solitudes.

> The first monuments to be erected by men were originally merely stones piled up, sometimes in the country to preserve the memory of victory, sometimes on a sepulcher to honor a private individual. Then industry gradually added to these crude constructions and occasionally the craftsman eventually succeeded in making himself more illustrious through the beauty of his own work than through the deed or the person whose memory he strove to memorialize. However numerous and sumptuous the monuments raised by the hands of men, they have no more privilege than the entire cities that *convert* to ruins and to deserts.

We will not dwell on the way in which this beautiful text offers an explicit formulation of the Enlightenment ideology regarding the progress of the arts and the glorification of artists rather than of the one they were to honor—the monarchic incarnation of state power. We will emphasize only the way in which the passage emphasizes the other semantic value of the monument—a value which the *Encyclopédie* links, incidentally, to the preromantic motif of the ruin. A *place of memory, the monument is also the place of death, the tomb.* It is in this sense that the term appears, in the text of the *Encyclopédie* as an architectural heading: "*Monument:* terme d'architecture, ce mot signifie en particulier un tombeau *quia monet mentem,* parce qu'il avertit l'esprit". [*Monument:* an architectural term, this word means in particular a tomb *quia monet mentem,* because it informs the mind]. Whence the reference to the mausoleum and to the pyramid which, as we know, will be in Hegel's *Aesthetics,* the figure of the moment of architecture as the moment of the symbolic beginning of art. It is the place of the Dead. The *Encyclopédie* already prefigures the Hegelian movement: the pyramid offers itself as inorganic nature (a pile of stones), but it already contains within it the beginning of an interiority. If it represents edification par excellence for Hegel, this is only because it is the dwelling allotted the dead: "It is from the dead which it contains that comes all its significance. Death then signifies the rough sketch of a spiritual interiority, of an internal invisible, but which exhibits itself only in the form of the edifice that serves as its shelter or its envelope and in which it remains invisibly hidden."[5] The *crypt* is thus for Hegel the first creation of art and architecture. It does indeed seem that some of Bernini's tombs erected for those absolutely absolute sovereigns, the Popes, offer a commentary on these passages from Hegel's *Aesthetics*, with however this important nuance—that a monumental architectural work, while obeying the "pyramiding" structure, neither indicates nor conceals any longer the *other* meaning and the *other* spirit hidden inside. Rather, it signifies and reveals it in its subterranean violence, while submitting that violence to the effigy of Peter's successor.

Now in the case of the King, we see an essential displacement of the meaning of the monument in a very interesting text, from the beginning of the seventeenth century (1602) by the curator of King Henry IV's Cabinet of Medals and Antiquities, Rascas de Bagarris. This discourse which concerns the establishment of the glory and the memory of great princes (in other words, the erection of their monuments) aims, in fact, at creating a history of the King through medals, "vraies et parfaites médailles." It is necessary, writes our author, "publier et perpétuer son histoire auguste et vive mémoire par le *Moniment* le plus parfait" [to publish and perpetuate [the king's] august history and vivid memory by the most perfect *Moniment*]. And he adds the following commentary to justify this neologism: "Le nom général de *Moniment* qui vient du latin *monitor* pour signifier toutes choses qui admonestent les absents ou de lieu ou de temps, de la mémoire de quelque sujet semble d'autant plus nécessaire d'être reçu dans ce discours que l'autre nom de *Monument* se trouve restreint par l'usage du vulgaire à signifier les sépulcres des morts qui sont aussi faits pour la mémoire." [It seems all the more necessary to include in this dis-

5. See Hegel, *Aesthetics*, trans. T. M. Knox (Oxford: Clarendon Press, 1975), vol. 2, 650 ff.

course the general name of *Moniment*—which comes from the latin *monitor*—and signifies any thing that admonishes the absent either in space or time, with the memory of a subject since the other name of Monument commonly refers only to the sepulchers of the dead, that are also meant as memorials]. The accomplished form of the Prince's glory must therefore be *like* a tomb. However unlike the sepulcher of the dead which marks his definitive passage to the past, and consecrates his death by its representation, this form must be "vivante et présente mémoire" [alive and present memory], that is to say, the presentation of the King, his real presence in a representation that is "publique et perpétuelle" [public and perpetual]. It is the monument to the glory of the King which defines the place and time of presence, understood as a transcendental permanence founding all presence. Thus in the future, it is not the Prince who will be absent, lost and dead in a past which would have to be brought back through representation: it is posterity that will have to be made by memory to think of itself as absent from the time and the place of the prince, from his stable presence, which authorizes this posterity to conceive of itself in the time and the place of its own history. What is this monument that, better than a tomb, might remind all those absent in time and space of the presence of the King? What monument would articulate the two dimensions of representation, both that of bringing back the dead in an imaginary presence and that of legitimately founding the presence of the present by giving it its symbolic dimension, by inscribing it under the regime of the sovereign and of the law?

This monument is his palace. Thus one must analyse the palace of the King as the architectural device whereby the body of the King appropriates geographic-urban space. Through the palace, space is transubstantiated into a monarchic body, as original principle and unique or absolute power. How, then, is one to submit space to this *monarchitectonics* of representing the Prince and specify his real presence, producing an exemplary symbolic place in the form of this representation?

IV-THE PALACE AT VERSAILLES: THE WORLD TRANSUBSTANTIATED INTO ROYAL BODY

In the representations that were done in the seventeenth century of the castle of Versailles, of its park and outbuildings, the functioning of this apparatus is revealed. It is not a matter here of undertaking a study of the history of Versailles and its meanings. We will confine ourselves, in conclusion, to comparing a few plans and topographic views of the castle which make apparent this appropriation of space and its trans-ubstantiation into royal body and to evoking briefly a few descriptive texts.

In the "general plan of the gardens, groves, and ornamental pools of the small park at Versailles" etched by Vanhoeck on the eve of Louis XIV's death there appears, in all its might, this central axis which, from the main part of the palace, itself central, articulates the symmetry of the gardens and dies out, beyond the fountain of Apollo, between the compact blocks of the legend on either side. This axis aims at a point which is literally undetermined, a point in infinity, which is however the rigorous structural equivalent of the place of the King. It aims, in fact, at his apartment and, in this apartment, at his bedchamber—the place of his body and on this body, of his head, his face, his eye. In other words, the layout of the small Park can be considered, if not as the matrix, at least as the projection, "tattooed" onto geographic space, of a steady, regulated network, equally quantified by lines which appropri-ate them to the King, make them "proper" like his property. Further-more it carries out the expansion of the body of the Prince according to the law of his gaze, the radius which already Alberti called the cen-trical radius, the radius of the prince, the radius of the Subject. This network around the central axis is the focal point of a regular grid-system hemmed in by two long diagonals, the Avenue du Trianon to the right, and its corresponding line to the left.

This first approach is confirmed with the "general plan of Ver-sailles, its park, its Louvre, its gardens, its groves and its town" drawn by Nicolas de Fer, geographer of His Royal Highness the Dauphin in 1705: (it will be noted that he is the author in 1693 of *La France triomphante sous le règne de Louis le Grand* and of the *Histoire des rois de France depuis Pharamond jusqu'à Louis XV* [1722], a collection of portraits). With the grand Park and the prolongation of the Grand Canal's central axis, the network continues and is amplified by the development of the grid-system around a star-shaped arrangement de-fined by diagonals. Yet if at the top of the map, the whole is enclosed by the wall of the Grand Park, Galie's point, which is the summit of this wall, marks out a compass card between the legends, which opens it, potentially, to universal space. But it is above all in the lower part of the plan that there occurs a remarkable conversion of the geo-metry and geo-graphy of state power, of its architectonics or more precisely of its "ichnography." Indeed, around a horizontal axis marked by the rue des Réservoirs and the rue de la Surintendance, between the Front-Courtyard and the Courtyard of the castle, there seems to be a drop in the guiding lines of the layout of the Grand and Petit Parcs, which, this time, would no longer articulate the space of Nature to subject it as power of the central gaze by transforming it into an expanding royal place, but would construct urban space as portrait of the Prince.

Here again, there is a central axis, the Avenue du Parc or the Grande Avenue directed toward Paris with the open cluster of the Avenues de Sceaux and de Saint Cloud (royal places) starting from the Place d'Armes. Its central axis is accompanied by a double grid-system, this time external to the two diagonal arms of the old Versailles and of the New Town. A double folding of the plan therefore inscribes its folds in cartographic space. One fold is central and defines the axis of the Prince's gaze from his apartment, from his bedchamber, and the other is horizontal, defining a lateral axis (a projection at the line of point of view, of the horizon) that determines the apportionment of the natural geographic world and of the cultural, urban, political world. It is this double folding that is repeated on the plan as a whole. But of course, in the general view, the royal gaze dominates from above the axis of its own gaze: the gaze of the Monarch cannot be tied to one point of view, but representation enables it, by its transcendent and reflexive position, to examine the great central folding of space and to master the semi-infinite cultural urban delimitated here by the palace's great horizontal line from an ideal point situated above the Grand Canal.

We see here the production of the symbolic place of power, of State power, of absolute power through the appropriation, by means of the gaze of universal space to this place. In contrast with Bernini's conception, seen in the colonnade of Saint Peter's, where universal space is caught in a kind of physical embrace as if by arms that would envelop it as they make the great ostentatious baroque gesture of Catholic and Roman charity, the King at Versailles is at once everywhere and nowhere. He is not in space or rather he is present in it only as a dominant gaze which "develops" its classic place. It is indeed the world in its entirety that finds itself architectured in the place of the King and transubstantiated into a monarchic body in the optical forms of his portrait, that is to say of his all-seeing gaze: the symbolic production of the exemplary royal place.

We will quote, in conclusion, two passages from a description of

Versailles by the great courtier, theoretician and art critic, Félibien. After arriving from Paris by the Grande Avenue, the Place d'Armes, the Front-Courtyard and the Courtyard, just before entering the castle, the visitor is given this instruction;

> Il est bon de remarquer que comme le Soleil est la devise du Roi et que les Poètes confondent Apollon et le Soleil, il n'y a rien dans cette superbe maison qui n'ait rapport à cette divinité: aussi toutes les figures et ornements qu'on y voit n'étant point placés au hasard, ils ont relation ou au soleil ou aux lieux où ils sont mis.

> It is appropriate to remark that since the Sun is the device of the King and since Poets connect Apollo and the Sun, there is nothing in this superb house that does not relate to this divinity: thus all the figures and ornaments that one sees there not having been placed at random, are linked either to the sun or to the places in which they have been put.

Nothing is left to chance, whether it be the architecture of the buildings and gardens or the ornamentation. The principle that rules them, the norm of their visibility and of their legibility is the king in his device. His body and type is the sun and the soul, the very legend of the incomparable absolute, *nec pluribus imper.* The principle of interpretation that provides the "narrative journey" with the instruction of its program ("Il faut partout lire le Soleil ou Apollon" [One must read the Sun or Apollo everywhere]) is thus rigorously identical to the imperious rule, that presided over the architecture of the stage and its representation—an identity that gives the visit its *total security* and offers it its *definitive certainty.* Through topographic representation, the architecturally visible is totally legible and the descriptively legible is visible; image and symbol are founded and merge in a same *reality* of discourses and places, that of a perfect simulacrum which manifests an identical prosography, the portrait of the Sun-King.

There is in this way a "theoretical" order of places which, in their silent monumental immobility, accompany and indeed even require of their structural gaze the "theoretization" of spaces that the visit brings about by its displacements in points of view and its contemplative vistas. The one represents the other, the second performs the first, and the monarch in his palace, visited by his subjects, is like an Argus with a hundred eyes that no gaze can escape; he is at one and the same time the castle that continuously expands in space and time, and that castle's center, the heart which gives it its meaning admitting structures that punctuate and articulate this space and this time, and legitimate its symbolic reality. And it is this legitimation that would be accomplished at Versailles, in the palace of the Monarch, the French "classic" replacement of the baroque powers of Berninian architecture.

Translated by Anna Lehman

CONSULTED OR QUOTED WORKS

F. Borsi, *Le Bernin,* trans. H. A. Baatsch and J. Robin (Paris: Hazan, 1984).

Michel de Certeau, *The Practice of Everyday Life,* trans. Steven Rendall (Berkeley: University of California Press, 1984).

N. Elias, *La Société de cour,* trans. P. Kamnitzer (Paris: Calmann-Levy, 1974).

A. Félibien, *Description sommaire du château de Versailles* (Paris, 1674).

R. E. Giesey, *The Royal Funeral Ceremony in Renaissance France* (Geneva: Droz, 1960).

G. W. F. Hegel, *Esthétique,* French trans. (Paris: Aubier Montaigne, 1969).

E. H. Kantorowicz, *The King's Two Bodies* (Princeton: Princeton University Press, 1957).

_____. "Mysteries of State: An absolute Concept," in *Harvard Theological Review* 48: (1955).

Louis XIV, *Mémoires,* ed. J. Corgnon (Paris: Taillandier, 1978).

Louis Marin, *Utopiques, jeux d'espaces* (Paris: Minuit, 1973).

_____. *Le Portrait du Roi* (Paris: Minuit, 1981). Trans. *The Portrait of the King* (Minnesota University Press, 1990).

Madeleine de Scudéry, *La Promenade de Versailles* (Paris, 1669).

B. Teyssèdre, *L'Art français au siècle de Louis XIV* (Paris: Le Livre de Poche, 1967).

Vitruvius, *Traité d'architecture,* trans. Charles Perrault (Paris, 1673).

CHRISTIAN JOUHAUD

Richelieu, or "Baroque" Power in Action

The adjective baroque is present in the title of this article only out of convenience. It would be all the same to me if I were to replace it by another: "classical," for example, or even "preclassical." The adjective refers here only to the attempt to circumscribe a specificity. For fewer than twenty years (1631–1642), if we choose to begin this story at the moment in which Cardinal Richelieu was able to eliminate the last truly dangerous opposition to his power, the power of the French state found a countenance, painted twenty-four times by Philippe de Champaigne or his imitators.[1] The surgeons who autopsied the cardinal say that behind this mask they found a brain of extraordinary form and development.[2] They pinpoint in this way the mystery of a political energy. With them, I would like to insist on the originality of a particular mode of the management of power, and thus refusing to admit that Richelieu was merely a very capable "ordinary minister".[3]

I was struck, a few years ago, by a strange affair, the accounts of which, at the end of 1633 and in 1634, were widespread.[4] This affair intrigued me, particularly because of the seeming discrepancy be-

1. Bernard Dorival, "Richelieu et Philippe de Champaigne", *Richelieu et le monde de l'esprit* (Paris, 1985), 129–34; J. Mclct Sanson, "L'Image de Richelieu", ibid., 135–48.

2. A. Aubery. *Histoire du cardinal duc de Richelieu* (Paris: 1660, 572); Scipion Dupleix, *Continuation de l'histoire du règne de Louis le Juste* (Paris: 1648), 354; Etienne de Jouy, *Trois documents inédits sur Urbain Grandier et un document peu connu sur le cardinal de Richelieu* (Paris: 1906).

3. Robert Descimon and A. Guery, "Un état des temps modernes?," in André Burguière and J. Revel, ed., *Histoire de la France*, volume 2, directed by Jacques Le Goff, *L'Etat et les pouvoirs* (Paris: Seuil 1989), 181–356, quotation 191.

4. Christian Jouhaud, "Le Duc et l'archevêque: action politique, représentations et pouvoir au temps de Richelieu," *Annales E.S.C.*, (1986), 5, 1017–39.

YFS 80, *Baroque Topographies*, ed. Timothy Hampton, © 1991 by Yale University.

tween the insignificance of the event behind it and the political importance which it later assumed.

On 10 November 1633, in Bordeaux, the archbishop Henri de Sourdis and the governor of the province, the old duke of Epernon, insulted
each other publicly and even came to blows. This local scandal quickly
took on the dimensions of a national scandal. The archbishop seemed
to possess none of the visible, tangible assets of his adversary (wealth,
authority, troops, the support of the local nobility, a central role in the
socio-political hierarchy of the province and the city, numerous en-
dorsements by the local clergy, etc.) yet he would carry off the victory
in a spectacular manner. The old duke was exiled and excommuni-
cated; he lost a significant share of his power. Through the intermediary Sourdis, it was Richelieu, or, if one prefers, "power," which made
him fall. The manner in which the trap functioned allows us to see at
once in this action the organization of the power of the state.

This state power in fact may be divided into two powers: a consecrated power which arbitrates and condemns (the king), and an *"absent"* power, with no institutional existence, which acts (the minister).
A recognizable duality. But more importantly, it is here that, for once,
we recognize the association functions: the royal perfection guaran-
tees to the acting force its freedom of action; in return, the acting force
gives this perfection the opportunity to manifest itself as such. Practical separation of roles forms part of the mystery of the State and of its
secrets.

This division of powers helped make the person of the king the
perfect incarnation of a function—the apparent center of the system, a
process which had been at work since the end of the religious uprisings
and the victory of Henry IV. But the *representatives* of the king, provincial governors, for example, received no direct benefit from this evolu-
tion (except when they, too, were princes of noble blood). As custodians
of a party delegated with public authority, they were also, in the French
system, living images of the monarch, without, however, having at
their disposal the symbolic means of assuring their function as reflection of a perfection. They found themselves to be prisoners of values
and of discourse. Whatever their actions, they would never represent
more than a pale reflection of these values and this discourse, whose
presence and grandeur they were nonetheless required to manifest.
Provoked by an acting force, Epernon invoked the person of the king
whom he represented in order to protect himself, but, by his acts and
the scandal that they brought on (and which his adversaries propagated

through the press), he showed that he was in contradiction with the royal perfection which he was supposed to reflect: the perfection condemned him.

From where does the "acting force" derive its energy? No political theory—and especially not those of sovereignty (Bodin)—, no judicial corpus comes to found its dominion. The citadel is well-guarded. It is only by guile, through the margins, through its weak points that it is penetrated. But it happens that these very weak points are to be sought in that which consecrates its success, in its very ostentation. Thus, the weakest point of the fortress of political mystery betrays itself perhaps by the detour of a corridor in the sumptuous château of Richelieu in Poitou. The energy belonging to power would come to incrust itself in stone, condense itself, and all but "trap" itself.

In 1621, on the death of his elder brother, Richelieu, who was not yet a cardinal, bought back the family fief. In 1624, then cardinal and minister, he undertook great works there, all the while systematically buying up contiguous or neighboring seigniorial domains. In 1631, after the great political crises at the end of the preceding year, the fief of Richelieu was elevated to the highest rank of aristocratic power after that of princes. From that time on, enormous works of construction were carried out: a château sprang from the earth; a city was mapped out and soon built.

One of the keys to this colossal accomplishment lies in the plan to render visible, to show through each other, two dimensions that are ordinarily mutually exclusive, representation and visibility:[5] to render the blueprint as visible as a great open book, to render the visible as thinkable as a system.

In a work which appeared in 1645, the *Traité des manières de graver en taille douce,* Abraham Bosse defined the finality of perspective in the following way: "c'est de disposer les choses non telles que l'œil les voit, mais telles que les lois de la perspective les imposent à la raison" [One must set things forth not in the way that the eye sees them; but rather in the way that the laws of perspective impose them upon reason].[6] The domain of Richelieu consisted of imposing a political reasoning upon a space. We find the logic of this reasoning in the

5. Philippe Boudon, *Richelieu, ville nouvelle. Essai d'architecturologie* (Paris, 1978). Hereafter cited in the text.
6. Quoted by Jacques Guillerme, in Philippe Boudon, J. Guillerme, R. Tabouret, *Figuration graphique en architecture,* fascicle 2 (Paris: 1976). Hereafter cited in the text.

blueprint, in the geometrical organization of the new city and of the subunits of the château and in the absence of center. The perfect center of the system city/park/château itself appears to the pedestrian only visibly. What is involved is a true geometric center, and therefore a unique one. Only from this point does one obtain a panoramic view of the whole of wholes in all four cardinal directions. A description written in 1676 defines this center as the *viewing point* in the following terms:

> on peut le dire unique et incomparable; de quelque côté qu'on se tourne, les portes de la ville, du château, du parc et de la grande avenue étant ouvertes, on voit à plus d'une grande lieue.[7]

> one may call it unique and incomparable; if the doors of the city, the château, the park and the great avenue are open, one can see for an entire league in every direction.

Thus from this point, one dominates the surrounding space. There, two lanes of honor meet: one, crossing the *avant-corps* and the *avant-cours* of the château, comes from the west, the other, crossing the city, comes from the north. Both of them extend visibly beyond the château toward the east, and across the forest to the south. The new city of Richelieu is therefore also a lane of honor which leads to the château as one arrives from Paris. And thus, in its own way, it performs the function of a gallery. On entry, at the north door, the visitor's gaze crisscrosses it: this is the *œillade* (Boudon, *Richelieu, ville nouvelle*); nothing obstructs this sight, for "dès l'entrée, la rue mène à la sortie" [as soon as one enters, the street leads to the exit]. It leads to the center which is outside the city. The architect Jacques Guillerme could write: "dans le regard qu'on porte sur le plan ou la maquette, le tout est généralement saisi avant la partie, l'édifice, à l'ordinaire, dans l'espace ambulatoire, se montre au contraire dans une continuité de flux d'images diversement détaillées et souvent l'œil se fixe à quelque particularité imprévue avant que de saisir l'ensemble, s'il le saisit jamais" [as one gazes at the blueprint or the clay model, one generally discerns the whole before the part; yet as one walks through it, the building reveals itself in a continuous flow of diversely detailed images, and often the eye fixes itself upon some unforeseen peculiarity before apprehending the whole, if indeed one ever apprehends it] (J. Guillerme, "Le Théâtre

---

7. B. Vignier, *Le Chasteau de Richelieu ou l'histoire des dieux et des héros de l'Antiquité avec des réflexions morales* (Saumur: chez Isaac & Henry Desbordes, 1676).

de la figuration," op cit.). To Richelieu, the plan to make the whole visible at once, to surpass and orient this spontaneity of perception is present in each of the motifs. As no part of the program must escape this process of taking charge of the production of meaning, it was necessary for the space to be saturated with signification and for each of these elements to enter, in one way or another, into a functional relation with that which surrounds it. Thus, the notion of the gallery as an organized space is fundamentally important.

The nodal gallery in this regard is found in the north wing of the castle, on the second floor. It is a gallery of battles composed of two series of ten paintings each. At each end, there is an equestrian portrait: on one side, that of Louis XIII; on the other, that of Richelieu. Each is surrounded by medallions, painted ovals, and scrolls. Under each painting are placed three details, three "overviews," if you will, of the scene represented. Above, corresponding to the exploit of the king's armies, a Roman military exploit somewhat analogous to it. Further above this, in the ovals, a mythological scene taken from Homer.

Each of these units (the painting and the motifs which complete it) is autonomous from the point of view of the production of a political meaning. Nonetheless they belong to a program, to a whole more vast in which they form a series. No space is left empty or is without use. Every element of the gallery-whole is linked to the others by Richelieu's monogram, the cardinal's hat and the ducal coronet which is affixed above each of the windows separating them. All of the signs and images may even be considered as linking the two portraits at the ends of the gallery. They justify the united presence of the portraits—a presence which is only an explicit projection of their implicit association in each of the battle scenes.

Thus, one finds in this room a series of works that from the point of view of signification, are autonomous. Yet each has a functional position in an even greater whole, an indispensable position in the construction of this whole. In its entirety, the gallery produces a discourse on power which only repeats on another scale the discourse of the wholes that constitute it. Hence the attempt to push this logic farther and to proceed to a series of enlargements of scale: taking as one's point of departure the ensemble tableau/motifs/emblems that characterizes the gallery, one must pass to the scale of the château, then to the domain, the duchy, and, why not, the kingdom. In other words, one must construct a political whole whose ideological coherence and functioning would follow the model of the smallest unity.

Both the city and the castle of Richelieu are marked by an element with no positive function: this is the structure of *dédoublement*, the obsessive presence of duality. Evidently it will be said, this doubling reflects the two-headed nature of power and in fact the two public squares of Richelieu were named, spontaneously, it seems, *place Royale* and *place Cardinale*. But what is the meaning of this statement? Is equality claimed? One would have to be Alexandre Dumas in the nineteenth century to have such thoughts. Rather, it is a question of concealing, by exhibiting, through exhibition, the secret of a political process—the very process revealed in the Duke of Epernon's defeat by the Archbishop Sourdis. This concealment works through the power, demonstrated in the very existence of the place, a "feudal" space, a newly created duchy which, paradoxically (does it not come from Richelieu who wanted to struggle, as he said, against "the nobles"?), produces a local remodeling of the space of the state.

But why such a meticulous plan; why such precisely chosen decor: a king's apartment, a cardinal's apartment in which neither one of them ever set foot?[8]

Power needs laboratories in which the coherence of the signs that it circulates are put to the test—that is its weakness: it cannot do without them. In these laboratories the ability of signs to form a system is posited (and is therefore accomplished); in them, the performativity of discourses, their ability to show themselves enacted in a representation, manifests itself. Nothing is certain, nothing is established before the monument is finished and functions, hence the importance of constructions, their progress, and their overseeing, attributed, as was the case at Richelieu, to trustworthy men. The success of the operation helps power to conceive of itself and, in particular, to conceive of itself as a force of action and persuasion in the fiction of a tabula rasa, a blank page, outside of the constraints of a society, outside of the burdens of entangled inheritances.

As Versailles would do later, Richelieu served as security and guaranteed the value of the images in circulation, if I may be permitted this monetary metaphor, of images put into circulation elsewhere, in public ceremonies, and particularly in print. It suffices to know that this place exists in its totality. The guarantee is this totality, even if no one ever sees it, just as no one ever sees the gold stock of the bank of France,

---

8. In fact, Richelieu never returned to his domain after its transformation: the proof, if needed, of the absence of all "consumer" ambition in this architectural ostentation.

a guarantee of coherence for signs which circulate everywhere and whose value is strong. This power is clearly demonstrated by an episode such as the revolt of the Nu-pieds in Rouen in 1639. The Jacobins of the city were the Cardinal of Richelieu's favorites: they placed his coat-of-arms above the entrance of their monastery. Out of fear of rioters and their rash actions, they had this coat-of-arms taken down. The parliament of Rouen devoted two sessions to the question of how to interpret this gesture and Grotius filled a page with meditations on it, addressed to the Swedish chancellor Oxensteirn.

The Jacobin monks of Rouen and the magistrates of the parliament were indeed encumbered by the stone engraved with the cardinal's coat-of-arms. The sign continued to refer to that which it designated, but in its solitariness in the middle of the city in revolt, it lost the power which it had symbolized: the pride of belonging, the manifestation of protection, the postulate of reverence. This sign no longer had its proper efficacity; its dimension of performative assertion had dissolved.[9] The performativity of political signs rests, not on the ostentation of force, but rather on the postulation of the presence of the force elsewhere. This postulation manifests the power of an absence which propels action.

In this sense, it is very different from the spectacle of royal perfection staged, for example, in the great rituals of State. One of these rituals, the solemn entry into a city, thus expressed the stipulations of an exchange within the very frame of absolutist power. Originally, it entailed the ceremonious repetition of a contract, the contract which linked the fidelity of the city with the respect of its privileges. This contractual dimension grew blurred, the ritual itself tended to become petrified as a sumptuous representation of the monarch's power alone. However, the exchange remained: parading into the city, the king discovered the emblems of his royalty which carpeted the streets and the triumphal arches. He saw his city gaze at him and the gaze of his city upon him, materialized by the decor, and the city saw him seeing himself in it. The mystical link between the person and the function thus found its expression. This horseman, this body, this face, were all, in fact, the king; the function resided in the person; but in return the successful exhibition of the person illustrated the function. It was

---

9. François Recanati, *Les Énoncés performatifs. Contribution à la pragmatique* (Paris: Minuit, 1981).

through this prism that the ritual staged and solemnized the pact which united the city to the king and which, having deserted the ritual heart of the ceremony, took refuge, transposed and euphemized—and thus watered-down—in the spectacles offered to the king in marginal moments: the ritual, emptied of its content, retained the strange power of ritualizing its peripheries. The moments which preceded or followed the ceremony, as soon as the king was present, were thus invested with an intensity of signification which did not exist before. At that time citizens were honored and conflicts were brought before the king. And printed narratives, ever more numerous, embraced with a single gaze both the ceremony itself and the moments which surrounded it.

The spectacular staging of the efficacious absence (the other face of power) can be created from the same ceremonial and decorative material. On 20 November 1632, Queen Anne of Austria made a solemn entrance into La Rochelle, four years after the siege and defeat of this Protestant city by the armies of the king. The cardinal of Richelieu meticulously organized this celebration, but he was not there, having fallen ill on the return road from Languedoc, where the revolt of Montmorency had just been crushed and the duke executed. As always in such a case, the city had been decorated and an entire program of festivities had been planned. The surprise lay in the central theme: the defeat of the city in 1628. On the triumphal arches could be seen grotesque representations of the famine caused by the siege which killed thousands. There were also diversions that replayed the battle of the siege and terrified spectators. They therefore accepted to play their role of vanquished with extreme good will; they commemorated their defeat by adhering to the image of themselves that the conquerors had spread everywhere. They assumed responsibility for the discourse of power upon themselves, and, in order to demonstrate their submission, pronounced it to the world and to the queen. That which power ordained was thus shown to be totally fulfilled; with no crack left through which a ferment of contestation, or, more simply, the manifestation of a remainder of reserve, could slip by. In the printed material which recounts the story of this entrance and describes it at length, the inhabitants of La Rochelle used the discourse of power upon themselves: they transformed it into a performative utterance.[10] The im-

10. Christian Jouhaud, "Imprimer l'événement: La Rochelle à Paris," in R. Chartier, ed., *Les Usages de l'imprimé* (Paris: Fayard 1987), 381–438. English translation: *The Culture of Print. Power and the Uses of Print in Early Modern Europe* (Oxford and Cambridge: Polity Press, 1989), 290–334.

position of belief is shown as already believed, through acts, by those very people whom one must make believe, as they play the role of the complacent vanquished.

The control of this process, the possibility of conceiving it and of realizing it, are debated in areas which might seem far removed from the concrete conditions of the exercise of domination. Literary theory is one of these areas. At stake in the debates which began to arise around the issue of the respect of theatrical rules were the effects of representation, of their control and therefore of their anticipation and reproduction. It is at the time of the Quarrel of *Le Cid* that Richelieu's interest in the matter appears most strikingly. He followed the affair very closely and reread line by line the text of the French Academy (which was supposed to settle the debate once and for all), requiring a number of changes and revisions. Jean Chapelain was the principal author of these *Sentiments de l'Académie française sur le Cid*. Today we possess several versions of this document which correspond to different stages of the elaboration of the text.[11] The differences between the initial and the final versions, published in 1638, are significant. We know that they are the result of Richelieu's specific demands. We may therefore believe that a comparison of these versions will bring to light the true mark of power.

In the first version, the author (allegedly collective) places himself in the position of judge, but of a judge of a civil trial in which two parties clash, and where justice could identify itself absolutely with either side. Given this situation, the author turns to one and then the other of the parties, regarding them with the same benevolence. The adversaries of *Le Cid* are asked to bear with his faults with indulgence; his unconditional supporters, to admit that Aristotle has more authority than they do and especially that there exist two kinds of pleasure, "l'un parfait qui se produit par les choses parfaites, l'autre imparfait qui est engendré par la nouveauté des choses plutôt que par leur beauté" [one, perfect, which is produced by perfect things, the other, imperfect, which is engendered by the novelty of things rather than by their beauty]. Theater has as its goal and its raison d'être this perfect pleasure alone. The disciples of pleasure at any price risk "[de] ressembler à la populace qui court aux prodiges et qui estime indigne de sa curiosité

---

11. C. Searles, "Les Sentiments de l'Académie française sur le Cid," *The University of Minnesota Studies in Language and Literature*, (March): 1916.

ce qu'il y a de mieux ordonné dans les ouvrages de la nature ou de l'art et qui, satisfaite de son ignorance, se fâche lorsqu'on la veut désabuser" [resembling the populace who runs after prodigies, who considers unworthy of its curiosity that which is most well-ordered in the works of nature or of art, and who, complacent in its ignorance, becomes angry when another would disabuse it].

The posture of the judge-arbitrator is a fiction, a staging of the promise kept, for, in reality, the pan of the balance clearly tips in favor of one side. This scenography of equitable judgment is endowed, like all fiction, with a particular efficacity. It makes of the two "parties" two respectable groups defending antagonistic positions with equal legitimacy: it presents the quarrel as a public debate of a literary matter. But behind this staging, Chapelain defends a position expressed by the distinction of two pleasures. Imperfect pleasure, qualified as popular, finds itself again on the side of illegitimacy, while perfect pleasure is perfect because it conforms to reason, which nothing expresses better than theatrical rules and their inventor Aristotle. Hence perfect pleasure finds itself on the side of utility, a notion presented in the fiction of the two parties as the antagonist of that of pleasure, and thus is identified with the camp of *Le Cid's* adversaries, for the claim to pleasure made possible the construction of the camp of Corneille's supporters.

In the definitive version of the *Sentiments,* the posture of enunciation has changed: it is no longer a question of trials, parties, or arbitration. Nor is it any longer a question of debate. The appearance of a third actor between the protagonists, the "people," orients the movement of the argumentation differently. The question of the reception of *Le Cid,* and its effects on the spectators, will henceforth be foregrounded. It is no longer a matter of arbitrating a public debate, but rather of explaining to the spectators why they liked the play. "Leur esprit, flatté par quelques endroits agréables, est devenu aisément flatteur de tout le reste" [Their minds, seduced by a few agreeable moments, easily became a flatterer of all the rest]. How? "Les passions violentes bien exprimées font souvent en ceux qui les voient une partie de l'effet qu'elles font en ceux qui les ressentent véritablement. Elles ôtent à tous la liberté de l'esprit, et font que les uns se plaisent à voir représenter les fautes que les autres se plaisent à commettre. Ce sont ces puissants mouvements qui ont tiré des spectateurs du Cid cette grande approbation et qui doivent aussi la faire excuser" [Well-expressed violent passions often create in those who see them a part of the effect that they create in those who truly feel them. They deprive everyone of freedom of thought, the result being that some men are pleased to see portrayed before them the faults that others are pleased to commit. It is these powerful movements which extracted such great approbation from the spectators of *Le Cid* and which must also cause it to be excused]. Excused: there is the key word. It is a question of excusing *Le Cid* because of its success, a fact which in no way legitimatizes the position of those who defend the play. The spectators were the victims of too sweet an illusion (victims of their pleasure). It is therefore necessary to call them back to reason. The Academy does not ask "qu'ils prononcent en public contre eux-mêmes; il lui suffit qu'ils se condamnent en particulier, et qu'ils se rendent en secret à leur propre raison; cette même raison leur dira ce que nous leur disons si tôt qu'elle pourra reprendre sa première liberté . . ." [that they testify publicly against themselves; it would suffice for them to condemn themselves privately, and to surrender themselves secretly to their own reason; this very same reason will tell them exactly what we are telling them, as soon as it can reclaim its own freedom . . .]. We have passed from the fiction of a judgment to this address to each of the readers, identified with each of the spectators of the play. The intimate disavowal of an initial enthusiasm—a disavowal which is demanded of them—will remain secret because the Academy asks for no public recognition. But we know that in reality there is no other stake in this text than publicly to recognize the new institution as the authority of legitimization, its authority extending, thanks to the operation produced by this text, to the secret of private reasoning opposed to the continued illusion of public defiance. The effect of writing places the text, exposed by its reader, in direct concurrence with the effects of *Le Cid*, but in another sphere. The distinction between two pleasures has itself completely disappeared.

We might tend to think at first that the second version, brought into focus and clarified by Chapelain after the finicky interventions of Richelieu, is, precisely because of these interventions, further removed from the real thoughts of its author.[12] Nothing is less certain. If we admit that the equilibrium ostentatiously advanced in the first

12. See, for example, the introduction of J. Hunter in his edition of the *Sentiments* in J. Chapelain, *Opuscules critiques*, J. Hunter ed. (Paris, 1936).

version had no other goal than that of its own staging, since in the end a stance against the partisans of *Le Cid* found itself expressed there, we can then say that this position is more clearly and more radically expressed in the second version and we may therefore believe that the intervention of power permitted Chapelain to express his own position more clearly. However, it is necessary to ask oneself, as counterverification, if the renunciation of the scenography of an equitable judgment between two parties did not consequently entail a loss for Chapelain.

In his letters throughout the preceding months, this author had abundantly expressed his fear of making himself odious in the eyes of the two parties by intervening under orders in the quarrel. His fear was a fear of neutralization, a fear of diverting onto himself the aggressiveness of the struggling adversaries. The scenography of arbitration can be thought of, in this framework, as a means of holding that aggressiveness at a distance. Now by his insistence on modifications, Richelieu had forced the Academy, and therefore Chapelain, to write openly, to risk a sort of gesture of force in the polemicotheoretical space of the man of letters, in a word, to impose himself. In this way, Richelieu pushed Chapelain all the nearer to the danger of neutralization, but at the same time he protected him from it by imposing an end to the polemics. Chapelain and the Academy finally benefited from their submission to the requirements of power. This case demonstrates how a sort of association between power and literature is erected.

Like all associations, this one is founded on an exchange.[13] Power intervenes in order to support, promote, condemn, or mobilize men and works. Writers who accept to serve it reap numerous benefits from it and accede to the function of classifying others. This aspect of the exchange is relatively well known. It is necessary to add to it the practices of writing. Writing in the sphere of power implies and supposes specific forms of service which are not limited to support by the pen or to fidelity. The ways of participating in politics are directly inspired by scriptuary strategies. This is exactly what Corneille expressed in his own way—allegorically—in the dedicatory epistle of *Horace* addressed to Richelieu: "lisant sur son visage (de Votre Eminence) ce qui lui plaît et ce qui ne lui plaît pas, nous nous intruisons

13. I developed this analysis in my paper "Pouvoir politique et littérature: les termes de l'échange (1624–1642)," given at the Davis Center, Princeton University, 13 April 1990.

avec certitude de ce qui est bon, et de ce qui est mauvais et tirons des règles infaillibles de ce qu'il faut faire et de ce qu'il faut éviter" [reading on his visage (of Your Eminence) that which pleases him and that which does not please him, we instruct ourselves with certainty on that which is good, and on that which is bad, and extract infallible rules for what we must do and what we must avoid].[14] This energy captured from power by the dramatic author or the critic is returned to it by works or by interpretations of works given freely to speculations of the politician, in a game of mirrors which it will perhaps *please* the minister to practice in the intimacy of private performances (circumstances which were very different from the ostentatious performances of court parties, such as the one at which *Mirame* was given in 1641).[15]

Chapelain thus theorizes the effects of the theatrical representation and the means of reproducing them ("mieux surprendre l'imagination du spectateur et le conduire sans obstacle à la créance que l'on veut qu'il prenne en ce qui lui est représenté . . . ôter aux regardants toutes les occasions de faire réflexion sur ce qu'ils voient et de douter de sa réalité" [the better to surprise the imagination of the spectator and to lead him without obstacle to the belief that one wants him to accept in that which is represented to him . . . to take away from the onlookers any opportunity to reflect on what they see and to question its reality].[16] In this way, he constructs a theory of persuasion and of the instigation of belief. Moreover, the reflection he proposes on the "marvel," that delectable surprise which must be caused by an implacable respect for verisimilitude (that is, from that which seems to rule out all possibility of surprise), and the definition that he gives of it (the criterion for perfection in theater), can be read at the same time as an inoffensive gloss on Aristotle and as an available model for conceiving of the *"coup d'état"* of the man of power. This same *coup d'état* was theorized at almost exactly the same time, just before his own entrance into the service of cardinal Richelieu, by Gabriel Naudé, in his scan-

14. Louis Marin. "Théâtralité et politique au XVIIe siècle: sur trois textes de Corneille," in Jean Serroy, ed. *La France et l'Italie au temps de Mazarin* (Grenoble: Presses universitaires de Grenoble, 1986), 399–407.

15. Timothy Murray, "Richelieu's Theater: the Mirror of a Prince," *Renaissance Drama* 8 (1977): 275–98 and the same author's *Theatrical Legitimation. Allegories of Genius in Seventeenth-Century England and France* (New York: Oxford University Press, 1987).

16. J. Chapelain, "Lettres sur la règle des vingt-quatre heures," op. cit., note 12, 113–26.

dalous *Considérations politiques sur les coups d'état* (of which only twelve copies were printed).[17]

On 3 February 1627, Richelieu delivered a speech before a delegation of magistrates from the Paris parliament. He ended with the following remarks; "il est à désirer que les mouvements des parlements soient semblables et uniformes à ceux du roi et de son conseil. Vous direz peut-être Messieurs que si vous saviez les motifs et la raison des conseils du roi, assurément vous les suivriez. Mais à cela j'ai à répondre que le maître du vaisseau ne rend point de raison de la façon avec laquelle il le conduit; qu'il y a des affaires dont le succès ne dépend que du secret, et beaucoup de moyens propres à une fin ne le sont plus lorsqu'ils sont divulgués . . ." [it is desirable for the movements of parliaments to be similar to and uniform with those of the king and of his counsel. You will perhaps say, Sirs, that if you knew the motives and the reasoning behind the councils of the king, you would assuredly follow them. But to that I must reply that the captain of the ship gives no reasons for the manner in which he sails it; that there are matters whose success depends only on secrecy, and many methods proper to one end are no longer useful once they are divulged . . .].[18] Many paths lead to the same end, some are good, that is to say, effective, others are not. And this is conceived in terms of movement, of displacement, and of dynamics which is underscored by the maritime metaphor. A science of circumstances which requires the secrecy and solitude of power. In response to those who demand the clarity and stability of choices, the participation of each of the organs of the political body in this transparency, here is a science of action which is enunciated in order to steal away, which invokes its rules in order the better to dissimulate its principles.

The downfall of the idea of Christendom, which had become evident since the bloody divisions of the wars of religion, provoked the sudden appearance of new forms of political rationality. In the reference to a City of God as model and ultimate guarantor of all legitimate political action, certain practices were attributed to a truth situated outside of history. Henceforth, it became necessary to find a motive for

17. Gabriel Naudé, *Considérations politiques sur les coups d'Etat*, preceded by Louis Marin, "Pour une théorie baroque de l'action politique" (Paris: Les Editions de Paris, 1989).

18. Published by Gabriel Hanotaux, *Maximes et papiers d'Etat du Cardinal de Richelieu* (Paris: 1880).

those practices that can replace the superannuated guarantee. This does not signify a pure and simple rupture between politics and theology: institutions continue to maintain the link in this time of loss of "the absolute object," to use Michel de Certeau's expression.[19] It is one of the probable stakes of the institutional position of great political actors within the Church. One thinks, for example, of Father Joseph, an eminent Capuchin friar, a cardinal, but also a mystic, principal collaborator of Richelieu and founder of a religious order, the Calvarians. Whatever his political duties, he devotes long hours to the direction of his female ordinates. He was the director and the "founder" of a place for the "seduction of God." This institution is evidence of a conjunction that replaced the clarity of a Christian society. An ultimate truth continued to be postulated, but, opaque, it needed places where it could vouch for itself by certain practices, where the lost guarantor, the ultimate reference of political action, continued to speak. This *separate* place was therefore the mark of a conception of politics that was still theological yet at the same time autonomous. But this equilibrium was fragile. To threaten it, it was sufficient for the institution (the guaranteeing machine) to find itself put into question in the very name of the truth which inhabited it. This threat took shape in the debates and the actions which were commonly characterized by a return to the source of the engagement on the part of those who dwelt in these institutions: let us call them the spirituals. "Jansenists" and "saintly" Jesuits, visionaries, denounced, in the name of an identity, a conformism, a loss of meaning. They sought an internal renewal to restore meaning to their own practices. In this way, they could reach positions beyond the political order. The danger of subversion which they represented depended first on the position which they occupied, institutionally and socially. The first "Jansenists," so clearly linked to the world of offices, up to and including the byways of power, would thus be immediately dangerous.

It was vital to the entire system that scruples about conscience not spread to the level of agents and executants. Soon compromises would be found.[20] In the meantime, the cardinal and his entourage carried the weight of the sin of the violence of the State. They relieved the king and

19. Michel de Certeau, *L'Écriture de l'histoire* (Paris: Gallimard 1975), in particular, chapter 4, "La Formalité des pratiques, du système religieux à l'éthique des Lumières", 152–212.

20. Michel de Certeau, "Politique et mystique. René d'Argenson (1596–1651)", *Revue d'ascétique et de mystique* 39, (1963): 45–82.

his servants of this sin, but they could only assume it by confiscating the living source of the theological guarantee. Alive, because it has been put to the test of daily action, which is very different from the theological founding of the divine right of kings. The simple bodies of the cardinal and of Father Joseph were the mistreated witnesses of the struggle and sacrifice.[21] This would later provide material for mockery and vengeance to Guez de Balzac, who could sneer at the ministers with "trop de ce qui élève et qui remue" [too much that elevates and agitates them], who dictate dispatches while dining and sleep with their eyes open: "je vous ferai dire," [I will have it told to you,] he writes in a transparent portrait of Father Joseph, "par un de ses domestiques qui vit encore, et qui couchait d'ordinaire dans sa chambre que de ses yeux ouverts, il sortait des rayons si affreux que souvent il en eut peur et il ne s'y accoutuma jamais bien" [by one of his servants who is still alive, and who ordinarily slept in his room, that from his open eyes, such awful rays of light came out that often he was afraid and never became accustomed to it].[22]

On 3 February 1627, the cardinal began his speech by evoking the *Tractatus de haeresi schismate apostasia* of the Roman Jesuit Santarelli, (which was, by the way, the cause for the convocation of the delegation of parliament). Because of its "mean and abominable" propositions, this book merited burning, he recalled, before adding: "on a estimé qu'il fallait parvenir à cette fin par une voie innocente et non telle qu'elle mît la personne du roi en plus grand péril que celui qu'on veut éviter. Vous savez Messieurs, qu'il y a beaucoup d'esprits mélancoliques, à qui il importe grandement d'ôter tout sujet de penser que le roi est mal avec Sa Sainteté . . . parce que l'excès et l'ignorance de leur zèle les fait quelquefois tomber en des passions d'autant plus dangereuses que leur frénésie les leur représente saintes" [it is necessary to do this innocently, and not in any way that might place the person of the king in greater peril than the one we wish to avoid. You know, Sirs, that there are many melancholy minds, and it is of the utmost importance that we rid them of all thoughts that the king is at odds with His Holiness . . . for the excess and ignorance of their zeal sometimes

---

21. The simple body of the minister as contrasted with the "King's two bodies" analyzed in the famous work of Kantorowicz (*The King's Two Bodies* [Princeton: Princeton University Press, 1957]) and greatly clarified and utilized by his students and followers. They in turn, have analyzed the ceremonies of the French monarchy. See also Alain Boureau, *Le Simple corps du roi* (Paris: Editions de Paris 1988).

22. J.-L. Guez de Balzac, *Aristippe ou de la cour* (Paris: 1658), 95.

makes them fall into passions all the more dangerous as their madness represents them as saintly]. Beyond the immediate context of the "peril" which would threaten the person of the king (Santarelli's book took up the famous theses of Bellarmine on the indirect power of popes on kings, that is to say, on the right of popes to release subjects from their fidelity to their monarch, a particularly sensitive question in France because these theses had served to justify tyrannicide and thus to arm the assassins of Henri III and Henri IV), the most striking element of this quotation is, of course, the manner in which the unnamed adversary is described: melancholy minds, fallen prey to the theater of passions. Passions which their madness represents to them as saintly. Who, other than zealous Catholics, the pious ultramontanes, could be designated in this way? In the excess and ignorance of their zeal they do not see what is at stake because, blinded by their passions, they vegetate in a world of illusion, of the irrational. How can one not notice as well that in the narratives of the final scene of the "day of dupes" which permitted Richelieu in November 1630 to rid himself of the pious opposition, the queen will be represented as abandoning herself to a crisis of anti-Richelieu madness, as if she wanted to illustrate the label of madness pinned on her supporters more than three years before by the cardinal.

The parliament of Paris immediately condemned Santarelli and summoned the Jesuits so that they might sign, in turn, a written condemnation of the work, not only of their Roman colleague, but also of the ideas of Bellarmine. Richelieu intervened in order to propose to the parliament a weakened form of the condemnation, which though explicit regarding Santarelli, was less hard on the French Jesuits, (who were led by Father Coton, the former confessor of Henry IV). The Jesuits signed.

The Sorbonne, with its theological Faculty, intervened in turn with a virulent condemnation of the book that gave it the opportunity to recall the extremist position of the Gallicans. The censure was published by the *Mercure françois*, which was controlled by those in power.

The general assembly of the clergy, meeting in Paris at the same time, debated the issue as well. It was divided between the moderate ultramontanes and the radical Gallicans. The parliament sided with the Gallican extremists and took advantage of the opportunity to condemn another work written by a Jesuit, *La Somme théologique* of Father Garasse. A generalized confrontation between the ultramontanes and the Gallicans seemed about to take place. At which point Richelieu intervened.

An intermediary between all involved parties was named, the master of "the French school of spirituality," Pierre de Bérulle. The king then raised the matter with his counselors, dismissed the parliament, forbade the Sorbonne to debate upon the issue any longer, and revoked its censure. He announced the formation of an ad hoc committee which, in fact, never met. All things considered, power placed itself as arbitrator between two "extreme" positions. The assembly of the clergy appeared to be profoundly divided. The action of Roman Jesuits succeeded only in weakening their French colleagues, who were threatened with expulsion from the kingdom by the parliament (following a precedent in 1594), but were finally saved by Richelieu, whose *Mémoires* note (V, 245): "il fallait réduire les jésuites en un état qu'ils ne puissent nuire par puissance mais tel aussi qu'ils ne se portassent pas à le faire par désespoir" [it was necessary to reduce the Jesuits to a condition from which they could neither do harm by force, nor through despair].

The cardinal began by allowing them actions and, perhaps, encouraging the most violent reactions against the Roman Jesuits and the papacy. He allowed into the arena hostile forces whose entry onto the scene itself instigated certain reactions and—*then*—he put himself in the position of peacemaker. He kept to the course of his politics and, at the same time, promoted mutual weakening of the two most powerful schools of thought of the preceding decades. All of which calls to mind La Fontaine's fable, *Le Chat, la belette et le petit lapin:* one can always play several forces against each other and, in this game, obtain their reciprocal neutralization.[23] Power could take neither the side of the Gallicans, nor that of the ultramontanes, both of whom presented a manifest danger in the radicalness of their reasoning. The novelty consisted of Richelieu's ability to utilize this antagonism to his own benefit. This does not mean, however, that he was really neutral toward the great debates of the times: he observed them from another point of view, that of a science of action.

On the death of Richelieu, the system of domination which he had put into place came undone. With the death of the king, it foundered completely. The unfettered absolutism of Louis XIV would have little

23. Louis Marin, *Le Récit est un piège* (Paris: Minuit 1978).

in common with the science of diversion so brilliantly practiced by the cardinal. Moreover, the intrinsic force of a two-faced system of government would be forgotten, first of all because, beginning in 1643, there was a child on the throne. The politics, the person of Richelieu, and his power to act would remain the models to which more or less all of the great political actors would refer, beginning with the great *Frondeurs*. However, the characteristically systematic dimension of the cardinal's position would escape all of these great actors. The two-headed nature of power would appear to them to be a bother and a danger. They would no longer calculate the extent to which Richelieu was protecting the sanctuary of naked legitimate violence—that sanctuary which would later seem a merely ornamental dissimulation. Theology and science of action: these two contradictory dynamics created the tension with which Richelieu moderated the violence of the State and turned Richelieu himself into the place where this tension became a political dynamic.

Translated by Suzanne Toczyski

OREST RANUM

Encrustation and Power in Early Modern French Baroque Culture

Baroque places? The three quite distinct historical meanings of the first word, and the three meanings of the second, may be thought of as possibilities for conceptual reinvention, a playfulness with words and an enhanced historical understanding. The word Baroque has quite recently fallen from being a concept into being merely a label for certain stylistic features, and a chronological moment that varies (particularly in music) in European culture. The history of attempts to rescue concepts that have lost their analytical force is yet to be written, though the volumes edited by O. Brunner, W. Conze, and R. Koselleck on *Begriffgeschichte* are a beginning.[1] The meanings of the word Baroque in text books and on the backs of record folders ought not to be disparaged; in historical discourse these serve well as short-hand signs to focus a debate, if not to advance or deepen understanding.

At this point the tiniest nominalist flinch is capable of destroying the possibility for conceptual reinvention. That dreaded English philosophical *quod libet* posing as mere common sense—"if you don't know what a word means, don't use it"—must explicitly be brought to mind in order that it may be rejected. A portent may inspire confidence. Philip Johnson's broken pediment on the new AT&T Building in New York gives this historian the feeling that there is a new cultural

I should like to thank my colleagues Nancy S. Struever and Gérard Defaux for their help.

1. O. Brunner, W. Conze, R. Koselleck, ed. *Geschichtliche Grundbegriff. Historische Lexikon zur Politisch-Sozialer Sprache in Deutschland* (Stuttgart: Eiklett, 1972), 5 volumes. See Melvin Richter, "Begriffgeschichte and the History of Ideas," *Journal of the History of Ideas* 48 (April, 1987): 1–17.

YFS 80, *Baroque Topographies*, ed. Timothy Hampton, © 1991 by Yale University.

moment coming along, and that this work might be a part of it.[2] Some critics have dismissed Johnson's work as a joke. For a historian of culture, thanks to Johann Huizinga, nothing can be more revealing about human mental furniture than toys and play. But to write about Baroque places in twentieth-century culture is not the assignment.

Options carefully chosen from the beginning can help to recover new meanings from the dialectical thickets of nineteenth-century Germanic thought. Reading French culture through German eyes has been the great adventure in French studies since World War II. The indispensable point of departure was Daniel Halévy's *Nietzsche*. After Nietzsche, Marx, Freud, and Heidegger, the time has come to try to recover something from Heinrich Wolfflin's Baroque.

After being semantically restricted, in the sixteenth and seventeenth centuries, to describing imperfect or bizarre natural objects such as peculiarly shaped or colored pearls, the word baroque became an epithet (not unlike gothic) for what was distorted, repulsive, and disconcerting in classical inspired works of architecture and art. Wolfflin invented the third semantic field for the word by making it into a concept just one hundred years ago, when he discerned a quite autonomous mood or spirit in the Baroque works of art that was, he posited, in dialectical opposition to the classical.

Thanks to Wolfflin's work, the Baroque generally ceased to be thought of as merely the classical gone awry. As we have it now, the Baroque alone, with or without places, is a *concept boîteux*, without the possibilities for reinvention by dialectic. This historian is left only to make inventories of "imperfect" physical objects and to discern a mood, or *Geist* that certainly is more not-conscious and routine than unconscious.[3] Without help from places, in some additional modifying, nondialectical sense, the results might be just *pastiche* of nine-

2. Historians are playfully wont to pick out an aspect of their subject for research in their own culture. "I am reminded of that matchless cartoon in the *New Yorker* showing the tracks of a skier, one track on each side of a trunk, with the skier unconcernedly going on. That is baroque." Carl J. Friedrich, *The Age of the Baroque* (New York: Harper and Row, 1952), 44 n. 9. The Baroque place lies somewhere between Jean Céard's *La Nature et les Prodiges* (Paris: 1977) and the *Néant*, or as J. Burckhardt put it, à propos of Rubens's *Fall of the Damned into Hell;* "But the incredible spatiality is brought out by a powerful light falling from the sky on to every ghastly group. If we survey the art and poetry of all times for a comparable imaginative power, we shall most probably recognize it in its exact opposite, namely in a horrible description of non-space." *Recollections of Rubens* trans. M. Hottinger (London: Phaidon, 1970), 77.

3. For the cultural history of memory, see Maurice Halbwachs, *The Collective Memory*, trans. Francis J. Ditter (New York: Harper and Row, 1980); Krzysztof Pomian, *Collec-*

Figure 1. Claude Mellan: *La Sainte Face.*

teenth-century cultural history, something that certainly ought not to be disparaged, but this historian lacks the erudition to write *pastiche*.

Places? The geophysical meaning, that is, the physical space of a place, jumbles immediately in our minds with the metaphorical meanings. This jumble of meanings might be thought of as a living artifact of language from ancient and early modern centuries. If the meaning of place in this essay were restricted to only the geophysical, the results would be a distortion, or an exaggeration, an over-emphasis on some aspects at the expense of others in a semantically recognized whole. A precise emphasis on the seventeenth-century meaning of the word baroque, and on places, may enhance the possibility of writing Baroque history.

The reason why this historian is willing to try to restore analytical force to the Baroque is that nominalist argumentation has destroyed almost all the concepts that can be found to enhance understanding in his field of research. Only the civic criticism of Absolutism, and the anticivic, Absolutism, survive in his field to interpret a rich, variegated, and playful culture. The poverty of conceptual analysis inevitably leads to pedantry and reductionism in studies of seventeenth-century France. Only a true skeptic, with quite special personality features, can live his whole scholarly life in tranquility by aggressively constructing meanings through saying what something does not mean.

Precious stones, crystals, mirrors, shells, city squares, grottoes, *reposoirs*, islands, eyes, androgynous and hermaphrodite bodies, monsters, execution sites, funerary *chapelles ardentes*, come readily to mind as Baroque sites. The physicality of each of these is different, and so they prompted different reflections and physical responses in their beholders. To ponder, to reflect on, or to wonder about, and to almost worship the ugly, strange, misshapen, geometrical, bizarre and even *néant* aspects of certain objects and places, was somewhat akin to a forbidden game in the early-modern centuries. In whatever archaeological dig, inventory of property, letter or memoir we pick up, there is evidence for a mental routine prompted by certain objects and places.

---

tionneurs, amateurs et curieux, Paris, Venice: XVIe–XVIIIe siècle (Paris: Gallimard, 1987); and Pierre Nora, *Lieux de Mémoire,* (Paris: 1984–1986), vols. 1–2. On the history of routine, Fernand Braudel, *Capitalism and Material Life, 1400–1800,* trans. Miriam Kochan (New York: Harper and Row, 1967).

The emotions might differ, and reflections might be moral or immoral, but each Baroque place, in its own predictable and novel way, both prompted and satisfied yearnings to be in the presence of some *thing* that left one filled with a sense of awe and a need to reflect upon its quality.

A single object such as a geometrically shaped pool, a crystal with its facets "carved" by nature, a mirror, a grotto of shell-covered walls, a public execution, the Place Royale or the funeral bier of the Grand Condé, might release a range of emotions in the beholder. Beautiful despite its oddity (for example, the dark, funereal paintings of exotic and imaginary plants), or geometrical although it had never been carved by human hands, or simply an emptiness framed by mirrors and natural objects such as polished tortoise shells or mother of pearl, the Baroque place brought tears to the eyes, chills, fevers, sexual arousal, lethargy, slow heart beat, rapid heart beat, dizziness, or sweating. As emotions welled up and the body responded to the place, the beholder had to choose whether to stay before it or in it, or to withdraw in order to calm down.

There is only minor value in attempting to interpret so rich and varied a phenomenon as the Baroque place as either religious, political, psychological, learned, or popular. While it is true that Furetière defines the *ineffable* as that speechlessness that comes only before the religious, his definition of the semantic field of effable, and its opposite ineffable, is restrictive: the words are used only to describe religious subjects, that is, the mysteries of the faith. How should this restrictive definition be interpreted? The matter-of-fact, or literal way would be to conclude that no one in the late seventeenth century ever spoke of the effable or the ineffable *except* about religious matters, the latter presumably being the institutionalized expression of the religious in the Roman church. Still, the usages of such emotionally charged words as awe, wonder, marvel, and ineffable cannot be strung out like an electrical circuit wired in series, with ineffable being the one that turns on all the lights. Instead, the restrictive usage ought to be interpreted as a clue to the fragility of a semantic field, and a fillip to explore meanings of words that convey intense emotional experiences outside the religious, as essentially the same as the religious. The bodily responses of early moderns to Baroque places, and their records of these responses, indicate that the dictionary usage was not respected. Indeed, like the religious experience of speechlessness before the divine, the Baroque place and the experience it prompted, unleashed torrents of words, provoked by the need to leave something of oneself before or in that place.

The Baroque place was never an entirely "natural" site in the seventeenth century; instead, the man-made grotto with rusticated stones and shell-encrusted walls that created the illusion of boundlessness between what is naturally human and what is simply natural, fascinated early moderns. Where nature seemed to be in mutation, unsure of itself, or very sure of itself (the geometrically shaped object such as a crystal), a sense of wonder and a welling up of feelings might come over the beholder. There could be feelings of disgust or repugnance, which might go hand in hand with a taunting attraction, an emotional satisfaction, a depression, an uplifting or a near ecstasy. All these feelings were most articulately and creatively expressed by the artistic and literary elite of the period, but there is no reason to assert that persons with more routine powers of self-scrutiny and bodily expression were insensitive to Baroque places. Chantelou noted that while he was looking at some shells with Bernini, "he showed us how spiral staircases, or 'snail stairs' as they are called in Italy, and twisted columns were based on some of the shells that he showed us. He said that he admired the infinite variety of nature, who expresses herself in these trifles, with as much power as in her larger creations."[4] That a seventeenth-century artist with enormous talent for teaching and self-promotion should think of creativity, divine creativity, while admiring a shell, is not surprising; but the almost religious sensibility expressed here by the word "admire" also suggests that being in the presence of the shells prompted and then satisfied some ill-defined, but felt, ontological *trouble*.

To assert that certain objects and places had special powers would be true, but it would oversimplify at just the point where early modern culture was complex. The characteristic that especially defined the Baroque place, the tracer to it, as it were, was the encrustation or layering and framing of the place by the beholder. Possibly as a result of centuries of religious education (or is the impulse to exchange primordial?), the beholder who experienced speechlessness, emotional upset, or bodily excitement wished to give something of himself in return. In institutionalized religious practice, this exchange between a place that

---

4. Paul Fréart de Chantelou, *Diary of the Cavaliere Bernini's Visit to France* ed. Anthony Blunt, trans. M. Corbett (Princeton: Princeton University Press, 1985) 299. ". . . for nature itself is devoid of both strength and beauty . . ." 166. Hereafter cited in text.

has given an emotional experience, and the beholder who has received it, had long since become quite routinized into donations for masses or the purchase of candles and indulgences, etc. For the Baroque place the token that was left also had to have something physical about it. The grotto had to have an environment of darkness, coolness, relative inaccessibility, damp atmospheric conditions, and perhaps some trees, all given to it by the humans who created it. Since the grotto was encrusted with special natural objects, the wonder felt by the beholder eventually extended from the grotto to its environment and, in the eighteenth century, altered the meaning of nature. It may be useful to glance at an important Europewide attraction, the rough-stone *santa casa* at Notre Dame of Loreto, in remote Ancona.

Barely 28 by 12½ by 13 feet, this single story dwelling had been the place where Saint Anne gave birth to the Virgin Mary. Borne by angels from Nazareth to Dalmatia, then on to Recanati, and finally to the place where it is now located, the *santa casa* became encrusted with tens of thousands of objects and was eventually encased in a veritable jewel box of architecture, sculpture, painting, metal work, and glass. The list of major artistic commissions for Loreto is too long to give here, but each was, in its own way, a testimony, a witness to the satisfaction felt at being in a place where the Virgin and her mother had been.

By the time Michel de Montaigne visited the *santa casa* in 1581, the medieval monument had nearly been submerged by more recent construction, an encrustation by contemporaries that he scarcely notes. What he deemed of importance to record was that at Loreto he had spent fifty sound *écus* on devotional objects, and he offers a brief description of the "brick" house which is the "place of the principal religion."[sic] Commenting that there was scarcely a space on the walls that was not covered with a plaque of gold or silver, he notes that after much *faveur* he acquired a preferential spot for the silver *tableau* that he had had made and affixed to the wall. It showed the Virgin and Montaigne, his wife and his daughter, "with Our Lady being higher and forward, and the others on their knees before Her."[5] The individual names, Montaigne's title, and the fact that his daughter was an only daughter were also engraved on the plaque. Montaigne says nothing about making a vow or special invocation to the Virgin at Loreto. Had

5. Michel de Montaigne, *Journal de Voyage en Italie en 1580 et 1581* ed. Maurice Rat (Paris: Garnier frères, 1942), 141. See for comparison, Louis Richeome, *Le Pèlerin de Lorete* (Bordeaux: S. Millangre, 1704). Hereafter cited in text.

he affixed such a plaque on the walls of some church in the Bordelais, the gesture might be interpreted as merely social. In far-off Ancona, and surrounded by thousands of other plaques and monuments offered by pilgrims from all over Europe, it is doubtful that this was an expression of status enhancement. Montaigne's travels were an exploration of religious feelings and beliefs in 1580–81: in Protestant areas he sought to talk with pastors and theologians; in Catholic ones he expressed more interest in devotional practices than in doctrine. In thinking of the concept "place" without the modifier Baroque, it is tempting to suggest that language occupied a physical space in Protestant culture that it did not in Catholic culture, and that the *santa casa* might have all the characteristics of a forbidden place for the Protestant, among them, perhaps, Montaigne's own Huguenot brother.

The *santa casa* was not like other late Medieval pilgrimage sites. There were no relics in the usual sense of the term, but only the place where the Virgin had been born—a place now empty. There were no dogmatic claims that she continued to be present there, though some pilgrims testified to feeling closer to her at Loreto than in their own homes. Montaigne's satisfaction at having a plaque affixed on the walls at Loreto testifies to the *néant* of the place. Would early modern fideists, agnostics, skeptics, and philologists have special affinities for objects and places in which feelings of being in a state of speechlessness might come in to play? Throwing coins in museum fountains today cannot be understood other than as, in some sense, a survival of the Baroque place that prompted feelings of reciprocity arising from feelings of wonderment.

In 1584 Henry III sent to Loreto a cup cut from an azure-colored sapphire of great size and value, covered with a rock-crystal lid bearing a solid gold angel carrying a diamond fleur de lys. Fifty years later, after the arrival of their first-born, Louis XIII and Anne of Austria sent two precious gold, bejeweled crowns. Included with the gift was a solid silver angel holding a solid gold infant lying on a silver pillow, with the inscription: *acceptum a virgine Delphinum Gallia Virgini reddit.* The infant was the *Dieu donné,* the future Louis XIV.[6]

Miniature replicas of the *santa casa,* some no bigger than a thumb nail, were made of every conceivable type of material. These garnished the dwellings of rich and poor alike all over Europe, or were worn as jewelry. The description of the one owned by the very rich princess,

---

6. Louis Moréri, *Le Grand Dictionnaire Historique* (Paris: Moreri, 1746), vol. 5, 556.

Mlle de Guise, occupies several pages of the inventory of her household effects, because of the many precious stones encrusted on it. More interesting than the gold and rubies on the house itself, however, were the miniature cooking utensils, the andirons, the bed, the lamp—all made of gold and silver—that furnished the house.[7] These chefs d'oeuvre of the silver and gold craft made it possible for the princess and her ladies in waiting to experience not ecstasy about the Virgin, but instead a playful wonderment prompted by the smallness, the beauty and the preciousness of these everyday household objects in miniature.

Just why enhanced feelings and reflections about certain objects and spaces occurred after about 1550 can only be quickly explored here by noting religious and political conditions prevailing in France, all familiar, and fairly well-established. During the civil and religious wars, people with archly stated certitudes from Rome, from Geneva, from the Sorbonne, or from Saumur obviously belonged to quite small and ill-confined but definable minorities. The faltering of three regency governments, the assassination of two kings and the strident, terrifying pronouncements from Rome celebrating the Massacre of St. Bartholomew's Day strengthened feelings of disquiet, fear, and terror. And, as theology came to occupy the physical space of liturgy in Roman Catholicism, it was no longer clear what the Host contained. The debates over whether the Word was more powerful than the things it represented, or vice versa, sustained and extended the need for satisfying the feeling of speechlessness before some thing or place.

Religious reform had undermined the liturgical, forcing the faithful, wittingly or unwittingly, to think about what they were saying or eating during religious services, instead of simply saying what everybody else said and eating what everybody else ate. The mysteries of the faith shifted toward words more than things, in the general religious life of the late sixteenth century. The Baroque place, more neutral, more empty, more unsaid than the theologically defined host and relic, prompted and satisfied yearnings to be in the presence of a divine creation that was especially comprehensible to human mental powers. And not to describe one's speechlessness in the Baroque place could only enhance disparities between feelings about words and feelings about things. The not-conscious taboo about speaking of one's emotions led to ever greater emphasis on the sensuality of the Baroque

7. Charles-V. Langlois, *Les Hôtels de Clisson, de Guise et de Rohan-Soubise au Marais* (Paris: Jean Schemit, 1922), 145.

place through still more encrustation. Historians can only speculate about the cultural effects of not speaking about feelings and must scrutinize actions and reciprocities that speak louder than unsaid words. The documents they consult are stone, paint, shrubs, gravel, and water forced into geometric forms. It would be very easy to challenge and refute these vague generalizations by citing exceptions to them, or by asserting that the previous, pre-1550 mood of relative optimism about the powers of human knowledge was but a veneer or an elite phenomenon. The latter it certainly was, and thin too, in its institutionalization. When Palissy pondered the shapes and the strength of mollusks, in order to recreate them in clay, he marveled at their ability to grow fortresses, as part of their own natures, to protect themselves against violence and murder. His wonderment before these miniature fortresses of nature can only be interpreted as a historically specific response to violence by a master artisan who was part of a persecuted minority, the Huguenots.[8] Imprisoned for heresy, Palissy would die in the Bastille.

It is difficult to think of the desire to be in a place that will prompt bodily reactions and feelings (something so bound up in the sciences of meaning and being) as something measurable, but by careful attention to the number of Baroque places created and inventoried, it might be possible to demonstrate that such places had increased in number or intensified in physical power across the early modern centuries. Would it be possible, at this point, to think the way we think Colbert thought and ask whether an inventory of all the Baroque places in France, 1550–1680, could be prepared in one big, neatly kept register, with the help of intendants, *eaux et forêts* officials, and the staff in the royal *garde meuble?* Under what categories would the specific places and objects be arranged? A historian writes for a deceased reader who might have special competence in his project.

Colbert would have no difficulty in accepting the Place Dauphine, the Place Royale, the Place des Victoires, and the Place Vendôme as a single category of *places* that inspire uplifted emotions and a sense of the grandeur and military force of the French Monarchy. Extravagant (out of place) and shocking to beholders in their geometric encrustation of the royal figures of the Bourbon kings, the triangle, the square, the ellipse, and the octagon were products of human ingenuity—form-

8. Neil Kamil, "War, Natural Philosophy and the Metaphysical Foundations of Artisanal Thought. . . , 1517–1730," Ph.D. dissertation, The Johns Hopkins University, 1988.

ing shapes divine in character out of stone, gravel, brick, glass, and slate.

Nor would Colbert have difficulty accepting grottoes such as those in the royal gardens as a category of places that convey special feelings and responses to their beholders. Might he recall the Grotte des Pins by Primaticcio (ca. 1543) at Fontainebleau as a very important early example? Still, he probably would have been unable to express his emotions or his reflections, on seeing the large male figures that guard the entrances to that grotto, deliberately made observable only at some distance. When close to the sculptures, the beholder sees only irregular rough carved stone, but as one moves away figures spring to the eye in/out of the stone. A sculpture that, in order to be seen, forces the beholder to move, is a Baroque place; the kings on their horses in the *places* oblige the viewer to move back, through the geometric space created for that purpose.

Colbert was not particularly articulate in describing his feelings about a work of art, nor were the French of his generation. In Félibien and Saint-Evremond there are surface meanings, iconographic and historical, but feelings and physical responses to works of art are almost entirely absent. When asked by Bernini what he thought of the great architect's proposal to leave blank spaces here and there in the foundation of the Louvre, all Chantelou could say was that he "thought the effect would be enhanced." (Bernini later agreed that the two-foot wide holes be made smaller for structural soundness, *Bernini's visit*, 300). Certainly one of the more subtle and informed observers of the arts of his generation, Chantelou perhaps did not wish to engage in discussion with the volatile Bernini, lest the discussion turn into a debate or an incident, but it is also just possible that he could not express his feelings and understandings of what was being proposed. Like Primaticcio's rough stone figures, the holes that Bernini proposed leaving between the great rusticated stone blocks in the Louvre foundation were intended to prompt observers to *wonder*. Clearly intentional, yet serving no structural purpose, the holes were decoration by absence, a *néant* of stonelessness that prompted reflection. The more learned beholder, seeking meaning rather than feeling, might imagine the semihuman creatures that were said to inhabit certain islands and might suddenly realize the obvious.[9] Bernini was proposing that the

9. See my "Islands in the South" in a volume edited in the *Continuum* series, by David Rubin (forthcoming), Irving Lavin, *Bernini and the Unity of the Visual Arts* (New York: Oxford University Press, 1980), passim, and Naomi Miller, *Heavenly Causes and the Garden Grotto* (New York: Braziller, 1982), passim.

illusion of an island be created in the new Louvre foundations, a special island where nature was in mutation and showing her powers to the fullest through enchantment by naiads and mermaids. Bernini did not propose placing sculptures in the holes so that the Louvre island would resemble a Roman foundation; instead he counted on the beholders' powers to interpret and to feel the spaces of stonelessness between the stones.

Colbert was untroubled by what he did not understand. A literalist, it was enough for him that both the Ancients and contemporary Italians had built grottoes and fountains. France had to have them too. Still, in his *Manière de Montrer les Jardins de Versailles*, Louis XIV does not tell the reader/spectator that the gigantic figure of Apollo by Girardon in the Thetis grotto had his own royal features behind the idealized features of the god. We never learn whether Louis XIV saw an idealized heroic image of Alexander the Great infused in Bernini's bust of him.[10] Conceits encrusted on surface meanings were simply not often talked about, yet they were there.

When Bernard Palissy describes the twelve precious stones that exist in the world (each a foundation in the Holy City Jerusalem), he places them in a more general theory of how waters (not just liquids) mutate in grottoes.[11] Jasper is congealed water that has flowed near an iron deposit before it congealed, giving it a yellowish color; an emerald is a clear strong water that has flowed near a brass deposit; a diamond is mere water, like crystal, but congealed by some rare salt. The shapes of stone reveal their watery past, for in grottoes one frequently finds stones that look like hanging ice. The fossils in stones are not only evidence of a vast flood, but they also show that living creatures may be turned to stone. For Palissy these mutations were by no means over; and, though he had no clear idea of when the crystals he found had been shaped, he thought the process could be rapid. His construction of a grotto for the Connétable de Montmorency confirmed for this intensely creative artisan the similarities between divine and human creative processes, a difference of degree, as it were, but not of essence. As he put it, "the sciences [that is knowledge] manifest themselves to those who look for them" (Palissy, 264). This dynamic process of creation and mutation prompted wonder, perhaps ineffability before nature's power.

Typical of the way Montaigne records things are his observations about the grotto of Pratolino, where he merely notes that "it has sev-

10. Rudolph Wittkower, *Bernini's Bust of Louis XIV* (London: 1951), passim.

11. Bernard Palissy, *Oeuvres Complètes*, ed. P. A. Cap (Paris: J. J. Dubochet, 1844), 51. Hereafter cited in text.

eral living areas and rooms, surpassing all [the grottoes] that I had seen
before" (Montaigne, *Voyage,* 83). Dare it be inferred from this that
Montaigne was a frequenter of grottoes, and that he was sensitive to
the phenomenon of scale? He records nothing about his feelings while
there. Only when referring to himself, and his work, the *Essays,* as
himself in his book, does he add an emotional valence. His essays are,
he says, like the paintings he has commissioned:

> . . . and the empty space all around [them] he fills with grotesques,
> which are fantastic paintings whose only charm lies in their variety and
> strangeness. And what are these things of mine, in truth, but gro-
> tesques and monstrous bodies, pieced together of divers members,
> without definite shape, having no order, sequence, or proportion other
> than accidental?
>
> A lovely woman tapers off into a fish.
>
> —Horace
>
> I do indeed go along with my painter in this second point, but I fall short
> in the first and better part: for my ability does not go far enough for me
> to dare to undertake a rich, polished picture, formed according to art.[12]

Montaigne starts with a metaphor, and then, on reflection, insists on
the real presence of the empty spaces to be filled by painters and by
essay writers and on his own inability to paint the "rich, polished
picture" that is framed by the grotesque and fantastic. He then "borrows" a picture from his friend, La Boétie, around which his reciprocities may be placed.[13] That the picture is a book should be no
surprise, and that the grotesques he adds to *La Servitude volontaire* are
encrustations to a friendship is only surprising if one insists that Montaigne is entirely in his book, a physicality that undermines the meaning of metaphor by extravagance and exaggeration. On the grotto at
Pratolino, Montaigne noted:

> [It] is encrusted and formed everywhere of some material that they say
> has been brought from some mountains, and [they] have fixed it to-
> gether with nails that are hidden. Not only music and harmony are
> made by the motion of the water, but also the movement of several
> statues and a door . . . , several animals dive in to drink . . . [and] in one

12. Michel de Montaigne, *Essays* trans. Donald Frame (Palo Alto: Stanford University Press, 1958), 205.
13. Gérard Defaux, *Marot, Rabelais, Montaigne: l'écriture comme présence* (Paris:
E. Champion, 1987), 195ff.

single motion the whole grotto is filled with water, with all the seats spraying water on the *fesses*. . . . [*Journal*, 83]

Furetière defines the grotesque as a "capricious figure in painting, engraving and sculpture, that has something ridiculous, extravagant and monstrous about it, like those with which grottoes are decorated." Again, no indication of what the beholder's bodily response may be. Still, writers could sometimes translate the expression of emotion in others, as expressed in another author's works. After translating the passage from the *Odyssey* describing the island and the woods around Calypso's grotto, Paul Pellisson-Fontanier says: "Finally, the poet [Homer] says, the place was so beautiful that even a god would certainly be moved by pleasure and admiration on arrival there."[14] Pellisson makes Homer say that a pleasure that moves a beholder comes from outside the self, it is a force or an affect on him. It is not ineffability, certainly, it is an emotional response to a place, in this instance a grotto.

Fénelon has Télémaque visit the same grotto and notes that its walls are covered with *rocailles* and *coquilles*, neither of which is mentioned in Homer. Fénelon includes Homer's vine, a "young vine that extends its supple branches symmetrically in every direction."[15] But in Homer this vine has vigorously growing branches heavy with grapes. Fénelon's encrustation of the place by symmetricality in the branches should not surprise us, nor should his addition of *rocailles* and *coquilles*. Calypso's grotto has become a Baroque place. In the translation of the same passage, Claude Boitet remarks that it is a vine "with several twists, and shoots covered with grapes . . . " (*Homère en France*, 441). This is also an encrustation of cultural specificity. One has only to think of the Baldachins at St. Peter's and at Val de Grâce, the Rubens *Head of Cyrus brought to Queen Tomyris* and the little twisted columns carved by local artisans for thousands of tabernacles on altars in parish churches.

La Valterie's translation of the same passage from Homer (1681) encrusts it with features that are post-Baroque. The branches have spread every direction with "chance or nature rather than art or industry . . . [to] make several little palaces of greenery in which shade and freshness reigned" (*Homère en France*, 441). Montaigne's description

14. Noémi Hepp, *Homère en France au XVIIe Siècle* (Paris: Klincksieck, 1968), 369. Hereafter cited in text.

15. Fénelon, *Les Aventures de Télémaque*, ed. Jeanne-Lydie Goré (Paris: 1987), 122.

of the Pratolino grotto scarcely calls to mind the *bosquet* or bower as a place where lovers meet, but La Valterie's translation speaks of "living areas and rooms" that are not of rock but of greenery, the point being that they are natural, not man-made. Palissy's faith that his work and God's were of the same essence, is almost explicitly rejected by La Valterie. And geometry has departed from the branches of the grape vine.

When Pierre Corneille's Cléandre is suffering the emotional effects of being in love and is momentarily unable to visit his beloved, he walks alone in the Place Royale. His friend Alidor's remark—"Encountering you in the Place Royale, alone, and so close to the sweet prison"[16]—is evidently a response to the place. It is not surprising that no expressions of royalism or of admiration for the geometric order imposed on urban space come from this love-sick young man. But is it not noteworthy that, in his emotionally upset condition, he chose to walk in the Place Royale? Not a true melancholic, for whom the geometric would have brought increased mental fatigue, Cléandre's state is within the bounds of the normal, unlike the extravagant abnormality of his friend Alidor.

Corneille chose sites for certain of his comedies that were already known for the emotional effects that they elicited, but at no point in his dedication or *examen* does he allude to this fact. Still, it is not the *extravagant* Alidor, with his possessiveness in love, whom Corneille shows walking in the Place Royale in an emotionally distraught state. For this playwright understood emotions to differ not only in essence (anger, love, courage) but in degree, and it is tempting to conjecture that, by having the normatively love-sick Cléandre walk alone in the place Royale, Corneille was articulating his general theory on the need for reason always to prevail, and to temper love.[17]

The placement of the equestrian statue of Henry IV where the curve of the Pont Neuf intersects the triangle of houses making up the Place Dauphine, and the statue of Louis XIII at the Place Royale in the Marais, seemed to require geometrically arranged spaces around them, the better to view and honor them. Equestrian sculptures of the powerful had rarely before prompted such elaborate geometrical environments. In the Israël Silvestre etching of the Place Royale, groups of people are sitting, standing, and riding around the square—going about their af-

16. P. Lierre, ed. *La Place Royale* (Paris: Gallimard, Pléiade, 1950), vol., IV.
17. Madeleine Bertaud "La Place Royale ou le jaloux Extravagant" *Pierre Corneille* (Paris: Presses Universitaires de France, 1986), 325–42.

fairs just like personages in the church interiors in seventeenth-century Dutch paintings. No one stands looking reverently at the royal majesty in bronze, in the way Claude Fleury encourages deference to royal portraits in interior settings.[18] Nor would feelings of reciprocity find an easy mode of expression at Place Royale, as they did at Loreto or in some other religious building.[19]

The thousands of cheap prints by Silvestre and his emulators who hawked images of the Place Royale cannot be said to account for the fact that the French peasantry and artisanry paid higher taxes in the 1630s than they had for half a century or more. Still, the royal squares became favorite visiting sites for provincials and foreign visitors alike, and not a few urban squares in provincial capitals were inspired by the Parisian models in that they were always king-focused and geometrical. More significant, perhaps, because measurable, are the encrustations on the subsequent squares designed to enhance the original feelings of being in a place that is truly worthy of, and essentially the same as royal majesty. The heaviness of the sculptures evoking French conquests, the hefty glory hovering over the king, the beacons and medallions of the Place des Victoires (like the fountains in generation after generation of shopping malls), all attempt to enhance the initial emotional affect that had historically first been felt in the Place Dauphine and the Place Royale. The prodigious size of the Girardon equestrian statue of the Sun King continued the effort at encrustation in the Place Vendôme. Feelings of marvel may or may not have been enhanced for the *habitués* of these places, but the encrustation from quite simple shapes and sculptures to increasingly larger-scale and more complex symbolism, assures the distant twentieth-century observer that each square, in its own way, met certain affective needs for the seventeenth-century French.

If not enhanced dignity for kings, there was at least an ambiguity that left beholders wondering about the meaning of the royal squares:

A la Place Royale on a placé ton père
Parmi les gens de qualité,
On voit sur le Pont Neuf, ton aieul débonnaire
Près du peuple qui fut l'objet de sa bonté,

18. See my "Courtesy, Absolutism, and the Rise of the French State, 1630–1660," *Journal of Modern History* 52 (1980): 426–51.

19. The same may be said for the *cours d'honneur* of *châteaux* and *hôtels*, and for the majestic staircases that led to the *étage noble,* as in the Hôtel Salé in the Marais. The letter bearing at the top the salutation, *Monseigneur,* separated from the first line of text by as much as half a page of empty paper, was also a Baroque place, in that a mental silence, a mark of respect, occurred in the reader's mind as his eyes moved down the page.

Pour toi, des partisans le prince tutélaire
A la Place Vendôme, entre eux on t'a placé.[20]

They placed your father on the Place Royale,
Among the persons of quality,
They see your easy-going grand-father on the Pont Neuf,
Near the people who were the object of his kindness.
As for you, titular prince of the tax contractors,
They placed you among them on the Place Vendôme.

Here is evidence, not of intentional and moment-specific encrustation, but of its near opposite, a historicist construction of meanings
that leads to a wondering about the social significance of a square's
environment, and the political implications for the Monarchy. Easy to
interpret on one level, impossible on another, the doggerel posits the
existence of an actor at work in history, an *on* [they] that seems to have
power quite independent from that of either God or kings. Nor was it
signed by the devil.

Jean Dupin proposed to Louis XIV, in 1662, that a wrought-iron grill
be built around the "effigy of Henry the Great" because of the scandal
of public filth (*ordure*) that there has been for a long time around the
Place Dauphine. Encrustation by public ordure? The historicist construction of Henry IV's persona as solicitous for the *peuple* is already
manifest in this description of a Parisian public space. For the *peuple*,
idle, littering, loud talking, and nonchalant, made the *place* public in a
sense that the word scarcely possessed in 1662.[21]

The same year Dupin came up with a grandiose project to turn the
Pré aux Clercs on the Left Bank into a vast military parade ground, a
place d'armes, from which, he informed Colbert, who was asked to
authorize funds from the royal treasury for the project:

> You will make it the most beautiful *place d'armes* in the world, and you
> will give the chateau of the Tuileries the richest and most agreeable
> view [*aspect*] that can be imagined, in as much as it is a *place* for the
> *peuple*, because they must be given *panem et circenses* [Dupin's Latin];
> you gave [the *peuple*] the former in time of necessity; they will ask for
> the other in times of peace. [Cauchie, 16]

---

20. *Le Nouveau Siècle de Louis XIV* III, 26, quoted by A. de Boislisle "Notices
historiques sur la Place des Victoires et sur la Place Vendôme" *Mémoires de la Société de
l'Histoire de Paris et de l'île de France* XV (1888) 170.

21. Maurice Cauchie, *Documents pour servir à l'Histoire Littéraire* (Paris: E. Champion, 1924), 12. Hereafter cited in text.

In the lengthy discussions over the location of the new Louvre façade, Colbert had argued that there ought to be sufficient space for a *place d'armes* between the Louvre and the parish church, St. Germain de l'Auxerrois. Dupin's project for the Pré aux Clercs may have been inspired by Colbert's ideas on the same subject for the Louvre, but it is noteworthy that a military parade ground with a view on a royal palace is a principal feature in both projects, an encrustation of manifest power in a space reserved for arms, from which the royal palace may be viewed.

For the cornerstone laying ceremony of the new Louvre, Bernini made it clear that, on the previous occasions where he had been the architect (St. Peter's and the Arsenal at Civitavecchia), the stone had been blessed and there had been a gun salute. He was immediately assured that, for this occasion, there would be fanfares and drums, and that a salute could be fired by a regiment of guards. Then the "Cavaliere [Bernini] suggested that a canopy would add more dignity to the occasion, as the king was to be there" (*Diary of Bernini*, 300). In the brief, staccatolike reporting of the plans, Bernini followed a typical seventeenth-century mental trajectory. He began by citing Roman precedents that he considered appropriate ceremony for someone of his stature as an architect; and he ended by recommending the use of a special dignity-enhancing device, the canopy, because the king would be present. Bernini's interlocutors had no trouble understanding either his precedents, his recommendations, or the trajectory of his thought.

Transferred from episcopal and imperial ceremonial to French royal coronations and other ceremonies, the *dais* at a cornerstone laying would be an encrustation for the royal dignity, and the emotional affects prompted by it. Were the canopies over the royal heads at various *fêtes* at Versailles also encrustations from high ceremonial such as a coronation, on such playful events as the *Plaisirs de l'île enchantée*? The Bernini recommendation suggests something quite revealing about Baroque places. Neither Charles Perrault nor Chantelou, who were Bernini's interlocutors, seems to have turned to French historical precedent in replying to the architect.[22] Their immediate response was not: Did Francis I and Henry II have canopies over them when they laid cornerstones at the Louvre? The presence or absence of canopies at previous cornerstone ceremonies presided over by kings, or the actual

---

22. There would be interest in precedents for the ceremony until Colbert gave the word to Perrault to arrange it according to Bernini's wishes.

occurrence of such ceremonies, is less important at this point than the *absence* of the precedental-historical reflex. It is tempting to assert that a flight from precedentalism occurred in the making of Baroque places—in the *places royales,* the grottoes, the cornerstone layings and, as we shall see, the funerals of important personages.

So many of the other places of early modern French culture, especially the endless rights and marks of respect for the church, the social orders, the monarch, the provinces, towns, universities, guilds, and sciences were locked in the temporalities of charters granted by one or another king, litigated over for centuries and transformed into an inchoate mass determining the routine thoughts and actions of the population, except for the most creative and thoughtful of each generation. The reading and translation of ancient authors (less frequently, the Bible and the fathers, with the exception of Augustine) could still unleash individuals from the moorings of custom, as did the pursuit of mystical experience; but it may well have been the Baroque place, with its powers of attraction and repulsion, that prompted the least historicized reciprocities from individuals. They were, and still are, the least historically meaningful aspect of French early modern culture.

Neither Perrault nor Chantelou seems to have taken umbrage at the Italian architect's implication that the king's dignity could, in fact, be enhanced, or that it needed enhancing. One might think that in 1665, after the prosecution of Fouquet in particular, the dignity and authority of the Sun King would have seemed firmly established. In point of fact, however, the political landscape was marked by various attempts to enhance the king's dignity and power. That dignity seemed most vulnerable in internal politics, and especially weak, since the civil wars of religion, at the execution place. The extreme caution that royal officials took to prevent onlookers from touching persons condemned to death, in order to capture some feeling from the act or collect drops of blood, body parts or the ashes of someone executed by royal justice, need not be described here. These objects were recognized as having some special power, one that was not described by any learned treatise of theology, natural philosophy, or astrology. The aspect of the execution that made it baroque was its uncertain outcome. Recent technologies have almost completely eliminated the accidental from capital punishment, but in the seventeenth century the trap could stick, the rope could break or become unknotted, or the blade could miss. If any accident spared the life of the condemned, the onlookers would rush up to free the condemned person and crush the royal guards in the melee, interpreting the life-saving accident as a sign from God of the condemned person's innocence. Isaac de Laffemas, royal intendant in Champagne in the 1630s, encrusted the execution place with a finality that was intended to enhance royal authority.

In most early modern trials that led to execution, there was really only one finality, the death of the guilty person. A guilty judgment might be rendered, and a death sentence as well, but until his last breath the guilty party would still be exhorted to make incriminating statements about accomplices or give secret information. The Chevalier de Jars was found guilty in the autumn of 1633 and was sentenced to death. Several requests to talk followed, but he always refused to cooperate, only repeating that he had been betrayed by women.[23] Laffemas then ordered the chevalier's public execution.

In point of fact, a decision had already been made to pardon de Jars, but instead of informing the prisoner, Laffemas decided to stage an execution. There were, Laffemas reports:

> More than 30,000 persons on the *place* or at their windows, and as he [de Jars] was on the scaffold, the judicial official in charge had the Jacobin priest and Sonbini climb up with him to admonish him to tell the truth, but without getting anything from him that he hadn't already said. Then two guards that I [Laffemas] had kept near the execution place, separated the crowd with their pikes, shouting loudly, "Pardon, pardon, Monsieur the Intendant has just received a dispatch from the king . . . to cancel the execution and bring the prisoner back to the Jacobin monastery. . . ." This action was received with such a great acclaim that never has something similar been seen, because in addition to admonishing the prisoner to give the king thanks, as he was doing, the whole *peuple* shouted "Long Live the King, and give him prosperity because he knows how to give mercy and justice."

The mock execution consolidated royal authority by encrusting the event, with its usual powers to inspire horror and fascination, with a certain rational and royal outcome. And the message of pardon was mediated by the intendant, that expresser of the royal will in the king's stead. In fact Laffemas sought more to enhance his own authority than the king's, but, like the addition of a canopy, the total effect of the Baroque place remained profoundly royal and authoritarian. The impulse to harness the force of a natural object, such as a dying person, an

23. Roland Mousnier, ed. *Lettres et Mémoires adressées au Chancelier Séguier* (Paris: Presses Universitaires de France, 1964), vol. 1, 211.

object or "thing thrown before the mind," only to harness it to royal authority, was an encrustation on older royal powers that had specific temporal and cultural meaning. It was Baroque in its exaggerated, sinister, emotive force of turning revulsion and the possibility of divine intervention into love for the monarch.

Any inventory of Baroque places would not only include execution places, with the drawing and quartering and burning of the guilty, but also the death scenes of the great, their last words and, especially, their funerals. Sébastien le Clerc's etching of the funeral of Chancellor Séguier, like his depiction of the Place Royale noted earlier, permitted thousands of beholders to share vicariously in the contrasts of light and dark, incense and silver, tears and dirges, of the great staged funeral. In the immediate foreground is a couple seeking admission to the ceremony and, if the gestures of the master of ceremonies are properly interpreted, being encouraged to enter the empty space around the great catafalque. The presence of halberd-bearing guards indicates how eagerly the Parisians pressed to attend the spectacle.

There was nothing new in the seventeenth century about eagerly attending funerals. Funerals had prompted enormous creative energies and had been manifestations of social power for centuries. But after about 1650, the more traditional focus on the special music, the eulogy, the fine tapestries hung in the church, and the vestments and candles for the service, gave way beneath the Italianate *chapelle ardente*. Like the *santa casa*, the funeral of the great became encrusted by everything precious, to enhance feelings of wonder, fear of death, and ineffability.

The *chapelle ardente* and the hangings for the Séguier funeral were designed by Charles Le Brun in the latest style, with a pyramid of blazing candles interspersed with silver-leaf stars (evoking Séguier's coat of arms) and surmounted by a great fiery urn that poured forth an angelic glory bearing the portrait (or arms) of the deceased, in the highest point of the vaulting in the Oratory Church.[24] This blazing pyramid seemed to be held up by pallbearing angels (actually, wires attached to the church walls held up the display), which hovered above the great pall-covered bier, on which was placed a ducal crown. The surrounding walls were covered with black velvet from which hung octagonal and circular silver-leafed medallions bearing the coat of

24. Jérôme de la Gorce, *Bérain* (Paris: Herscher, 1986), 131 ff. Hereafter cited in text.

arms of the deceased and scenes of his great deeds resumed into virtues. Still more candles and torches blazed below the level of the coffin, creating a visual effect of movement and silver-black light. The heat from all the flames must have caused wavy, shimmering effects for the beholders—movement upward through silver-black light.

The lighted *chapelle ardente* had the effect of a canopy of light rising heavenward, with the bier bearing the body following in its wake. On the right, in a small, simple pulpit, a preacher gestures, but it is clear from Le Clerc's etching of the scene that it was the image of the *chapelle ardent*, not the words of the preacher, that conveyed to the beholder awe and a sense of grandeur, vulnerability and wonder.

For seventeenth-century French Catholicism, the donations for masses, the donations to charity, and the lights, music, words, and eminence of those who attended such funerals, all manifested the deceased person's rightful place in the afterlife. The Protestant contention that the individual's actions and thoughts were solely responsible for his fate on Judgment Day had never really undermined familial and communitarian duty, so central to Catholicism, to assure God's favorable opinion of the deceased. Temporal and divine justice were two distinct spheres of judicial authority, but man and God had their hand in both. Occasional protests about the expense and ostentation of funerals notwithstanding, there was general agreement that a grand send-off would deeply and favorably impress God. The same habit was at work in the royal *entrées* and other ceremonies not exclusively reserved for the royal family.

The work of Le Brun and Jean I. Bérain, supported by writers such as Menestrier and Charpentier and preachers such as Bossuet, Bourdaloue, and Massillon, encrusted the funeral into a Baroque place. The tear-covered palls of silver gauze, ermine and crepe that draped from the suspended canopies in immense swags in the nave, with its decor of black velvet and silver candelabra and medallions, skulls, blazons and flaming urns, filled the empty spaces of churches surrounding the body of the deceased, as if grotesques had come off the walls. The funeral decor for the ceremonies marking the deaths of such persons as the Grande Mademoiselle, Turenne, the Grand Condé, Queen Marie-Thérèse, or the Grand Dauphin were especially created Baroque places that both prompted and satisfied feelings of being in the presence of things neither entirely divine nor entirely human, natural yet artificial, terrestrial yet heavenly, transcendent and exaggerated. The effects were so powerful that occasionally even theologians and philosophers—men preoccupied by the power of words—had to recognize or express something about the emotional affects of the *chapelles ardentes*. Thus in his eulogy of the Grand Condé, Bossuet said to the assembled mourners:

> Glance in every direction: here is everything that magnificence and piety can do to honor a hero. Titles, epitaphs, futile marks of what is no longer, figures who seem to weep around a tomb, and fragile images of a suffering that time carries away with all the rest, columns that seem to bear witness to Heaven of our *néant;* nothing is missing from all these honors except the one to whom they are rendered. . . . [*Bérain*, 136]

Bossuet had not earned his reputation for eloquence by describing the physicality and the emotional force of Baroque places. His prose is, in fact, rather reductionist in the sense that he only mentions banal iconographic meanings and their obvious emotional implications. We have noted before how seventeenth-century Frenchmen were not particularly adept at expressing their feelings and physical responses to encrusted places made precious by human artifice. Light, music, voice, non-light black and mirrors seconded the presence of the deceased person's body to carry it upward. While each art was stretched to its technical limitations, it reached toward the others in a unison grounded on the supposition that the body of the beholder could and did incarnate the same affects and meanings in similar ways. Like a *santa casa*, the body of the deceased was empty, that is soulless, but its emptiness retained the strength to inspire awe.

Were all human bodies the same? In what ways did the body of a nobleman differ from that of a peasant? Or a woman's from a man's? The balances and imbalances of an individual's humor created different affections.[25] One person was more sensitive to light, another to music, another to words, but these variations were usually not of such magnitude that persons became totally insensitive to one or another form of encrustation. If one felt disgust or loathing for one aspect of a Baroque place, these were nonetheless emotionally strong responses.[26]

Around the irregularly shaped, minute, blank paper spot that constitutes the reflection into the eye, there is a minuscule black-brown

25. See Roger Duchêne's succinct review of the issues, taking Cureau de la Chambre's *Les Caractères des Passions* as his point of departure, "Éros chez le Médecin," *Quaderni del Seicento Francese* 8 (1981): 177–86.

26. The dissection chamber could well be described as a Baroque place, for despite all the work done by Galen, Vesalius, and others, there was always the possibility for

spot for the pupil in a Nanteuil portrait. Then, encrusting geo-metrically around the pupil, are concentric circles divided by straight lines drawn as if from every point on a circle to the focal point in the blank paper spot, making the iris of the eye a series of conic sections, each less than a millimeter in width.[27] Encrusted by geometrically created space around a blank spot, the Nanteuil eye is a very special geometer's gameboard exclusively reserved for the "window to the soul," an encrustation that signals the beholder that this is a Baroque place. This geometer's game was not played on any other surface of the human body, as if to suggest that the eye was the only external bodily place for rationality.

And what of the face of Christ, etched by Claude Mellan, with all the features made by a single, unending spiral line? Simply a tour de force by an artisan-artist? Of course, but it still prompts wonder in the beholder today, as a physical object at once obvious and ineffable, as it did when it was first engraved. And repugnance too, for beholders were offended by human attempts to capture through the exaggerated re-liance on one element of the engraver's skill something that cannot be captured in geometry, the face of Christ. Not remembering Mellan's name, Bernini asked Chantelou about an engraver who had come to see him early on during his stay in Paris but who had not called again. Chantelou recalled immediately that it had been Mellan, adding:

> I said [to Bernini] that he was not doing much at present; there were others better at his profession than he; I had never thought much of his work, for he was too preoccupied with a good line. He [Bernini] replied that he had seen some wonderful engraving by him, notably some of Signor Poussin's works . . . . [I replied that] M. Mellan only produced a sort of shell with no half-tones or shadows for fear of hiding the outline. The Cavaliere said that he thought it fine and well engraved. [*Bernini's Visit*, 280]

A foreshortened view of the Mellan Christ yields only a spiral. Only at a certain distance does the head of Christ appear. Chantelou was un-willing to recognize the brilliant results that Mellan achieved by exag-

---

surprise when the human body was opened. A special room for the event, a special place, was therefore created, and its walls encrusted with meaningful sayings. No one could exactly predict from the outside what the inside might hold, no matter how closely the outside was scrutinized by the doctor, or artistically represented.

27. I am indebted to H. Diane Russell, curator of prints, the National Gallery, Washington, for this point. The eyes in the portrait of Peiresc by Mellan complete concentric circles around a black point.

gerating only one feature of the engraver's art. The figures in the Primaticcio grotto would certainly not have come to his mind, nor would the distance between the equestrian statues of the kings of France on their *places* have been qualitatively perceived as the same as that between the beholder and the portrait of Christ by Mellan. The creators of Baroque places in France had very few contemporaries who understood the deeper emotional, artistic, geometric, and religious intentions that prompted the reciprocities in their works. Bernini was one of these few, yet he was rejected in Paris even though he was being enormously influential on those very places in French culture that could scarcely be imagined, let alone expressed.[28]

28. "In the domain of architectural theory [Claude] Perrault mapped out a space into which the Bourbon crown moved, a space constructed for the societal function of defining aesthetic conventions whose authority derived neither from nature nor God but from the king of France," Hilary Ballon, "Constructions of the Bourbon State: Classical Architecture in Seventeenth-Century France," *Cultural Differentiation and Cultural Identity in the Visual Arts, Studies in the History of Art* 27, National Gallery of Art, 1989, 142.

GILLES DELEUZE

The Fold*

MATERIAL COILS[1]

The Baroque does not refer to an essence, but rather to an operative function, to a characteristic. It endlessly creates folds. It does not invent the thing: there are all the folds that come from the Orient— Greek, Roman, Romanesque, Gothic, classical folds. . . . But it twists and turns the folds, takes them to infinity, fold upon fold, fold after fold. The characteristic of the Baroque is the fold that goes on to infinity. And from the beginning it differentiates them along two lines, according to two infinities, as if the infinite had two levels: the coils of matter, and the folds in the soul. Below, matter is amassed according to an initial type of fold, then organized according to a second type, insofar as its parts constitute organs "differently folded and more or less developed."[2] Above, the soul sings the glory of God by running along its own folds, though without succeeding in entirely developing them, "for they reach into the infinite." ("Monadology," § 61, in Philosoph-

---

* With the permission of Gilles Deleuze and Georges Borchardt, Inc.

1. Deleuze distinguishes, not entirely consistently, between the "replis" of inorganic matter and the "plis" of the organic. "Pli" and "repli" both have a primary meaning of "fold" and are otherwise largely synonymous, although the form of the latter suggests an idea of repetition. An introverted person is furthermore said to be "replié sur soi," and the word "repli" consequently has a connotation of turning inward, or invagination. To maintain a distinction in English, I have translated "pli" as "fold" and "repli" as "coil," since the latter evokes the movements of a reptile (referred to in French as replis but not plis), the idea of folding in on oneself and the springs [ressorts] which Deleuze says underlie Leibnizian matter. —Translator's note.

2. "A New System of the Nature and the Communication of Substances," § 7, in Gottfried Wilhelm Leibniz, Philosophical Papers and Letters, vol. 2 trans. and ed. and introduction by Leroy E. Loemker (Chicago: University of Chicago Press, 1956), 743. Hereafter cited in the text.

YFS 80, Baroque Topographies, ed. Timothy Hampton, © 1991 by Yale University.

ical Papers and Letters, 1055, and cf., also "The Principles of Nature and of Grace Based On Reason," § 13, 1040–41). A labyrinth is said to be multiple, etymologically, because it has many folds. The multiple is not merely that which has many parts, but that which is folded in many ways. Each level corresponds perfectly to a labyrinth: the labyrinth of the coextensive content of matter and its parts, the labyrinth of liberty in the soul and its predicates ("On Freedom," vol. 1, 404–10). If Descartes was unable to reconcile them, it is because, unaware of the soul's inclination and the curvature of matter, he tried to find content's secret running along straight lines and liberty's secret in a rectitude of the soul. A "cryptography" is needed which would both enumerate nature and decipher the soul, see into the coils of matter and read in the folds of the soul.[3]

It is certain that there is communication between the two levels (which is why content rises up into the soul). There are souls below—animal, open to sensation—or even bottom levels in souls, and the coils of matter surround them, envelop them. When we discover that souls can have no windows to the outside, we will need, at least at first, to think of this in reference to the souls above, the rational souls, which have risen to the other level ("elevation"). It is the upper level which has no window: a darkened compartment or study, furnished only with a stretched cloth "diversified by folds," like the bottom layer of skin exposed. These folds, ropes, or springs set up on the opaque cloth represent innate knowledge, but an innate knowledge which passes into action when called upon by matter. For the latter unleashes the "vibrations or oscillations" at the lower extremity of the ropes by means of "small openings" which do exist on the lower level. It is a great Baroque apparatus which Leibniz sets up between the lower level, pierced by windows, and the upper story, sealed and sightless but in return resonant, like a sounding box which would render audible the visible movements coming from below.[4] It will be objected that this text is not an expression of Leibniz's thought, but rather the limit of his

3. On cryptography as the "art of inventing the key to an enveloped thing," cf., Fragment "De Arte Combinatoria" in *Opuscules et fragments inédits de Leibniz: Extraits des manuscrits de la Bibliothèque Royale de Hanovre,* ed. Louis Couturat (Paris: Les Belles Lettres, 1934), 563; John Locke, *New Essays on Human Understanding,* ed. and trans. Peter Remnant and Jonathan Bennet (Cambridge: Cambridge University Press, 1981), vol. 4, chap. 17, § 8: the coils of Nature and the "abstracts [*abrégés*]." Hereafter cited in the text.

4. Gottfried Wilhelm Leibniz, *New Essays,* 144–45. In this book, Leibniz "reworks" Locke's *Essays;* the darkened compartment has been referred to by Locke, but not the folds. Hereafter cited in the text.

possible agreement with Locke. That does not hinder it in the least from offering a way of representing what Leibniz will continually assert: a correspondence, even a communication between the two levels, between the two labyrinths, between the coils of matter and the folds in the soul. A fold between the two folds? And the same image—of veins of marble—is applied to both in different contexts; sometimes the veins are the twisted coils of matter which surround the living beings caught in a block, so that a bank of marble is like an undulating lake full of fish. Sometimes the veins are the innate ideas in the soul, like the bent figures or the potential statues caught in a block of marble. Matter is marbled, and the soul is marbled, in two different ways.

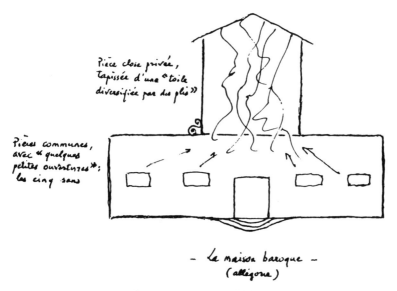

The Baroque House—(allegory)

[diagram: a closed, private room, draped with a 'cloth diversified by folds' / common rooms with 'a few small openings': the five senses]

Wölfflin has noted a certain number of material characteristics of the Baroque: the horizontal extension of the bottom sections, the lowering of the pediment, the forward movement of low, curved steps; the treatment of matter by masses or aggregates, the rounding off of angles and the avoidance of straight lines, the substitution of the rounded acanthus for the jagged acanthus, the use of travertine to produce spongy, cavernous forms, or the elaboration of a whorl that feeds endlessly on new turbulences and ends only in the way a horse's mane or wavefroth does; the tendency of matter to overflow space, to be reconciled with fluidity, at the same time that the waters themselves divide into masses.[5]

It is Huyghens who develops a Baroque mathematical physics whose object is the curve. And with Leibniz, the curvature of the universe extends in accordance with three other fundamental notions: the fluidity of matter, the elasticity of bodies, the spring as mechanism. In the first place, it is certain that matter would not of itself move in a curved line: it would follow the tangent (Preface to the *New Essays*). But the universe is, as it were, compressed by an active force which gives a curvilinear or swirling movement to matter, following to its end a curve with no tangent. And the infinite division of matter means that the compressive force relates each portion of matter to its surroundings, to the surrounding parts which bathe and penetrate the body in question, determining its curvature. Ceaselessly dividing, the parts of matter form little swirls within a swirl, and in them there are other, smaller ones, and still more in the concave intervals of the swirls which touch one another. Matter thus offers a texture that is infinitely porous, that is spongy or cavernous without empty parts, since there is always a cavern in the cavern: each body, however small it may be, contains a world insofar as it is perforated by uneven passageways, and the world, surrounded and penetrated by an increasingly subtle fluid, was like a "pond of matter in which there are different currents and waves" ("Letter to Des Billettes, December 1696," *Philosophical Papers and Letters*, vol. 2, 772). It is not, however, to be concluded that in the second place even the subtlest matter is perfectly fluid and losing thereby its texture, in accordance with a thesis that Leibniz attributes to Descartes. It is undoubtedly Descartes's mistake, which one finds in various areas, to have thought that the real distinction between parts entailed separability; what defines an absolute fluid is precisely the absence of coherence or cohesion, that is to say, the separability of the parts, which is only applicable to an abstract and passive matter (Leibniz, "Table de définitions," in *Opuscules et fragments*, 486. And *New Essays*, 2, chap. 23, § 23, 222–23). According to Leibniz, two truly distinct parts of matter can be inseparable, as is shown not only in the action of the surroundings—which determine the curvilinear movement of a body—but also by the ambient pressure, which determines its hardness (coherence, cohesion) or the inseparability of its parts. One would thus have to say that a body has a degree of hardness as well as a degree of fluidity, or that it is essentially elastic, the elastic force of

5. Cf., Heinrich Wölfflin, *Renaissance and Baroque*, trans. Katherine Simon (Ithaca: Cornell University Press, 1984).

bodies being the expression of the active compressive force which works on matter—once a boat reaches a certain speed, a wave becomes as hard as a marble wall. The atomistic hypothesis of an absolute hardness and the Cartesian hypothesis of an absolute fluidity converge all the more easily because they share the same error, positing separable minima, either in the form of finite bodies, or, infinitely, in the form of points (the Cartesian line as the site of these points, the punctual analytic equation).

This is what Leibniz sets forth in an extraordinary text: a flexible or elastic body still has coherent parts which form a fold, with the result that they do not separate into parts of parts, but rather divide infinitely into smaller and smaller folds that always retain a certain cohesion. What is more, the labyrinth of continuity is not a line which would dissolve into independent points, like sand flowing in grains, but is like a piece of fabric or a sheet of paper which divides into an infinite number of folds or disintegrates into curved movements, each one determined by the consistency or the participation of its setting. "The division of the continuous ought not to be considered as that of sand into grains, but as that of a sheet of paper or of a tunic into folds, in such a way that there can be an infinite number of folds, one smaller than the next, without the body ever dissolving into points or minima" ("Placidius Philalethi," *Opuscules*, 614–15). Always a fold within the fold, like a cavern within the cavern. The unit of matter, the smallest element of the labyrinth, is the fold, not the point, which is never a part, but only an extremity of the line. That is why the parts of matter are masses or aggregates, as corollary to the compressive elastic force. The unfold is thus not the opposite of the fold, but follows one fold until the next. "Particles twisted into folds," and which a "contrary effort changes and changes again" ("Letter to Des Billettes," 773). Folds of the winds, of fire and the earth, and the subterranean folds of lodes in the mine. The solid creases of "natural geography" can be attributed to the initial action of fire, followed by that of the winds and waters on the earth in a system of complex interactions; and lodes are like the curves of conic sections, ending now in a circle or an ellipse, now extending into a hyperbola or a parabola.[6] Material science, the Japanese philosopher would say, has as its model "origami," or the art of the paper fold.

* * *

6. G. W. Leibniz, "Protogaea," *Opera Omnia*, ed. L. Dutens (Geneva: Fratres de Tournes, 1768), vol. 2.

WHAT IS BAROQUE?

Monads "have no windows by which something might enter or leave them," they have "neither holes nor doors."[7] If we do not try to reach a precise understanding of the situation, we run the risk of understanding it too abstractly. A picture still has an external model, is still a window. The modern reader might call to mind a film shown in the dark, but the film was nonetheless shot. Is one then to imagine numerical images, that have no model, the products of a calculation? Or more simply, a line of infinite inflection, which works for a surface, as we find in the works of Pollock or Rauschenberg? It has in fact been said that with Rauschenberg the picture's surface is no longer a window onto the world but becomes an opaque table of information on which a numbered line is inscribed.[8] In place of the picture/window there is substituted tabulation, the table on which are inscribed lines, numbers, changing characters (object-matter).[9] Leibniz ceaselessly draws up linear and numerical tables with which to furnish the interior surfaces of the monad. In place of holes there are folds. Against the system window/countryside is opposed the pair city/information-table.[10] The Liebnizian monad would be such a table, or rather a room, an apartment entirely covered with lines of variable inflection. It would be the dark room of the *New Essays*, furnished with a stretched cloth diversified by moving, living folds. The essential point about the monad is that it is background: it draws everything from this, and nothing comes from outside and nothing goes outside.

In this respect, there is no need to refer to overly modern developments, except insofar as they aid in understanding what the Baroque enterprise already was. For a long time there have been places where what is on view is inside: the cell, the sacristy, the crypt, the church, the theater, the reading-room, or print collection. These are the places which the Baroque privileged in order to draw from them their power

7. Leibniz, *Monadology,* § 7; Letter to Princess Sophie, June 1700, *Philosophischen Schriften,* vol. 1, 554.

8. Leo Steinberg, *Other Criteria,* (New York: Oxford University Press, 1972): "the flatbed picture plane."

9. *Objectile* [object-matter] is a neologism apparently based on the model of *subjectile,* which means the material support, such as canvas, board, wall, that underlies a painting.—Translator's note.

10. On the Baroque city, and the importance of the city in the Baroque, cf., Lewis Mumford, *The Culture of Cities* (New York: Harcourt, Brace and Co., 1938) and Severo Sarduy, "El Caravaggio / la ciudad barroco" in *Ensayos generales sobre el Barroco* (Mexico: Fondo de Cultura Económico, 1987), 179–82.

and glory. At first, the dark room has only a small, high opening, through which light enters, passing through two mirrors, the second of which is tilted to follow a page, onto which the light will project the unseen objects that are to be drawn.[11] Then come the transformational decors, painted skies, all types of *trompe-l'œil* which adorn walls: all the monad's furniture and objects are in *trompe-l'œil*. Finally, there is the architectural idea of a room in black marble, where light penetrates only through orifices so artfully twisted that they allow not the slightest glimpse of the outside but illuminate or color the decorations of a pure inside (is it not the Baroque spirit which, in this sense, inspires Le Corbusier in the La Tourette abbey?). It is impossible to understand the Leibnizian monad, and its system of light/mirror/ point of view/interior decoration without relating them to Baroque architecture. The latter sets up chapels and chambers whose glancing light comes from openings invisible even to their inhabitants. One of its first acts is the Studiolo in Florence, with its secret, windowless room. The monad is a cell, more a sacristy than an atom: a room with neither door nor window, where all actions are internal.

The monad is the autonomy of the interior, an interior without exterior. Yet it has as a correlative the independence of the facade, an exterior without interior. It—the facade—can have doors and windows, it is full of holes, although there is no such thing as an empty space, a hole being nothing more than the site of a more subtle matter. The doors and windows of matter open and even close only from the outside and on the outside. Naturally, organic matter already suggests an interiorization, but a relative one, always in progress and never complete. Consequently, a fold runs through that which is living, but in such a way that it separates the absolute interiority of the monad and the infinite exteriority of matter respectively into the metaphysical principle of life and the physical law of phenomena. Two infinite sets which never meet: "The infinite division of exteriority extends endlessly and remains open, so that it is necessary to leave the exterior and posit a punctual, interior unity. . . . The realm of the physical, the natural, the phenomenal, the contingent is completely flung into the infinite iteration of open chains: in this respect it is not metaphysical. The realm of the metaphysical lies beyond, and brings a close to the iteration . . . the monad is that fixed point which infinite

11. Cf., "L'Usage de la chambre obscure" at Gravesande, in Sarah Kofman, *Camera obscura* (Paris: Galilée, 1973), 79–97.

partitioning never attains and which closes off infinitely divided space."[12] Baroque architecture can be defined by that scission of the facade and the inside, of the interior and the exterior, the autonomy of the interior and the independence of the exterior effected in such a way that each one sets off the other. Wölfflin, too, said this in his own way, ("it is precisely the contrast between the aggravated language of the facade and the serene peacefulness of the interior which constitutes one of the most powerful effects that Baroque art has on us"), although he is wrong in thinking that the excess of interior decoration ultimately obscures the contrast, or that the absolute interior is peaceful in itself. Similarly, Jean Rousset defines the Baroque by the scission between the facade and the interior, although he too believes that its decoration risks "exploding" the interior. Still, the interior remains perfectly unified when viewed from the perspective or mirror imposed on the viewer by the decoration, however complicated. Between the interior and the exterior, between the spontaneity of the inside and the determination of the outside a new mode of correspondence is needed, one which was totally unknown to pre-Baroque architects: "What direct and necessary connection is there between the interior of Saint-Agnes and its facade? . . . Far from being adapted to the structure, the Baroque facade has a tendency to express nothing but itself," while, for its part, the interior falls back on itself, remains sealed, tends to offer itself to the viewer who discovers it in its entirety from a single viewpoint, as a "jewel-box in which the absolute resides."[13]

The new harmony will be made possible, first of all, by the distinction between the two stories, insofar as it resolves tension or distributes scission. It is the lower story which is charged with the facade, and which extends by puncturing itself, which curves back in accordance with the determinate coils of a heavy matter, thereby constituting an infinite reception room, or room of receptivity. It is the upper story that is closed, a pure interior without exterior, an interiority sealed in weightlessness, lined in spontaneous folds which are now only those of a soul or a spirit. Consequently, the Baroque world, as Wölfflin has shown, is organized according to two vectors: a sinking downward and an upward pull. It is Leibniz who permits the coexis-

---

12. Michel Serres, *Le système de Leibniz* (Paris: Presses Universitaires de France, 1968), 762.

13. Jean Rousset, *La Littérature de l'âge baroque en France: Circé et le paon* (Paris: J. Corti, 1968), 168–71. And, by the same author, *L'Intérieur et l'extérieur* (Paris: J. Corti, 1976).

tence of the heavy system's tendency to find its equilibrium at the lowest possible point, there where the sum of masses can descend no farther, with the tendency to rise, the highest aspiration of a weightless system, to that place where souls are destined to become reasonable, as in a painting by Tintoretto. The fact that one is metaphysical and concerns the soul, and that the other is physical and concerns bodies, does not prevent the two vectors from composing one and the same world, one and the same house. And not only are they separated off as functions of an ideal line actualized in one story and realized in the other, but a higher correspondence ceaselessly relates them to each other. This kind of house architecture is not a constant of art or thought. What is specifically Baroque is this distinction, this partition-ing into two stories. The Platonic tradition knew a distinction between two worlds. It knew the world of innumerable stories, tracing a descent and a climb that confronted each other on every step of a stairway which lost itself in the eminence of the One and fell apart into the sea of the multiple—the stairway-universe of the neo-Platonic tradition. But the world of only two stories, separated by a fold which reverbe-rates on both sides in accordance with different orders, is the preemi-nent Baroque innovation. It expresses the transformation of the cos-mos into "mundus."

Among the so-called Baroque painters, Tintoretto and El Greco stand out, incomparable. And yet they share this characteristic of the Baroque. The *Entombment of the Count of Orgaz* is, for example, divided in two by a horizontal line, and below the bodies squeeze up against one another, while above the soul rises, in a thin coil, awaited by holy monads each of which is endowed with its own spontaneity. In the works of Tintoretto, the lower level shows bodies bowed down by their own heaviness, the souls stumbling, bending and falling in the coils of matter; in contrast, the upper half acts like a powerful magnet drawing them up, making them straddle the yellow folds of light, the folds of fire which revive the bodies, infecting them with a vertigo, but a "vertigo of the heights." So it is with the two halves of the *Last Judgement*.[14]

The scission of interior and exterior thus refers back to the distinc-

14. Régis Debray, "Le Tintoret ou le sentiment panique de la vie," in *Eloges* (Paris: Gallimard, 1986), 13–57. (Debray criticizes Sartre for having seen only the lower level of Tintoretto's works). And Jean Paris, *L'Espace et le regard* (Paris: Seuil, 1965): the analysis of the "ascensional space" in El Greco's works, 226–28 ("like Cartesian divers men thus balance earthly gravity and divine attraction").

tion of the two stories, but this in turn refers to the Fold, actualized in the intimate folds that the soul encloses in the upper story, and realized in the coils, under the influence of matter, and generated from one another, always on the exterior, on the lower level. The ideal fold is thus a *Zwiefalt*, a fold which differentiates and self-differentiates. When Heidegger refers to the *Zwiefalt* as the differential of difference (*le différenciant de la différence*), he means above all that the differentiation does not refer to undifferentiated origin, but to a Difference which ceaselessly unfolds and folds back from both sides and which only unfolds one by folding back the other in a coextensivity of the unveiling and veiling of Being, of the presence and withdrawal of the being.[15] The "duplicity" of the fold is necessarily reproduced on both of the sides which it distinguishes and which it sets into a mutual relation by distinguishing them: a scission in which each term sets off the other, a tension in which each fold is extended into the other.

The fold is undoubtedly the most important notion of Mallarmé— not only the notion, but rather the operation, the operatory act which makes of him a great Baroque poet. *Hérodiade* is already the poem of the fold. The fold of the world is the fan, or "l'unanime pli" [unanimous fold]. And sometimes the open fan makes all the grains of matter rise and fall, ashes and mists through which one perceives the visible as if through the holes in a veil, according to the way the folds [*replis*] offer glimpses of the stone in the indentation of their inflections, "fold following fold," revealing the city, but also its absence or withdrawal, a conglomerate of dust, hollow collectivities, hallucinatory armies and assemblies. In the long run, it is characteristic of the sensual side of the

15. André Scala has examined the genesis of the fold in Heidegger's works (*La Genèse du pli chez Heidegger* [forthcoming]). The notion arises between 1946 and 1953, especially in "Moira," *Early Greek Thinking*, trans. David Farrell Krell and Frank A. Capuzzi (San Francisco: Harper & Row, 1984); it succeeds the Intermediary or Incident, *Zwischen-fall*, which indicated more of a fall. It is the "Greek" fold par excellence, attributed to Parmenides. Scala points to a commentary of Riezler, who, as early as 1933, found in Parmenides a "folding of being," "a fold of the one in being and non-being, both drawn intimately into one another" (*Faltung*); Kurt Goldstein, when he discovers himself to be Parmenidian in his understanding of the living, draws on Riezler (*La Structure de l'organisme*, [Paris: Gallimard, 1983], 325–29). Another source, according to Scala, would play on problems of new perspective, and on the method of projection which already appears in Dürer's works, under the name of "zwiefalten cubum": cf., Panofsky, *The Life and Art of Albert Dürer*, (Princeton: Princeton University Press, 1955), 259: ("an original and, if one may say so, proto-topological method of developing them [solids] in such a way that the facets form a coherent "net" which, when cut out of paper and properly folded where two facets adjoin, will form an actual, three-dimensional model of the solid in question"). Analogous problems resurface in contemporary painting.

fan, of the sensual itself, to stir up the dust through which one sees and which betrays its inanity. But sometimes too, from the other, now closed, side of the fan ("le sceptre des rivages roses . . . ce blanc vol fermé que tu poses . . ."[the scepter of rosy shores . . . that closed white flight which you set down . . .]), the fold no longer moves toward a pulverization, but surpasses itself or finds its finality in an inclusion, "a heaping of thickness, offering the miniscule tomb, clearly, of the soul." The fold is inseparable from the wind. Ventilated by the wind, it is no longer the fold of matter through which one sees, but the fold of the soul in which one reads, "yellow folds of thought," the Book or the monad with multiple leaves. So it contains all folds, since the set of possible combinations of its leaves is infinite; but it includes them within its enclosure and all of its actions are internal. And yet, they are not two different worlds; the fold found in a newspaper, dust or mist, inanity, is a circumstantial fold which must have its own, novel mode of correspondence with the book, the fold of the Event, the unity which gives being, an inclusive multiplicity, a collectivity that has taken on consistency.

With Leibniz, it is not the folds of a fan but the veins of marble. On one hand there are all those coils of matter by which one sees living organisms in the microscope, collectivities (such as armies and herds) through the folds of dusts which they themselves stir up, green through the dust of yellow and blue, inanities or fictions, teeming holes which ceaselessly feed our uneasiness, our lassitude, or our dullness of spirit. And then, on the other hand, there are those folds in the soul, where inflection becomes inclusion (just as Mallarmé said that folding becomes heaping): one no longer sees, one reads. Leibniz begins using the word "read" both for the act within the privileged region of the monad and for the act of God throughout the monad itself.[16] It is well known that the total book is as much the dream of Leibniz as it is of Mallarmé, although they themselves never gave up working fragments. Our error lies in believing that they did not achieve what they wanted to—in circumstantial letters and opuscules, they perfected this unique Book, this book of monads, which could bear all dispersion as well as all combinations. The monad is the book or reading room. The visible and the legible, the exterior and the interior, the facade and the room: they are not two different worlds, for the visible has its own way of being

16. *Monadology*, § 61: "He who sees all could read in each everything that happens everywhere and even what has happened and will happen . . . but a soul can read within itself only what it represents distinctly."

read (like the newspaper for Mallarmé), and the legible has its own kind of theater (its theater of reading, in both Leibniz and Mallarmé). The combinations of the visible and the legible constitute the "emblems" or the allegories that were dear to the Baroque. We are always being led back to a new kind of correspondence or mutual expression, "inter-expression," fold following fold.

The Baroque is inseparable from a new regime of light and colors. One can at first think of light and darkness as 1 and 0, as the two levels of the world separated by a thin line of waters: the Happy and the Damned.[17] It is not a question however of an opposition. If one moves into the upper story, in a room without door or window, one recognizes that it is already very dark, almost lined with black, "fuscum sub-nigrum." This is a Baroque innovation: in place of the white chalk or plaster ground which prepared a picture, Tintoretto and Caravagio substitute a dark reddish-brown on which they place the deepest shad-ows, painting directly onto it and shading off towards the shadows.[18] The status of the painting changes, things surge up from the back-ground, colors well up from a common depth which attests to their obscure nature, the figures are defined more by their covering than by their contour. But this is not in opposition to light, this is, on the contrary, by virtue of the new regime of light. Leibniz says in the *Profession of Faith of the Philosopher:* "It slips, as though through a slit in the midst of shadows." Is one to understand it as coming from a basement window, from a narrow, bent or folded opening, by the inter-mediary of mirrors, the white consisting "of a great number of small, reflective mirrors"? More strictly speaking, the monads being without slits, a luminosity has been "sealed in," which lights up in each of them when it is raised up to reason, and which produces white through all the little interior mirrors. The light gives off white, but it also gives off shadow as well; it gives off white, which blends with the lighted section of the monad, but which darkens or shades off toward the dim background, "fuscum," from which things emerge "through well ex-ecuted shadows and hues in varying degrees of intensity." As with

17. On the Leibnizian invention of binary arithmetic, on its two characters, 1 and 0, on the link with the "Chinese figures of Fohy," cf., *Invention de l'arithmétique binaire, Explication de l'arithmétique binaire* in Leibniz *Mathematische Schriften,* ed. C. I. Gerhardt (Berlin: A. Asher, 1849–63), vol. 7. The reader is referred to the annotated edition by Christiane Frémont, Leibniz, *Discours sur la théologie naturelle des Chinois* (Paris: L'Herne, 1987).

18. Cf., Goethe's *Theory of Colours,* trans. and notes by C. L. Eastlake (London: Frank Cass & Co., 1967), §§ 902–09.

Desargues, it is enough to invert perspective or to put "the luminous in place of the eye, the opaque in place of the object, and shadow in place of projection" ("Préceptes pour avancer les sciences," *Philosophischen Schriften*), vol. 7, 169; *New Essays*, 2, chap. 9, § 8). Wölfflin stressed the lesson of the progressivity of a light which waxes and wanes, transmitted by degrees. It is the relativity of light (as much as of movement), the inseparability of light and dark, the effacement of contour, in short, a rebuttal to Descartes, who remained a man of the Renaissance, from the double perspective of a physics of light and of a logic of the idea. What is light plunges ceaselessly into shadow. Chiaroscuro fills the monad according to a series which can be followed in both directions: at one end the dark background, at the other sealed light; the latter, when it lights up, produces white in the section set aside for it, but the white grows dimmer and dimmer, yields to darkness and deepening shadow as it spreads out towards the dark background throughout the monad. Beyond this series there is on the one hand God, who commanded that there be light, and with it the mirror-white, but on the other hand there are shadows, an absolute black, which consist in an infinite number of holes which do not reflect the rays that fall on them, an infinitely spongy and cavernous matter which ultimately consists of all these holes.[19] Does the line of light, or the fold of the two stories, pass between the shadows and the dark background which it draws from them? In the final analysis it does, insofar as the lower story is nothing but a basement hollowed out by basements, and matter, pushed away beneath the waters, is reduced almost to nothing. But concrete matter is above, its holes already filled with an increasingly subtle matter, so that the fold of the two stories is more like the common limit between two kinds of full folds.

The entry of Germany onto the philosophical scene implies the whole German soul, which, according to Nietzsche, shows itself to be less "profound" than full of folds and coils.[20] How is one to paint the portrait of Leibniz the person without including in it the extreme tension between an open facade and a closed interior, each independent and both regulated by a strange, preestablished correspondence? It is an almost schizophrenic tension. Leibniz is depicted in terms of the Baroque. "Leibniz is more interesting than Kant as the type of the German: easy-going, full of noble words, sly, supple, malleable, a medi-

19. Black, the somber background ("fuscum subnigrum"), colors, white and light are defined in Leibniz, "Table de définitions" in *Opuscules et fragments*, 489.
20. Friedrich Nietzsche, *Beyond Good and Evil*, 8, § 244.

ator (between Christianity and mechanist philosophy), with, except for his own person, an enormous audacity, hidden under a mask and courteously importunate, modest in appearance. . . . Leibniz is dangerous, a good German who needs facades and philosophies of facades, but rash and, in himself, as mysterious as can be".[21] The courtly wig is a facade, an entrance, like the wish never to shock established feelings in any way, and the art of presenting his system from varying viewpoints, in such or such a mirror, according to the presumed intelligence of a correspondent or of a contradictor who appears at the door, while the System itself lies above, turning on itself, losing absolutely nothing in the compromises below, in the lower level whose secret it holds, taking rather the "best of all sides" to deepen itself or to create yet another fold, in the room of closed doors and walled-in windows where Leibniz has enclosed himself, saying: Everything is "always the same thing— once the degrees of perfection have been set aside."

The finest inventors, the finest commentators of the Baroque, dismayed by the way that, despite them, the notion threatened to extend arbitrarily, have had doubts about its consistency. The Baroque was thus restricted to a single genre (architecture), or to an increasingly restrictive determination of periods and locations, or even to a radical denial. The Baroque never existed. Still, it is odd to deny the existence of the Baroque in the same way as one denies the existence of unicorns or pink elephants. For in the latter case the concept is already a given, while in the case of the Baroque it is a question of knowing whether one can invent a concept capable (or not) of giving it existence. Irregular pearls exist, but the Baroque has no reason to exist without a concept which forms that very reason. It is easy to deprive the Baroque of its existence, it is enough not to propose its concept. There is no fundamental difference between wondering if Leibniz is the Baroque philosopher par excellence, or if he formulates a concept capable of bringing the Baroque itself into existence. In this respect, those who have linked Leibniz and the Baroque have done so by virtue of an excessively broad concept, as with Knecht and the "coincidence of opposites." Christine Buci-Glucksmann proposes a much more interesting criterion, a dialectic between sight and seeing [*voir et regard*], but this criterion is perhaps too restrictive as well and would only allow for the definition of an optical fold.[22] For us, however, the criteri-

21. Cited by Ernst Bertram, *Nietzsche*, (Rieder edition), 233.
22. Herbert Knecht, *La Logique de Leibniz, essai sur le rationalisme baroque*, (Lausanne: L'âge d'homme, 1981); Christine Buci-Glucksmann, *La Folie du voir, de*

on or the operative concept of the Baroque is the Fold, in its full comprehension and extension: fold upon fold. If one can extend the Baroque beyond precise historical limits, it seems to us that it is always by virtue of this criterion, which allows us to recognize Michaux when he writes "To live in the folds," or Boulez when he invokes Mallarmé and composes "Fold upon fold," or Hantaï when he creates a method out of folding. And if, on the contrary, we go back further into the past, how might we already have to find the Baroque in, for example, Uccello? Because he is not content to paint blue and pink horses, and to draw lances like streaks of light directed toward all the points of sky; he is forever drawing "*mazocchi,* which are circles of wood covered with cloth and placed on the head, such that the folds of the fabric, when pulled back, surround the entire face"; he runs up against the incomprehension of his contemporaries, because "the power of *developing absolutely* all things and the strange series of folded hoods seem more revealing than the magnificent marble figures of the great Donatello."[23] There would thus be a Baroque line, passed down in strict accordance with the fold and which could bring together architects, painters, musicians, poets, philosophers. Of course, it could be objected that the concept of the fold itself remains too broad: to speak only of the plastic arts, what period and what style could fail to see in the fold a painted or sculpted line? And it is not only clothing, but also the body, rocks, the waters, the earth, line itself. Baltrusaitis defines the fold in general by scission, but a scission which causes each of the two split terms to set each other off anew. It is in this sense that he defines the romanesque fold by the scission/setting-off of the figurative and geometry.[24] Could one not as well define the Oriental fold by the scission/setting-off of empty and full? And all the others will have to be defined in turn by a comparative analysis. Uccello's folds are not truly Baroque because they remain caught in geometrical solids, polygonal, inflexible structures, however ambiguous they may be. If we wish to maintain the operative identity of the Baroque and the fold, we must then show that in all other cases the fold remains limited while in the Baroque it experiences a limitless release, whose conditions can

---

l'esthétique baroque, (Paris: Galilée, 1986): the author develops a conception of the Baroque that draws on Lacan and Merleau-Ponty.

23. Marcel Schwob, *Vies imaginaires,* (Paris: 10/18), 229–31.

24. Jurgis Baltrusaitis, *Formations, déformations,* (Paris: Flammarion, 1986), chap. 9.

be determined. The folds seem to take leave of their supports, cloth, granite, and cloud, to enter into an infinite competition, as in the *Christ in the Garden of Gethsemane* of El Greco (the one in the National Gallery). Or else, notably in the *Baptism of Christ*, the counterfold of calf and knee, where the knee seems the inversion of the calf, lends an infinite undulation to the leg, while the pinching of the cloud in the center transforms it into a double fan. . . . It is these characteristics rigorously interpreted that must account for the extreme specificity of the Baroque and for the possibility of expanding it, without arbitrary extension, beyond its historical limits: the Baroque's contribution to art in general, Leibniz's contribution to philosophy.

1. *The Fold:* The Baroque invents the infinite work or operation. The problem is not how to finish a fold, but how to continue it, make it go through the roof, take it to infinity. For the fold affects not only all kinds of materials, which thus become matter of expression in accordance with different scales and speeds and vectors (the mountains and the waters, papers, fabrics, living tissues, the brain), but it also determines and brings form into being and into appearance, it makes of it a form of expression, *Gestaltung*, the genetic element or the line of infinite inflexion, the curve of a single variable.

2. *The Interior and the Exterior:* The infinite fold separates, or passes between matter and the soul, the facade and the sealed room, the interior and the exterior. For the line of inflection is a virtuality ceaselessly differentiating itself: actualized in the soul it is realized in its own way in matter. It is the Baroque characteristic: an exterior always on the exterior, an interior always on the interior. It is characterized as an infinite "receptivity," and an infinite "spontaneity"—the exterior facade for receiving, the interior chambers for action. Even up through our own time Baroque architecture continues to place two principles in confrontation: a weight-bearing principle and a covering or facing principle (whether in Gropius or in Loos).[25] The conciliation of the two will not be direct but necessarily harmonious, inspiring a new harmony; the same thing, the line, is expressed in the rising of the interior song of the soul, by memory or by heart, as in the extrinsic creation of the material of the musical score, from cause to cause. But,

25. Bernard Cache, *L'Ameublement du territoire*.

the fact is precisely that—the expressed does not exist beyond its expressions.

3. *The High and the Low:* The perfect harmony of the scission, or the resolution of tension, is effected by the distribution of two stories, which both belong to one and the same world (the line of the universe). The matter-facade tends downwards while the soul-chamber rises. The infinite fold thus passes between two stories. But in differentiating itself, it swarms over both sides: the fold differentiates itself into folds, which insinuate themselves into the interior and overflow onto the exterior, articulating themselves into the high and the low. Coils of matter when conditioned by exteriority, folds of the soul when conditioned by enclosure. Coils of the musical score and folds of the song. The Baroque is the preeminent informal art: on the ground, at ground level, at hand, it comprises the textures of matter (the great modern Baroque painters, from Paul Klee to Fautrier, Dubuffet, Bettencourt . . .). But the informal is not the negation of form; it posits form as folded, as existing only as "mental landscape," in the soul or the mind, at a height; it thus includes immaterial folds as well. The kinds of matter constitute the base, but the folded shapes are its forms. One moves from materials to forms. From grounds and terrains to habitats and salons. From *Texturology* to *Logology.* These are the two orders, the two stories of Dubuffet, and the discovery of their harmony, which must go all the way to the point of indiscernability: is it a texture, or a fold of the soul, of thought?[26] Matter which reveals its texture becomes material, in the way that form which reveals its folds becomes power. It is the pair material-power which, in the Baroque, replaces matter and form (the primitive forces being those of the soul).

4. *The Unfold:* certainly not the opposite of the fold, nor its effacement, but the continuation or the extension of its act, the condition of its manifestation. When the fold ceases to be represented and becomes a "method," an operation, an act, the unfold becomes the result of the act which is expressed in precisely that way. Hantaï begins by repre-

---

26. On "the two orders," material and immaterial, cf., Jean Dubuffet, *Prospectus et tous écrits suivants,* collected and presented by Hubert Damisch, (Paris: Gallimard, 1967), vol. 2, 79–81. Cf., also the *Catalogue des travaux de Jean Dubuffet,* ed. Max Loreau (Paris: Minuit, 1964): "Tables paysagées, paysages du mental"; and "Habitats, Closerie Falbala, Salon d'été" (the Logological cabinet is a veritable interior of a monad).

senting the fold—tubular, teeming—but soon folds the cloth or paper.
Then there are, as it were, two poles, the one of the "Studies" and the
one of the "Tables." Sometimes, the surface is locally and irregularly
folded, and the exterior sides of the opened fold are painted, so that the
spreading-out, the opening, the unfolding cause the fields of color and
the zones of white to alternate, modulating one with the other. At
other times, it is the solid which projects its internal planes onto a flat
surface, regularly folded in accordance with the edges: now the fold has
a resting point, it is knotted and closed at each intersection and unfolds
to set the interior white into circulation.[27] Here, setting the color in
the coils of matter to vibrate, there setting the light in the folds of an
immaterial surface to vibrate. And yet, why is it that the Baroque line
is only a possibility for Hantaï? Because he never stops running up
against another possibility, which is the line of the Orient. The painted
and the non-painted are not distributed as form and background, but as
fullness and emptiness in a reciprocal becoming. Which is why Hantaï
leaves the eye of the fold empty and only paints the sides (line of the
Orient); and yet it sometimes happens that in the same region he will
make a succession of folds which no longer leave any empty spaces (the
full Baroque line). Perhaps it is profoundly characteristic of the Baroque
to set itself in confrontation with the Orient. It is already the case with
Leibniz's undertaking in binary arithmetics: in one and zero Leibniz
recognizes fullness and emptiness in a typically Chinese manner, but
the Baroque Leibniz does not believe in emptiness, which always
seems to him full of a coiled matter, and consequently his binary
arithmetics superposes the folds which the decimal system, and
Nature herself, conceals in apparently empty spaces. For Leibniz and
the Baroque, folds are always full.[28]

5. *Textures:* Leibnizian physics comprises two principal headings,
one concerning the active, or so-called derivative, forces which relate
to matter, the other the passive forces, the resistance of the material:
texture (On textures, cf., Letter to Des Bosses, August 1715. Leibniz's

27. On Hantaï and the method of folding, cf., Marcelin Pleynet, *Identité de la
lumière*, catalogue (Arca Marseille). And also Dominique Fourcade, *Un coup de pinceau
c'est la pensée*, catalogue, (Paris: Centre Pompidou); Yves Michaud, *Métaphysique de
Hantaï*, catalogue (Venice): Geneviève Bonnefoi, *Hantaï, Paintings, Watercolors 1971–
1975* (New York: Pierre Matisse, 1975).

28. Leibniz counted on his binary arithmetics to reveal a periodicity in the number
series (a periodicity which Nature perhaps concealed "in its coils") as well as for the
primary numbers (*New Essays*, 4, chap. 17, § 13).

physics testifies to a consistent interest in problems of the resistance of materials). It is perhaps at its limit that texture is best revealed, just before rupture or tearing, when spreading is no longer opposed to the fold but expresses it in its pure state, in accordance with a Baroque figure indicated by Bernard Cache (hysteresis more than spreading). Here again, the fold pushes back groove and hole; it does not belong to the same pictorial vision. As a general rule, it is the way in which matter

folds that constitute its texture: it is defined less by its heterogeneous and genuinely distinct parts than by the manner in which, by virtue of particular folds, these parts become inseparable. From that one gets the concept of Mannerism in its operatory relation to the Baroque. And this is what Leibniz was talking about when he referred to "paper or tunic." Everything folds in its own way, the rope and the stick as well as colors, which separate out in accordance with the concavity or convexity of the ray of light, and sounds, which rise in pitch in accordance as "the trembling parts are shorter and tighter." Texture thus depends not on the parts themselves, but on the strata which determine their "cohesion": the new status of the object, its object-matter [*objectile*], is inseparable from the various strata which dilate, like so many opportunities for detours and coils. Relative to the folds within its power, matter becomes matter of expression. In this respect, the fold of matter or texture must be seen in relation to several factors, first of all light, *chiaroscuro*, the way in which the fold catches light, the way it varies according to the time of day and the sort of illumination (the contemporary research of Tromeur and Nicole Grenot). But also in relation to depth: how the fold itself determines a "shallow depth" which can be superposed. Here, the paper fold defines a minimum of depth on our scale, as is seen in the Baroque *trompe-l'œil* letter holders, where the representation of a dog-eared card throws what lies on this side of the wall into depth. So it is with the soft and superposed depth of fabrics which has served as an unending inspiration to painting and which Helga Heinzen has, in our time, carried to a new power when, the body consigned to absence, the representation of striped and folded cloth covers an entire painting in falls and elevations, in swells and suns, following a line that comes, this time, from Islam. Or again the theater

of materials, when a material caught, hardened in its spread-out state or its hysteresis, can assume a felicity of expression in itself the folds of another matter, as in the wood sculptures of Renonciat, where cedar of Lebanon turns into plastic drop-cloth, or Paraña pine into "cotton and feathers." In short, the way in which all these textures of matter tend toward a higher point, a spiritual point which envelops form, which holds it enveloped and which alone contains the secret of the material folds below. Where do these latter flow from, given that they cannot be accounted for by the constituant parts and that the "teeming," the perceptual displacement of contours, comes from the projection onto matter of something spiritual, of a fantasmagoria on the order of thought, as Dubuffet says. Though in another way, the sculptor Jeanclos nonetheless treads an analogous path when he moves from the infinitely coiled, knotted, and crimped physical leaves of cabbage, or from sheets infinitely spread out, to metaphysical peas, spiritual sleepers or monad heads who give full meaning to the expression "the folds of sleep".[29] Active or passive, the derivative forces of matter refer back to the primitive forces, those of the soul. Always the two stories, and their harmony, their harmonization.

6. *The Paradigm:* The search for a model of the fold proceeds by way of a choice of matter. Is it the paper fold, as the Orient suggests, or the fold of cloth, which seems to predominate in the Occident? The crux of the question is that the material components of the fold (the texture) must not hide the formal element or the form of expression. In this regard the Greek fold is unsatisfactory, though it rightly aspires to currency in the highest realms, political power, the power of thought—the Platonic paradigm of weaving as a mesh remains on the level of textures but does not draw out the formal elements of the fold. For the Greek fold, as the *Politics* and the *Timaeus* demonstrate, presupposes a common measure between two terms that mix and therefore operates by means of circular movements which correspond to the repetition of the proportion. This is the reason that the Platonic forms fold, but never reach the formal element of the fold. The latter can only appear with the infinite, in the incommensurable and the extravagant, when the variable curve has unseated the circle (On the presence or

29. Jeanclos-Mossé, *Sculptures et dessins*, (Orléans: Maison de la culture).

absence of "common measure," cf., Leibniz, "On Freedom" in *Philosophical Papers and Letters,* vol. 1, 404–10). So it goes with the Baroque fold, with its corresponding status as power of thought and political force.

—Translated by Jonathan Strauss

Contributors

GILLES DELEUZE, the distinguished French philosopher, taught at the University of Paris in Vincennes until his recent retirement.

MADELEINE DOBIE is a Ph.D candidate in the Department of French at Yale University.

KEVIN DUNN teaches English at Yale University. He is currently finishing a book on Renaissance prefatory rhetoric and its relation to the history of authorship.

EDWIN M. DUVAL is Professor of French and Renaissance Studies at Yale University. Author of *Poesis and Poetic Tradition in the Early Works of Saint-Amant* (1981), *The Design of Rabelais's Pantagruel* (1991), and many articles on Rabelais, Montaigne, and sixteenth-century French poetry, he is currently completing books on Rabelais's *Tiers Livre* and *Quart Livre.*

TIMOTHY HAMPTON is Associate Professor of French at the University of California at Berkeley. He is the author of *Writing from History: The Rhetoric of Exemplarity in Renaissance Literature* (1990).

ERICA HARTH of Brandeis University is the author of *Ideology and Culture in Seventeenth-Century France* and *Cyrano de Bergerac and the Polemics of Modernity.* Her contribution to this issue is part of her forthcoming book, *Cartesian Women.*

CHRISTIAN JOUHAUD is a researcher at the Centre National de la Recherche Scientifique in Paris. He is the author of *Les Mazarinades: La Fronde des mots,* and the recently published *La Main de Richelieu ou le pouvoir cardinal.*

ANNA LEHMAN is a Ph.D. candidate in the Department of French at Yale University.

JACQUELINE LICHTENSTEIN is Associate Professor of French at Berkeley. She is the author of *La Couleur éloquente.*

KATHERINE LYDON is a Ph.D. candidate in the Department of French at Yale University.

JOHN D. LYONS is Professor of French at the University of Virginia. His most recent book is *Exemplum. The Rhetoric of Example in Early Modern France and Italy* (1989). He is currently writing a book on the relationship between tragedy and history in Corneille's theatre.

LOUIS MARIN, currently Directeur d'Etudes at the Ecole des Hautes Etudes in Paris, has written widely on literature, philosophy and art, with special attention to the seventeenth century in France.

GISÈLE MATHIEU-CASTELLANI teaches at the University of Paris, St. Denis, and has written widely on sixteenth- and seventeenth-century French literature. Her most recent book is *Montaigne: l'écriture de l'essai.*

OREST RANUM is Professor of History at the Johns Hopkins University. His *The Fronde, a French Revolution: 1648–1652* is forthcoming at W. W. Norton and Company.

TIMOTHY J. REISS is Professor and Chair of Comparative Literature at New York University. His most recent book, *The Uncertainty of Analysis. The Meaning of Literature* is currently in press. The essay in this issue is connected with research leading to a book on its subject.

JONATHAN STRAUSS is a Ph.D. candidate in the Department of French at Yale and is currently writing a dissertation on Gérard de Nerval, Mallarmé, and Georges Bataille.

SUZANNE TOCZYSKI is a Ph.D. candidate in the Department of French at Yale University. She is currently writing a dissertation entitled "On n'y agit qu'en parlant: Reading Corneille through Speech Act Theory."

The following issues are available through **Yale University Press,** Customer Service Department, 92A Yale Station, New Haven, CT 06520.

63 The Pedagogical Imperative:
   Teaching as a Literary Genre
   (1982) $15.95
64 Montaigne: Essays in Reading
   (1983) $15.95
65 The Language of Difference:
   Writing in QUEBEC(ois)
   (1983) $15.95
66 The Anxiety of Anticipation
   (1984) $15.95
67 Concepts of Closure
   (1984) $15.95
68 Sartre after Sartre
   (1985) $15.95
69 The Lesson of Paul de Man
   (1985) $15.95

70 Images of Power:
   Medieval History/Discourse/
   Literature
   (1986) $15.95
71 Men/Women of Letters:
   Correspondence
   (1986) $15.95
72 Simone de Beauvoir:
   Witness to a Century
   (1987) $15.95
73 Everyday Life
   (1987) $15.95
74 Phantom Proxies
   (1988) $15.95
75 The Politics of Tradition:
   Placing Women in French
   Literature
   (1988) $15.95

Special Issue: After the
   Age of Suspicion: The
   French Novel Today
   (1989) $15.95
76 Autour de Racine:
   Studies in Intertextuality
   (1989) $15.95
77 Reading the Archive: On
   Texts and Institutions
   (1990) $15.95
78 On Bataille
   (1990) $15.95
79 Literature and the Ethical
   Question
   (1991) $15.95
Special Issue: Contexts:
   Style and Values in
   Medieval Art and
   Literature
   (1991) $15.95

Special subscription rates are available on a calendar year basis (2 issues per year):

Individual subscriptions $24.00   Institutional subscriptions $28.00

- -

ORDER FORM   Yale University Press, 92A Yale Station, New Haven, CT 06520

Please enter my subscription for the calendar year
☐ **Special Issue (1991)**   ☐ **1991 (Nos. 79 and 80)**   ☐ **1992 (Nos. 81 and 82)**

I would like to purchase the following individual issues:

_____

_____

For individual issues, please add postage and handling:
Single issue, United States $2.75   Single issue, foreign countries $5.00
Each additional issue $.50   Each additional issue $1.00
Connecticut residents please add sales tax of 8%.

Payment of $ _____ is enclosed (including sales tax if applicable).

Mastercard no. _____

4-digit bank no. _____ Expiration date _____

VISA no. _____ Expiration date _____

Signature _____

SHIP TO: _____

_____

_____

- -

See the next page for ordering issues 1–59 and 61–62. **Yale French Studies** is also available through Xerox University Microfilms, 300 North Zeeb Road, Ann Arbor, MI 48106.

The following issues are still available through the **Yale French Studies** Office, 2504A Yale Station, New Haven, CT 06520.

Add for postage & handling

Single issue, United States $1.75
Each additional issue $ .50

Single issue, foreign countries $2.50
Each additional issue $1.50

- -

YALE FRENCH STUDIES, 2504A Yale Station, New Haven, Connecticut 06520

A check made payable to YFS is enclosed. Please send me the following issue(s):

Issue no.	Title	Price
_____	_____	_____
_____	_____	_____
_____	_____	_____
	Postage & handling	_____
	Total	_____

Name _____

Number/Street _____

City _____ State _____ Zip _____

The following issues are now available through Kraus Reprint Company, Route 100, Millwood, N.Y. 10546.

36/37 Structuralism has been reprinted by Doubleday as an Anchor Book.
55/56 Literature and Psychoanalysis has been reprinted by Johns Hopkins University Press, and can be ordered through Customer Service, Johns Hopkins University Press, Baltimore, MD 21218.